PRAISE FOR *PICKS AND SHOVELS*

"Prashant has channeled his thirty-plus years of experience in developer marketing and turned it into the definitive guide for technical marketers everywhere. Level-up your marketing with Prashant's guidance."

—Dick Costolo, managing partner, 01 Advisors, and former CEO, Twitter

"If you are marketing to developers, you are going to love this book. Regardless of your role, technology, or organizational maturity, you will find entire chapters that speak to your situation."

—Jeff Barr, VP and chief evangelist, Amazon Web Services

"I've seen the impact Prashant's work has had. This book will help you replicate that in your own company."

—Paul Copplestone, founder and CEO, Supabase

"If you're building the picks and shovels that power the next generation of developers, this book is your playbook."

—Astasia Myers, general partner, Felicis

"Prashant and I have spent our careers helping developers—working together across multiple companies and platform shifts. This book captures the strategy we've lived and now reimagined for the AI era. It's thoughtful, practical, and grounded in real experience. Prashant deeply understands how to connect with developers, and this is the playbook for today."

—Jeff Sandquist, VP and head of product (generative AI), Walmart

"I've worked across some of the world's biggest platforms, and I wish this book existed years ago. Prashant breaks it down with clarity and heart."

—Katie Penn, VP of marketing, Planet

"Prashant has worked on every side of the dev tools market. That perspective shines through on every page."

—Hemal Shah, product manager, OpenAI

"This is the most complete playbook I've seen for anyone marketing to developers—tactically deep, philosophically right, and grounded in both unit economics as well as how modern developer products actually grow in an AI-first world."

—Aaron Cort, operating partner, Craft Ventures, and first head of marketing and former VP of operations, ClickUp

"Every early-stage dev-tools company should keep this book within arm's reach."

—Bryan Clark, VP of product, Neon

"Prashant captures exactly what developers care about, from building trust through technical credibility and a genuine 'Help First' approach to creating tight, hands-on product feedback loops. This should be required reading for anyone interested in marketing to developers."

—Waqas Makhdum, ex-developer GTM, Snowflake and OpenAI

PICKS AND SHOVELS

Marketing to Developers During the AI Gold Rush

PRASHANT SRIDHARAN

STRATEGICNERDS
<!--PRESS-->

Published by Strategic Nerds Press, San Francisco, CA
www.strategicnerds.com

GIRL FRIDAY
PRODUCTIONS

Edited and designed by Girl Friday Productions
www.girlfridayproductions.com

Cover design: Brad Foltz and Paul Barrett
Project management: Abi Pollokoff
Editorial production: Kylee Hayes

Image credits: Rawf8/iStock (pickaxe and shovel),
Kevin Sanderson/Pixabay (emoji)

ISBN (paperback): 979-8-9991111-0-4
ISBN (ebook): 979-8-9991111-1-1

Library of Congress Control Number: 2025914077

First edition

For Melody & Bodhi, the loves of my life.

CONTENTS

SECTION 1: DEVELOPER RELATIONS

SECTION 2: PRODUCT MARKETING

SECTION 3: MARKETING LEADERSHIP

FOREWORD

If you are marketing to developers, you are going to love this book. Regardless of your role, technology, or organizational maturity, you will find entire chapters that speak to your situation and provide detailed guidance on how to organize and work toward a successful outcome.

When we launched AWS in 2006, cloud computing was a radical idea. We gave developers instant access to compute, storage, and databases without having to rack and stack servers. What started as a way to help startups move faster quickly became the foundation for enterprises, governments, and builders of all kinds. Over the years I've seen firsthand how developers can create entirely new categories of technology and business when armed with the right tools and services. The challenge, of course, is how to find those developers and, after you do, how to artfully persuade them that your products are the best fit for their needs.

The impact of developer tools built on AWS has been staggering. Kubernetes, Terraform, Datadog, and a generation of frameworks, platforms, and automation tools have transformed how software is built and operated. Today, AI and serverless technologies are pushing the boundaries even further, giving developers superpowers and the ability to scale to any conceivable level of traffic. But while technology keeps evolving, one thing hasn't changed: great products don't succeed on technology alone. The best developer tools win because they meet developers where they are, earn their trust, and make it easy to start, scale, and succeed.

Prashant was there in the early days of AWS, helping shape how we engaged with developers, and brought cloud computing to the world. Since then, he's been on all sides of the industry, from BigTech to startups to scale-ups, and everything in between. He has a rare perspective on what it takes to build and market products that developers actually adopt. This book distills decades of his hard-earned knowledge into a playbook for anyone building in this space. If you want developers to discover, trust, use, and even champion your product, keep on reading!

Jeff Barr, VP and Chief Evangelist

Amazon Web Services

AI STATEMENT

This book represents the knowledge and experience I've gained over my career. It was not written by AI. I did use ChatGPT to help me turn my thoughts into coherent chapter outlines, check passages for grammar, and analyze the text as I wrote to minimize redundancy.

This book contains only hand-crafted, artisanal em dashes that were added during the editing process. Let's all pour an em dash out for the Chicago Manual of Style.

CHAPTER 0

How Can I Help?

"In a gold rush, sell picks and shovels."

Samuel Brannan, California's first millionaire, didn't mine for gold during the California Gold Rush in the 1840s. He made a good deal of his fortune selling supplies to miners.

Since the dawn of the modern tech age in the 1990s, the metaphor of selling picks and shovels to miners has inspired many entrepreneurs to focus on building tools for software developers.

I'm fortunate to have built my entire thirty-plus-year career marketing picks and shovels to developers. I've had a front-row seat at several modern gold rushes:

- **The internet** at both Sun Microsystems and Microsoft, working on the Java programming language and web development tools, eventually leading product management and product marketing for Visual Studio.
- **The cloud** at Amazon Web Services, as the first director of marketing for that transformative product, at Microsoft as the principal manager for developer relations on Microsoft Azure, and at numerous high-scale cloud-native database startups, including Supabase and Timescale.
- **Mobile development** at both Facebook and Twitter, building mobile platforms.

I'm one of the few who have driven these gold rushes from leadership positions as CMO and in product management, product marketing, developer advocacy, and business development. I've compiled my experience and knowledge in this book for you.

And now here we are at the beginning of perhaps the most important platform movement of all: **artificial intelligence.**

Watching my beautiful adopted hometown of San Francisco light up with the energy of thousands of startups building AI products, I find myself, once again, excited most by those selling picks and shovels. I naturally gravitate to products made for builders, and I simultaneously admire and romanticize the builder in all of us.

And there are a lot more builders now than there used to be. In fact, there are twice as many computer science graduates today as there were a decade ago, and that number continues to increase. Every single company on the planet is now a technology company, and every single company needs software engineers to build, deploy, and manage the core infrastructure that is the foundation of the business.

With the rise and prominence of developers comes a veritable glut of picks and shovels. Today, 30 percent of the latest Y Combinator batch are companies building tools for software developers, mostly centered around artificial intelligence. There are more developer tools, and thanks to the resource-heavy needs of artificial intelligence companies, they are funded at much higher rates than before.

As a founder, executive, product marketing manager, or developer advocate tasked with taking a product in a crowded field of picks and shovels to a rapidly growing market of software developers, you probably feel more than a little bit overwhelmed.

This is the field of developer marketing.

The primary goals of developer marketing are to drive awareness of developer-focused products among developers, convince developers to adopt your product, and nurture developers so they feel comfortable using your product, providing helpful feedback, and doing business with you. That shouldn't be too controversial, as it's the same marketing challenge with any product: awareness to adoption to conversion.

But developers are different.

Developers want truth and integrity. They don't want marketing puffery and will turn away from companies that engage in sales and marketing pitches and bombastic claims. They want to know if a product will really work for them, and they are more than willing to use a product themselves and evaluate it without any help from outsiders. Only after a successful self-guided evaluation will they consider working with sales or, as is increasingly common, purchasing on their own.

However, developers are different in another way: They are willing to try new tools quickly. The consideration cycle for developer products is much shorter than for traditional IT products. Developers love shiny objects, and while they will insist on evaluating a product on their own, they are very amenable to the prospect of finding new picks and shovels.

All of this gets to my fundamental philosophy for working with developers:

Help First.

In everything you do, seek to teach and be helpful. In the act of doing so, you also set broader context. If your company becomes known for just one thing, be known for being helpful. Being helpful confers a brand promise of "trust" that you simply cannot buy through ads or event sponsorships.

- When you write a feature-launch blog post, think about the broader context and the problem you're trying to solve. Teach developers about the history of that problem, the many attempted solutions over time, the kind of solution necessary to solve the problem, and the myriad benefits of solving it. And then talk about how you solved it.
- When you speak at a conference, don't do a product pitch session. Pick a problem that your product solves and dive deep into it. Or pick a problem that you solved in the act of building your product, and talk about how your engineering team overcame it.
- When you attend a meetup, ask the event organizer if there's anything they need. Don't assume it's pizza or a box of T-shirts. It may well be! But start by asking how you can help.

In my years selling picks and shovels, I've made mistakes. I've had successes. But I've never lost sight of the primary mission: Help First.

Help First is my overarching principle of developer marketing, and in this book I cover the many ways Help First manifests itself in building a full developer marketing program.

By reading this book, you can expect to learn the following directly from my thirty-plus years of experience:

- how to use **developer advocacy** to drive awareness and trust through content, community, and events
- how **developer marketing** drives brand perception and growth
- how **product marketing** builds positioning, messaging, and go-to-market strategies for your product or service

My name is Prashant, and I'm here to help.

CHAPTER 1

Getting Started

Every successful company or organization has three core elements dialed in:

1. a **deep understanding** of the market and customer and a *specific* problem that they have a *burning need* to solve
2. a **product strategy** that solves this problem in a unique, differentiated way
3. a **go-to-market motion** that, in a repeatable and scalable way, identifies potential customers and convinces them to try your product

Fundamentally, marketing and developer relations exist to serve the go-to-market motion and ensure that the entire organization understands the market, customer, and problems being solved. With some notable exceptions around synthesizing and delivering product feedback, our job is to make it easier for the company to sell its products and services. Plucky startups may spend most of their time focused on customer discovery and finding awareness channels. Established organizations with mature product lines and large installed bases may focus on product feedback channels and sales activation. As marketing leaders, it's our job to understand what our organization needs most from us.

The key to any marketing strategy is a thorough understanding of the customer. Developers are opinionated, thorough in their analysis, and enthusiastic about trying new products and services. They may harbor healthy skepticism over a product's promises, but they'll nonetheless give it a fair shake. We must be the Voice of the Customer, an advocate for the customer's needs throughout the organization.

I once worked at a startup that could never decide who their customer was. One quarter it was developers, the next it was data engineers. And because it couldn't decide on the customer, it couldn't land on a single, focused go-to-market strategy. One quarter it was product-led growth to developers, the next it was sales-led growth to engineers. Bad developer marketing is often a symptom of a greater problem. Clarity on your customer target is step zero, and of paramount importance.

Developer marketing layers knowledge of the developer persona atop traditional B2B SaaS go-to-market strategies, sharpening our approach to reaching the market and customer with greater candor, focusing our product strategy on features that solve complex problems, and building a go-to-market motion that simultaneously reaches the technical user and economic buyer. It's difficult to take a traditional marketer and throw them at a technical product. It's less difficult, but still hard, to take a technical user (or founder) and ask them to run go-to-market functions.

This book bridges that gap. It's designed to help seasoned marketers understand how their tried-and-true tactics can be adapted for the developer market. It also helps technical people start from things they inherently understand, such as content and communities, and scale them into marketing strategies.

I've organized the book into three sections:

- **Developer relations:** how to reach developers where they are with interesting content, events, and other materials that help your customers learn, grow, and understand what you're offering
- **Product marketing:** how to talk about your product, define pricing, run launches, and ensure everyone in sales and product is aligned
- **Marketing leadership:** how to grow your career and your people as you build successful developer marketing programs

In many ways, this book is the distillation of my career. I hope you enjoy it.

Section 1

DEVELOPER RELATIONS

CHAPTER 2

The Developer Marketing Organization

As we've discussed, the guiding principle of the developer marketing organization is to Help First. We aim to help developers (and adjacent technical professionals) succeed in their jobs and careers. We do this primarily by listening to their problems, finding solutions, and teaching them how to use the latest technologies (including, but not limited to, products that we are responsible for) to solve those problems.

Many in our industry use the shorthand "developer relations," or DevRel. It's typical to think of developer relations solely as developer advocacy: people who speak at conferences, write blog posts, and record videos. But as the name implies, developer relations forges a bond with the communities or segments within the developer world, ensuring mutual respect and understanding. This bond is based on technical knowledge and credibility. The outward-facing products of developer relations—the punchy videos, exotic travel, prolific social media presence, and so on—are all functions of this respect and understanding.

Developer marketing applies B2B SaaS fundamentals to the developer space. Everything from measurement and metrics to content marketing to product marketing to traditional business models, all morphed to fit a developer persona. To be successful, it's critical to gain a deep understanding of the developer.

Thus, developer relations is the essential component of a more expansive developer marketing organization. It's the team responsible for the entirety of the go-to-market motion for a developer-focused product or company. The developer marketing organization comprises the following distinct functional areas:

- **Developer advocates:** They're the heart of your developer relations program. They're technical experts, content machines, top-gun spokespeople, and the main community interface. As I always say, "Trust and integrity, not your products or services, are your primary currency." Developer advocates (sometimes called DevRels) ooze trust and integrity, always speaking honestly and on behalf of (advocating for) the developer community.
- **Developer marketing:** Campaigns, programs, SEO, digital marketing, events, social media, comms, and content program management.
- **Developer product marketing:** The ringleaders of the circus. They coordinate consistent positioning and messaging, launches, and customer feedback and discovery, and they imbue the rest of the organization with mission and purpose.
- **Developer education:** Documentation, training, and (if you're big enough) certification.

Throughout this book, we will dive into these functional areas with greater detail on executing strategies and tactics more effectively.

WHERE TO START?

The answer to this question depends on the size and scope of your organization. If you're a ten-person startup composed of nearly all engineers, who should be your first hire? If you're an established organization within a big company looking to bring a developer-focused API or service to market, should you bother hiring a marketing team? And if you're a BigTech company with many of these assets in place, should you organize yourself as one developer go-to-market team?

Early-stage startups

Let's start with the early-stage startup. You are pre-revenue, and maybe on the cusp of product-market fit. In these initial stages, your founders and engineers must be content machines. It will bring you closer to the customer and infuse the organization with a Socratic culture of clear thinking and debate.

At the same time, you need someone who can hit the road and represent your company at meetups and events. They can also coordinate content and work with the community to amplify it. It's a bonus if they can contribute quality posts as well.

If you're an early-stage startup, my advice is to find someone fairly junior but very eager and with a strong program-management orientation (read: hyperorganized and disciplined, a checklist junkie, with a penchant for getting things done). This person will coordinate content creation across your small engineering team, reach out to meetup organizers, and be tenacious about getting responses; they will be eager to connect with podcasters, bloggers, and YouTubers to find ways to place your founders for maximum amplification and awareness. If they're also technical, they can author a few blog posts and, at minimum, author case studies and interface with your customers. They can help organize customer feedback sessions with your team. Thus, your first hire is for developer marketing.

As the organization grows, this person's skill set as a polymath will be invaluable. They'll also grow up having built out much of how your internal culture operates daily. How do people collaborate? How do you address people who need to follow through on their verbal commitments? How do you make sure people are listening to customer feedback?

Your second hire should be your first true developer advocate. You will know you're ready for one when you (forgive the facetiousness) have a product worth advocating for. Before you hire your first developer advocate, your product should be in customers' hands, and they should be actively using it and providing feedback. The sentiment has been positive and close to product-market fit. Your first few blog posts were successful, and you're in something of a groove regarding the tone and quality of your content. Maybe you've spoken at a few meetups or events and found the experience positive. At this point, you've built a strong foundation for developer advocacy.

From here, as you gain confidence, think about hiring your first developer growth person. Start building systems around digital growth, using content from your developer advocate and programs from your developer marketing hire.

It might be too early to hire a product marketing manager (PMM). In the early stages, your best PMMs will be the founders. They're the ones who can bridge customer feedback and product vision to identify messaging. You won't need a dedicated PMM until you have a sales team or a predictable engineering ship schedule. Right now you're looking for someone who can translate founder-driven vision and messaging into a sales-enablement program or launch process. Eventually you will need a PMM to support messaging and customer-behavior research, but in the early stages these activities will be most effective when driven by the founders.

Scale-up startups

In this scenario, you have a larger organization, you probably have a handful of marketing hires on board, and you've found product-market fit and your tribe through a combination of hustle and grit. There is already a ton of internal knowledge about how to reach customers, and you're looking to scale that up and drive top-of-funnel growth using a developer go-to-market motion.

In this case, I advise looking for experienced hires with a hands-on, operational attitude. You are too early for the professional managerial class. You need people who can put in a modicum of process but still be aggressive in rolling up their sleeves and doing the work.

You will need a developer advocate (or a few) who can build content and docs; a marketing manager who combines content management, community development, and website content as their total purview; and a leader who can put together the entire strategy (this book is a great start!).

You can think about growing as you prove that this team has the right stuff. If you are convinced that events will be a growth vector for you and you've already run a handful of experiments to prove it, you will need a full-time events manager with some interest in field marketing.

If you are simultaneously building a sales organization, you will need a product marketing manager focused on sales enablement. At this stage, positioning and messaging are still the near-exclusive purviews of the founders, so a PMM that has no issues focusing on building collateral, running launches, and training sales will be an effective addition to your team.

Established organizations

At this point your biggest question will be the degree to which you should organize your developer go-to-market operation as one team. In many companies, a PMM reports directly to product, while developer relations can sometimes report to the CTO or engineering.

Depending on the challenges you're facing, you may want to either maintain a separation of concerns or unify your team. Part of the equation is whether you have a leader in place who can bridge product marketing, marketing, growth, and developer advocacy. This is not an easy role to fill. I do it daily, but it is complicated at scale.

Developer side projects

If you're an organization whose primary business is not developer focused, yet you want to ship an API or service for developers to consume, your best bet is to hire a single developer advocate and give them the task of growing awareness and usage of the product. They will need the full support and awareness of the marketing organization. For example, they may want to attend a meetup and require swag from the marketing team. Or maybe they want to secure speaking slots at conferences, so your comms team might need to approve their speeches quickly.

The bottom line is that a lone developer advocate can get a lot done in these situations, but they will require the understanding and support of their marketing organization to be most effective. (This book makes a great gift for marketing organizations that have a developer side project!)

TYPES OF DEVELOPER RELATIONS TACTICS

As I've said, developer advocates are the heart of your developer marketing team. You must first determine what your overarching goals are as a developer marketing organization before identifying how you will use your developer advocates. This will dictate many of your decisions, including whom you hire and when, what work you prioritize, and of course what you measure.

Growth first, growth forever

With this approach, you are focused on attracting and onboarding new users by demonstrating how your product or platform can solve real-world developer challenges. Advocates create technical content (blogs, videos, tutorials, sample code, and webinars) that showcases the product's capabilities while educating developers. By sharing knowledge and best practices, developer advocates lower the barrier to entry, making it easier for developers to get started with the product. The goal is to engage developers early and often, building a steady stream of new users who can convert into long-term advocates themselves.

The growth approach also leverages metrics to guide and scale outreach. By tracking how developers engage with content, products, and community resources, teams can see which topics, formats, and channels are most effective in driving awareness and adoption. Successful growth tactics require agility; they must adapt to new trends, emerging needs, and developer feedback to stay relevant. This form of advocacy positions the company as a thought leader while keeping the focus on developers' needs, making them more likely to adopt the product and share it within their networks.

Developer advocates are held accountable for growth and revenue metrics. This is my default mode of operation for early-stage startups.

Build the community around the product

With this approach, you will emphasize building a genuine, supportive network around your product or platform. Developer advocates serve as connectors, bringing developers together to share knowledge, solve problems, and grow as a group. They help create spaces for developers to interact, such as forums, Discord channels, meetups, and events, fostering a sense of belonging that encourages long-term loyalty. This approach is about investing in relationships, positioning the developer advocate as the face of the company and a peer within the community.

Authenticity is key to community-focused advocacy. Developer advocates should prioritize transparent, credible engagement, actively helping developers solve issues without overt sales pressure. This is how advocates become trusted voices within the community, which leads to greater brand affinity. The community becomes an asset, as it attracts other developers who see the support and resources available. This self-sustaining ecosystem also serves as a feedback loop for product improvement.

As a community tactic, developer advocates are held accountable for metrics such as Net Promoter Scores. This is my default mode of operation for BigTech companies.

Support engineering and build better products

Here, you are deeply ingrained into the product development life cycle, ensuring that the developer experience is optimized from the ground up. Developer advocates provide direct technical feedback to product teams based on their interactions with the developer community. They identify pain points, usability issues, and feature requests that help engineers refine the product, resulting in a tool or platform that aligns more closely with developers' needs and expectations.

This engineering-focused role requires developer advocates to have strong technical knowledge and an understanding of both the product and the end user. They often work closely with product management and engineering teams to prioritize enhancements that make the product more accessible, flexible, and powerful for developers. By integrating developer feedback into the product roadmap, developer advocates help create a developer-centric product development cycle, where each iteration reflects real-world usage and needs, ultimately resulting in a more compelling and user-friendly product.

As you will see later in this book, I ask all developer advocates to be engineering focused. Still, with this tactic as a controlling idea, developer advocates become accountable for actionable product feedback.

Support sales and drive revenue

Few things in this space are more controversial than employing developer advocates in a sales capacity. Larger organizations will have sales engineers and other presales technical roles to support sales. Smaller organizations may ask developer advocates to guide developers through the buying journey with a focus on educating and empowering rather than hard selling. Developer advocates are uniquely positioned to engage with developers at various stages of their journey—answering technical questions, providing hands-on support, and sharing in-depth knowledge about the product's value in specific-use cases. By positioning themselves as knowledgeable allies, developer advocates help developers overcome technical barriers that might prevent them from advocating for a product within their organization.

In this role, developer advocates act as technical consultants who can bridge the gap between technical users and sales teams. Their insights into both the technical and business aspects of the product help align it with the developer's goals, providing concrete examples and case studies that illustrate how the product fits into larger workflows or solves specific challenges. This advocacy approach doesn't just convert developers into customers; it also sets a foundation for long-term relationships where developers become internal champions, driving adoption within their organizations.

I have been in larger organizations where developer advocates have been co-opted into the sales process. The results can be unpleasant for all involved. Developer advocates are, by nature, brutally honest and direct (like all engineers). Having them participate in sales calls may be more than you bargained for.

We will talk later about ways developer advocates can be useful in the sales process. However, sales leaders need to recognize that even if someone is technical and knows the product well, they still need to be temperamentally suited to be a sales representative.

SUMMARY

Developer marketing is more than just advocacy. It's a holistic go-to-market function for developer-focused products.

- **The Help First principle:** Your primary job is to help developers succeed in their jobs and careers.
- **The four core functions of developer marketing:** These are the areas responsible for bringing developer products to market.
- **Advocacy:** The heart of developer relations. Developer advocates build trust, write content, and engage deeply with the community.
- **Marketing:** The engine of growth. This team focuses on SEO, content programs, campaigns, and digital marketing.
- **Product marketing:** The ringleaders of the circus. They align messaging, positioning, and launch execution.
- **Education:** The backbone of adoption. Documentation, training, and certification programs make onboarding easier.
- **Where to start in different company stages:** Priorities change depending on whether you are in an early-stage startup, a scale-up, or an established company.

Now that we know how to organize our team, let's discuss how to set up its measurement systems.

CHAPTER 3

You Are What You Measure

The modern developer marketing organization is driven by data. In the old days, you could get away with running marketing using key performance indicators (KPIs) that were delayed several days. Today you run marketing using real-time data that enables you to make fast, effective decisions. But getting your organization to a point where you can obtain and act on data in real time can be a challenge.

This book will teach you how to use data to make better decisions about your marketing efforts. Thus, we will focus on building measurement systems first.

THE GOLDEN METRIC

There is only one metric that matters for marketing teams: revenue.

Yes, there are other metrics we can identify and measure. But our mission is to drive revenue. It isn't marketing qualified leads (MQLs) or sales qualified leads (SQLs) or number of sign-ups.

Our first priority is to drive revenue, and our mission as a marketing team is to do everything we can to support sales and bridge the gap between product and the entire go-to-market organization in the service of driving revenue. Pipeline is a function of revenue, but revenue (and revenue growth) is key.

If revenue is down, marketing leaders get fired first, sales leaders get fired soon after, and then everything goes to hell.

Now, with that out of the way, what are the secondary metrics or KPIs that we can measure and manipulate? Let's dive in and look.

DEFINE YOUR MARKETING KPIS

Your marketing KPIs are your leading-indicator metrics that show if you are doing the right things to drive revenue. They'll tell you if your strategies are generating the results you need. While specific KPIs can vary based on the organization, every developer marketing team should measure the following:

Is our work effective in driving awareness of our company?

Awareness is the first step in the funnel. Track unique website visits, social media reach, and engagement rates. Awareness metrics tell you if your messages are reaching developers and resonating.

Is our work effective in driving revenue growth?

Revenue-related KPIs are the ultimate measure of success. They show if your awareness efforts are converting into paying users or customers. Track conversions from developer-focused campaigns, calculate revenue attribution, and understand the downstream impact of every engagement.

How much money do we spend to make money?

Calculating customer acquisition costs (CAC) for developer marketing is critical. Track your CAC per campaign and channel, and monitor the return on each dollar spent. A lower CAC with stable or growing revenue means your team is spending effectively.

Which tactics are most effective at driving these metrics?

Measuring channel and campaign effectiveness is essential to allocating resources where they will make the most impact. Attribution (which I cover in detail later) will help you understand which tactics, from email marketing to content creation, deliver the best ROI.

How is our product perceived in the market?

Mature product lines have large customer bases. If you want to grow your base, it's important to measure how your company or product is perceived; the level of satisfaction customers have not just with your product features, but also with your documentation and marketing tactics; and your customers' willingness to recommend you to others.

THE ACES FRAMEWORK

When I begin to build out metrics for any organization, I break it down into four components:

- **Awareness:** How do you drive awareness of your product or service, and how do you get people to visit your website?
- **Conversion:** How do you turn site visitors into sign-ups or users, and from there, how do you convert them into active users?
- **Expansion:** How do you convince existing customers to use more of your product—more consumption, additional features, complementary products, and so on? How are your company and product perceived?
- **Systems:** What systems do you put in place to measure everything?

BUILDING THE RIGHT MEASUREMENT SYSTEMS

Let's start with systems. To track these KPIs effectively, you'll need robust data-collection systems. In a world of distributed teams and hybrid data flows, your measurement systems should do the following:

1. **Integrate with all major marketing channels and tools:** Ensure your customer relationship management (CRM), analytics platform, email marketing software, social channels, and ad networks work together. If data sources are siloed, you'll only get partial insights. Choose platforms with good API support, or use tools that unify data streams to create a comprehensive view.

2. **Support real-time data ingestion and reporting:** Real-time insights make all the difference. Opt for platforms that provide live dashboards, where you can track campaign performance and react without delay. Regular automated reports are fine for quarterly analysis but inadequate for daily decision making.

3. **Allow for segmentation and attribution:** Knowing overall performance isn't enough. Segmentation by channels, regions, or developer personas will show which tactics work best for each audience. Attribution is the key to understanding your ROI on individual campaigns.

4. **Enable experimentation and learning:** Every new campaign is an opportunity to learn. Your system should support easy A/B testing of messaging, formats, or timing. Record findings and apply them to future efforts. A good measurement system helps you iterate and improve constantly.

5. **Provide a feedback loop for continuous improvement:** Set up a regular review cadence. Make data the basis for every adjustment to strategy, content, or outreach. An effective feedback loop will help you spot trends, correct course, and align your tactics with your objectives.

Tips for integrating data

One of the things I like to do is modify my CRM (e.g., HubSpot or Salesforce) to include a custom field labeled Touchpoints. This field is a multiselect box that allows me to establish which of the following channels a customer used to interact with my company: Webinar, Event, Meetup, Sign-up, and so on. I can then build a cohort analysis of users to identify the most common touchpoints for common behavior. For example, "of all quality sign-ups, what were the most common touchpoints?"

This gives me a high-level understanding of the most effective channels. And of course you can always dive deeper and analyze *which* webinar topics were most associated with certain cohorts.

The other thing I love to do is funnel product-usage data into my CRM. For every developer product, there are some "golden actions" that you want users to take. For example, a database product may want customers to ingest data and run a query. I can build Python scripts to aggregate data in my product-analytics database and sync them to each contact in my CRM.

In doing so I can identify and segment users based on specific actions they took within the product.

> **TIP:** Work with your product team to identify these golden actions. Sometimes, a golden action is something a user does *not* do. For example, you may want to know all users who opened a dialog box but did not complete the action. That gives you some information about what they found interesting in your product and helps you formulate an outreach campaign to show users what they're missing and incentivize them to complete the action.

Finally, make sure that you aggregate data at both an individual level and a team level. You want to know not only if an individual took an action, but also if someone else on their team (or organization) did.

Developer products and services are typically a team sport. Teams of developers work together to create software. As we will see later in the chapter on product-led growth (PLG), team activation is a very important signal to identify and act upon.

Real-time dashboards I like to use

Real-time dashboards allow you to see what's happening across your campaigns at any given moment. Here are some dashboards worth building:

1. **Campaign-performance dashboard:** Identifies whether a given campaign works. Tracks top-line metrics like visits, click-throughs, conversions, and revenue per campaign.
2. **Content-engagement dashboard:** Measures which articles, videos, or social posts perform best. Identifies the source of inbound referrals. Helps you identify what topics resonate most with developers.
3. **Revenue-attribution dashboard:** Maps conversions back to their original touchpoints so you can see which channels are most effective at generating paying customers.
4. **Engagement dashboard by segment:** Breaks down your engagement by developer personas or industry segments to understand how each group interacts with your brand.

For a company with a PLG motion, I typically like to break things down further into personal email (Gmail, Hotmail, etc.) vs. business email.

I also like to segment sign-ups vs. "quality" sign-ups. In this context, a quality sign-up is someone who uses the product within the first seven days of signing up. You will typically see some ratio of sign-ups who do nothing with your product (at least initially). These aren't lost sign-ups—later we will learn techniques for reactivating these users through email marketing and our PLG funnel—but I like to see which users actively use the product vs. those just looking around.

> **TIP:** With developer products, it is very often the case that someone will learn about you, sign up for the product, and mentally file you away for later. They may not have your use case yet, you may not yet have a feature they really need, or the use case you solve may be temporarily deprioritized. But they know you exist, and they want to keep you in mind when they need you. This is where email marketing can really shine. We will talk more about that in later chapters.

Attribution is the holy grail of marketing

Attribution tells you which marketing activities are driving results and connects marketing spend to revenue. In developer marketing, attribution is crucial (and also inordinately difficult) because there are multiple vectors into your product that are difficult to measure.

As I mentioned earlier when we discussed the developer consideration funnel, developers may hear about your product through a number of sources. For example, they could learn about your product via GitHub and your open-source project. They may install your product using a package manager like brew or pip. They may hear about your product in a Reddit discussion or on a random Discord. A delighted customer may be raving about your product in a vertical-specific niche community that you aren't even aware of yet.

When you know where your leads, engagements, and conversions are coming from, you can make informed decisions about budget allocation, messaging, and channel prioritization. With developer products, it's not always easy to know these things. That shouldn't dissuade you from doing the basics though.

Attribution tracking

In general, you want to track attribution for three core areas:

- **Lead generation:** Identify where your leads originate, such as through paid ads, blog posts, social media, or community events. Tag every entry point with UTM parameters or similar tracking codes to gain a granular view of which channels and content pieces drive the highest volume of leads. (We will discuss this more in chapter 4, *Developer Advocacy*.)
- **Content engagement:** Track how users interact with content throughout their journey. Engagement metrics like time on page, downloads, and shares help you determine which content types are most effective. By assigning value to each interaction, you'll better understand which assets contribute most to brand awareness and consideration.
- **Conversions:** Track the final steps developers take before committing, whether that's signing up for a trial, joining a webinar, or downloading a tool. Identify what influenced that action and which earlier touchpoints contributed. This approach highlights high-impact channels and activities.

Attribution in these areas helps clarify where to invest more (or less) effort. It's about identifying the highest-value interactions that move developers down the funnel.

Common attribution models

Several attribution models can help you track this information. Each has its strengths and limitations. Here's a breakdown of the main methods:

1. **First-touch attribution:** Credits the first interaction a developer has with your brand. This method is useful for measuring top-of-funnel activities and can indicate which channels are best for initial awareness. However, it misses the bigger picture of interactions after the first touch.

2. **Last-touch attribution:** Credits the last interaction before a conversion. It's useful when you need to know what drives developers to take the final step, but it ignores all previous interactions, so it won't give you insights into the journey.

3. **Multitouch attribution:** Allocates value across multiple touchpoints in the developer's journey. Here are common variations within multitouch:

   ○ **Linear attribution:** Distributes equal credit across all touchpoints, giving you a broad view but often lacking precision.

   ○ **Time-decay attribution:** Gives more weight to touch-points closer to the conversion, emphasizing the role of more recent interactions.

   ○ **U-shaped attribution:** Splits most of the credit be-tween the first and last touches, with minor credit to middle interactions. This model works well when the first and last interactions are pivotal.

   ○ **W-shaped attribution:** Expands on U-shaped by split-ting credit among three primary touchpoints: first touch, lead conversion, and opportunity creation. This is ideal for longer sales cycles with multiple decisive in-teractions.

4. **Data-driven attribution:** Uses machine learning to assign value to each touchpoint based on historical data. DDA adapts based on what the data suggests, but it requires

significant interaction volume to yield accurate insights and is often available only on advanced platforms.

Each model has its tradeoffs, and you may use various models in different circumstances. Your top-of-funnel marketing activities may be best measured by first-touch attribution models. After all, if a tactic is driving people to your website who consequently sign up, maybe it's worth continuing. Last-touch attribution is useful for tweaking your website. Maybe it's worth studying why a particular web page is resulting in more signups than others. And multitouch attribution is great for predicting the relative quality of leads, especially for complex developer products where your best prospects may spend several different sessions researching your product before deciding to jump in.

If you are collecting the right data, you can apply different attribution models to different circumstances.

Tools for tracking and measuring attribution

Several tools are available to track attribution, from basic to advanced. The marketing-technology (MarTech) space is ever evolving, and newer tools take full advantage of artificial intelligence and machine learning to deliver even more insight. You can get bogged down with analysis paralysis when it comes to your MarTech stack. The time you spend evaluating tools should be directly correlated to the sophistication of your organization. Early-stage startups should just pick HubSpot and move on. Later-stage startups and BigTech organizations will likely need to do a more thorough analysis.

Nevertheless, here are a few options that I have used:

1. **Google Analytics:** Provides free multitouch attribution modeling, allowing you to view channel performance in both first- and last-touch terms. GA also includes data-driven attribution but may lack granularity for very complex funnels.
2. **HubSpot:** Works well for smaller or midsized teams, providing multitouch attribution through CRM data, UTM tags, and engagement metrics. Its reporting is straightforward and integrates well with email and social channels.
3. **Marketo:** Offers advanced attribution tracking and is more suitable for high-touch campaigns. Marketo's attribution modeler lets you assign values across touchpoints and analyze which campaigns are most effective for each stage of the buyer journey.
4. **Salesforce Marketing Cloud:** Useful for advanced B2B attribution. It allows customized attribution models based on lead stages and integrates deeply with Salesforce's CRM. With add-ons, it can support complex, data-driven attribution.
5. **Attribution App:** A modern attribution tool that combines and organizes all customer touchpoints to help you understand which channels work best. It integrates with Salesforce and HubSpot seamlessly.

Each tool has strengths, so select one that aligns with your team's data volume, budget, and technical requirements. In all honesty, I've spent way too many hours of my life fighting attribution tools in a vain attempt to get the insight they claim to give. Your mileage may vary.

When "good enough" is good enough

Perfect attribution is elusive. Multiple touchpoints, device switching, and different lead sources make it nearly impossible to achieve 100 percent accuracy. Developers also tend to decline cookies and trackers when presented with cookie banners. Therefore marketing attribution, especially in developer marketing, is an estimate at best.

Instead of aiming for perfection, focus on what gives you actionable insights. Work with a "good enough" standard. Look for an attribution model that captures your highest-value interactions without overwhelming your team with complexity. If you can see clear trends and know where to invest next, your model is serving its purpose. Achieving *directional guidance* is a far more achievable goal.

The goal of attribution isn't perfection; it's to help you spend wisely, target accurately, and ultimately drive better results.

Continuous testing and learning

Optimization is valuable, but it has a time and place. If your organization is in the early stages, focus on gathering data and building a basic measurement system. Testing at this stage will yield limited insights due to low volume. When you're ready, start small. Run A/B tests for content formats, subject lines, or call-to-action wording. As your volume grows, expand tests to include landing-page layouts, targeting parameters, and multichannel campaigns. Keep a log of what you learn for future campaigns.

MEASURING AWARENESS

Awareness is foundational. You want to measure your reach and mentions on social media; the conversations about you happening on forums, Discords, and Slacks; the number of job descriptions that mention you; the meetups that cover you; and a host of other places where people can talk about you and others can learn about you. Some examples of metrics could include . . .

- mentions on community platforms such as Stack Overflow, Reddit, GitHub, and relevant Discord servers
- impressions and engagement rates on social media platforms
- newsletter mentions and citations in developer-focused blogs
- number of talks at relevant conferences
- mentions in job descriptions

In addition, you'll want to use tools like Google Analytics to evaluate your website traffic and behavior. Key metrics include the following:

- **Traffic sources:** Where are visitors coming from (organic, direct, social, paid)?
- **Bounce rate:** How quickly do visitors leave your site? High bounce rates can signal misaligned messaging or poor site navigation.
- **Page views:** Which pages are most visited? Focus on those and make sure they're optimized.
- **Time on page:** How long do visitors spend on key pages? Track time spent on product or case-study pages as an indicator of engagement.

An important point: we will spend an entire chapter in this book on documentation, because while you may *think* of documentation as part of the *product*, in reality, documentation is going to be your single most important *sign-up vector*. When you take the time to craft exceptional documentation that is both easy to navigate and easy to read, you will help customers envision using your product in their daily flow. And from there, the most interested customers will self-select into one of your calls to action.

Along those lines, I like using tools like Common Room and Koala (and even HubSpot if you're not ready to spend on another tool) to identify site visitors who show the most promise. If a site visitor goes to your homepage, /pricing page, and any page under /docs, then I score the visitor higher than those that do not. With tools like Common Room and Koala, you gain visibility into *who* is on your page (e.g.,

"Jane Doe from Ford Motor Company" or "Anonymous Visitor from Royal Caribbean Cruises"), which can significantly inform your go-to-market motion, regardless of whether the visitor signs up.

Awareness doesn't always correlate with conversion. Indeed, if you are engaging with low-quality sources, you will drive traffic to your site, but that traffic will not convert. Thus these metrics cannot be taken in isolation. You must test tactics that drive awareness, and ensure that your systems can tell you whether those tactics are driving quality traffic.

MEASURING CONVERSION

The goal is to turn your site visitors into sign-ups or users. If awareness is all about getting developers to your site, conversion is all about tuning your site to drive a sign-up.

Looking beyond website metrics, you want to understand what people *do* on your page. Heatmap tools are moderately helpful in identifying which links and buttons are most effective. At some point you will realize that the obvious ones (Try for Free, Request a Demo) are the most effective by far.

Even better, model the flow of visitors across your site to your ultimate CTAs. For developer products, I've typically found that people view the homepage (expect them to scroll, at most, two-thirds of the way through the page); then click on Pricing in your top navigation bar; and finally end up in your docs. Your site may be different, but in my experience, this flow is consistent across our industry.

Use tools like Amplitude, Mixpanel, or even Google Analytics to understand the types of developers who visit your site and the actions they take when they arrive.

As we will discuss in a later chapter on product-led growth (PLG), you'll want to track not just sign-ups but *quality* sign-ups, a metric that tells you who has signed up and actually uses your product. For this reason I also recommend building dashboards that combine both your website metrics and your product metrics, so that you can get a full picture of site visitors, sign-ups, and product activity.

Beyond the product, you should also look for ways to add more "lead magnets" to your site. A lead magnet is a tool that entices a developer to give you their contact information. It could be an ebook (super common, though less popular among developers); an invitation to a webinar or live-coding stream; an open-source tool; or something else you've built that complements your product.

Think about the last time you bought a car. At first you did research online. Then you scheduled test drives. Then you consulted with your partner or a friend. And then you made a decision. There are many touchpoints along the way to the final decision, and giving developers opportunities to raise their hand to ask for and receive information on their journey to a decision is a good thing. We will talk about lead-magnet opportunities in detail in our chapter on content, but stay open to the prospect of adding more than product sign-ups to your repertoire.

MEASURING EXPANSION

Expansion is all about increasing usage among existing customers. You'll want to keep close track of your existing customers and identify those with expansion potential. While this is largely a function of sales and customer-success organizations, as a marketing team you're critical to identifying scenarios and playbooks that turn existing customers into even more successful customers.

You also can identify usage patterns that indicate a user is ready to move up to a higher tier of service. Helping your team understand these patterns, building playbooks with personalized outreach, and coaching/monitoring sales for progress is a crucial part of the marketing role.

In addition, work cross functionally within your organization to set up in-product nudges, referral programs, and customer-success insight that will drive even greater awareness among everyone in the team.

We will cover much of this in later chapters on product marketing and sales-led growth.

WATCH YOUR CAC

Customer acquisition cost (CAC) is a vital measure of efficiency. To calculate CAC for developer marketing, add up all campaign costs, including creative, ad spend, and platform fees, and divide by the number of conversions. Common definitions of CAC focus on per-channel or per-campaign CAC. A good target is to keep your CAC lower than the average revenue per customer. In some cases, you may want to lose money to gain users (this was particularly the case during the zero-interest-rate era in the early 2020s).

What is CAC, and why does it matter?

CAC represents the total cost of acquiring a new customer. It includes all sales and marketing expenses, such as . . .

- advertising spend (Google Ads, LinkedIn, Twitter, etc.)
- creative production costs (videos, tutorials, landing pages)
- salaries and overhead for marketing and sales teams
- event sponsorships, swag, and community-engagement budgets
- software and tools used for marketing automation, CRM, and analytics

CAC is vital because it directly impacts the profitability of your business. A high CAC relative to the average revenue per customer (ARPC) or customer lifetime value (LTV) can indicate inefficiency, while a low CAC can signal strong ROI and scalability.

How to calculate CAC

To calculate CAC, use the following formula:

$$CAC = \frac{Total\ Sales\ and\ Marketing\ Costs}{Number\ of\ New\ Customers\ Acquired}$$

For example, if you want to analyze your CAC for a quarter and you spent $100,000 on marketing and sales and acquired 500 new customers, here's the formula:

$$CAC = \frac{\$100,000}{500} = \$200 \, per \, customer$$

If your customer's average lifetime value (LTV) is over $200, you're in the black and in good shape. If you're spending $200 per customer and their LTV is below $200, you're losing money. If that wasn't your intention, you need to adjust your marketing tactics to be more cost-efficient.

An ideal CAC-to-revenue ratio is around 1:3, but this varies by industry.

Segmenting CAC for developer marketing

In developer-focused businesses, CAC varies significantly across acquisition channels and customer segments. Breaking down CAC by these dimensions provides actionable insights:

> **Per-channel CAC:** Measure CAC across individual channels like paid ads, webinars, content marketing, or sponsorships. Example: LinkedIn ads might generate 50 customers at a CAC of $400, while organic blog traffic might generate 200 customers at a CAC of $50.

> **Per-campaign CAC:** Analyze specific campaigns (e.g., "Q3 Webinar Series") to assess their effectiveness. Include all associated costs, such as design, promotion, and hosting.

> **Segment-specific CAC:** Developer segments (e.g., front-end vs. back-end) or organizational segments (e.g., small-medium businesses vs. enterprises) may have differing CACs. Enterprise customers may have a higher CAC but offer greater LTV, justifying the investment.

Strategies to optimize CAC

Here are some time-tested ideas for adjusting tactics and improving your CAC:

- **Focus on high-intent channels:** Prioritize channels with a proven track record of high-quality leads, such as SEO; developer communities (e.g., Stack Overflow, GitHub); and industry newsletters. Make sure you're measuring everything so that you can identify which of these channels is most effective for you. Discard low-performing ones with prejudice.
- **Leverage product-led growth:** Use free trials or freemium models to encourage organic adoption, reducing reliance on costly outbound or paid acquisition strategies. See the chapters on PLG and SLG for more information. We'll discuss the pros and cons of free vs. free trial later in this book as well.
- **Enhance targeting and segmentation:** Use tools like Clearbit, LinkedIn, or Common Room to build highly targeted lists and minimize wasted ad spend.
- **Improve conversion rates:** Optimize your landing pages, documentation, and onboarding flows to turn more visitors into active users, effectively lowering CAC. You're already spending money getting people to your site. Now make sure they're converting.
- **Track attribution more accurately:** Implement multi-touch attribution to better understand which channels and touchpoints are driving conversions, ensuring you're investing in the right areas. Be careful not to go overboard with it though!
- **Incentivize referrals:** Build referral programs that encourage current users to bring in new customers, reducing acquisition costs while leveraging social proof.

BUILDING TRACKING SYSTEMS FOR DEVELOPER PRODUCTS

So far we've covered a number of concepts related to what data to collect and what to do with that data. Now let's talk about how to collect data. This is another area that changes frequently as new products and features come to market. I encourage everyone to ask questions in forums. In general, however, there are a few concepts worth covering that transcend technology.

Developers do not like tracking

It's important to correctly and consistently ask developers for consent before using analytics tools. The GDPR cookie dialog is something that many developers take seriously. Not only do they take it seriously, but they also have the wherewithal to determine if you are implementing it correctly.

I like to set up server-side Google Tag Manager (GTM), in which I add all third-party data trackers, such as Google Ads, Meta, and LinkedIn tracking pixels; heatmap tools; and so on. If you want to add a new tracking tool, you simply go into the GTM interface and configure it. You don't need to go back to your development team. Implementing GTM on the server side offers maximum resistance to ad blockers, and it's great for products that have heavy server-side workflows.

> **TIP:** As we will discuss later, technical SEO is important. Technical SEO includes site performance. The more trackers you add to GTM, the slower your site will be. Keep a close eye on your technical SEO performance as you add new tracking tools to GTM.

Customer data platforms, the developer way

A customer data platform (CDP) enables you to systematically track events that customers take in your application. You can collect data anonymously before a customer identifies themselves. Then, once they do identify themselves by signing up for a product, logging in to your product using an existing account, filling out a form, and so on, you can merge the anonymous data with the identified data. With CDPs, you can collect standard actions like pages visited and buttons clicked, but also custom actions like "created a workspace," "ingested data," or "called an API."

With developer products, some of these actions will happen in the web or mobile version of your product. That's pretty standard in terms of tracking scripts. Where things get dicey is when you add a command-line interface or APIs to your application. Now you have logged-in users taking actions in your product outside the context of a web page or mobile application. This is why I recommend server-side tracking in addition to more traditional client-side tracking.

> **TIP:** A consistent theme throughout this book is collaboration across roles. Marketing working with sales, marketing working with customer success, and especially marketing working with product and engineering. When it comes to server-side tracking, it is essential that marketing works in concert with product and engineering to devise and implement the CDP properly.

Also, with a CDP you can route tracking information to multiple downstream systems. In other words, you collect once and consistently, route anywhere and consistently. As such, CDPs are your most important first-party behavioral analytics, and you typically want to funnel all tracking activity through it.

Most CDPs are priced for consumer products or typical B2B SaaS products. They aren't usually priced favorably for developer products, which tend to generate many events, all of which you probably want to track. I've used and like Rudderstack, a well-priced CDP that is great for developer-focused products. But be aware: Rudderstack doesn't include a data warehouse. You'll need to supply your own data storage. That may not be a bad thing. I prefer working directly with a database and writing my own SQL queries, and I suspect most technical people do as well.

How to use tracking data effectively

One fantastic thing about using a CDP to consistently track and store data is that regardless of where developers engage with your website and your product, the CDP can merge the data. For example, if a developer first visits your website on their mobile phone and submits a form to sign up for a webinar, they've identified themselves. Later, if they come to your website and sign up for the product, they've once again identified themselves, and the CDP unifies the two profiles in its tracking database.

Ultimately, by tracking this information, you will gain a complete view of your customer, and be able to segment them into cohorts, such as "Customers who registered but did nothing," "Customers who were active but no longer are," "Customers who are using legacy features but haven't touched any feature released in the last six months," and so on. With this information, you can build personalized email outreach and ad campaigns.

There are a number of CDPs to choose from, and it's worth starting by building your tracking plan (a spreadsheet that lists all the actions you want to track); estimating the number of events and size of data warehouse you'll need; and then finding the right product with the right price. The good news is that the tracking scripts you install on your site and in your product are all pretty much standardized now.

Once you have a tracking plan, it's important to think about a data-storage plan. Data will flow through your CDP or analytics stack from multiple sources. It's important that this data ends up not only in destinations where action can be taken, but also in a central repository where all of it can be combined. Magical things happen when you can see website metrics and product analytics together.

> **TIP:** Don't be afraid of SQL! You should be very comfortable with all your data flowing into a database such as ClickHouse or Postgres so that you can run your own sophisticated queries. I often implore founders to hire "reformed developers" to their marketing team. Take the time to learn the basics of SQL and learn how to use LLMs to turn your basic skills into black belt skills.

Using AI to measure intent signals

As this tracking data is stored, you'll want to act on what you learn. You can score sign-ups based on intent information. For example, users may bounce right away. They may click on the Pricing page (usually a good sign); they may dive into your Products page (another good sign); or they may visit your documentation (an excellent sign). In all these instances, they are signaling to you how serious they are about learning more about your product.

In the past, lead scoring was rudimentary—what pages were viewed, what actions were taken in the product, and so on. Now you can use AI to create models that predict future performance based on past results.

There are several tools that are useful in this context. Koala is wonderful for turning intent signals into actions for your sales team. Common Room can combine intent signals on your website with (inferred) data about what that user is doing on Reddit, GitHub, and other platforms, to add more detail for sales.

You can work closely with your sales development representative (SDR) team to build "plays" (prescriptive guidance) they can run based on the intent signals that have been accumulated and the subsequent priority assigned to leads.

A USE CASE FOR METRICS

Let's pull it all together and examine how to use these metrics. This is a real-world-use case based on a startup I worked with recently. This startup has a developer API for which they would like to drive greater usage. They believe that when their users customize their product and integrate with their existing workflow and tools, the product will be stickier and it will more easily drive expansion. This startup has a product-led growth model (we will discuss PLG in a later chapter).

This startup sees thousands of sign-ups per month for its API, but only a fraction of those users actively engage with the API in a meaningful way.

Through their activation and engagement dashboard, they can see the following metrics:

- **Sign-up trends:** Total sign-ups per day/week/month.
- **Quality sign-ups:** Sign-ups that perform a key "golden action" within the first seven days (e.g., deploying an API request, executing a query, or setting up a workspace).
- **Drop-off analysis:** Where users abandon the onboarding flow.
- **Feature engagement:** Which core features are used most in the first seven days.
- **Cohort retention:** How many sign-ups return to use the product in week two, week four, and beyond.
- **Source attribution:** Which marketing channels (SEO, social, events, partnerships) bring in the most-engaged users.

In this dashboard, we are able to see these trends:

- Nearly 73 percent of sign-ups dropped off before completing their first successful API request.
- Users coming from paid ads had a much, much lower activation rate than those coming from organic channels.
- Users who activated as a result of an email campaign to existing users or sign-ups were more likely to use the API.

- When we dove into the product analytics, we saw that the most common point of drop-off in the onboarding flow was in generating the private key for the API. The product was built in a way that the private key was shown only once, and if the user wanted to see it again, they had to reset the project and generate a new key (an overly zealous antipattern for security, if you ask me).
- The most commonly visited page in documentation was related to resetting an API key.

We took this data and made a few changes:

- We shifted money away from paid ads to organic. We saw a similar correlation between low-quality users and paid ads elsewhere in the product. It became obvious that while paid ads were generating sign-ups, they weren't high quality. We documented our findings, and the startup will revisit this information in a couple of years when they layer in a sales-led motion to their go-to-market strategy.
- We optimized the onboarding flow and made changes to the product to make it easier to generate and re-obtain the private API key.
- We doubled down on our email campaign to existing users, choosing to showcase not only the existence of the API but also customer scenarios where the API would be useful.
- We included an email about the API in the post-sign-up onboarding drip campaign.

These are the kinds of well-informed changes you can make if you're collecting the right data and have the means to bring all the data together quickly across numerous sources.

THINKING AHEAD TO AI AGENTS

AI agents are autonomous software programs that can perceive their environment, make decisions, and take actions to achieve specific goals. Unlike simple scripts or rules-based systems, agents are designed to handle complex workflows, adapt to new information, and collaborate with other agents or humans to complete multistep tasks.

In a marketing context, you could use an AI agent to continuously monitor multiple data sources, including customer call transcripts, product usage data, customer CRM records, support tickets, and even email or meeting logs. You'd then use that data to identify users or accounts that show strong signals for upsell. For example, an agent might notice that a particular customer has activated new features, exceeded usage thresholds, or recently engaged with documentation related to premium capabilities. It could then enrich that signal with firmographic data from Clearbit or similar, score the account's propensity to buy using historical conversion data, and automatically notify a customer success manager via Slack or create a task in Salesforce.

AI agents won't replace your team, but they will run 24/7, combining data that lives in silos and proactively suggesting actions that drive revenue. For the marketing teams who figure this out early, the leverage will be enormous.

SUMMARY

In this chapter, we established the core principle of modern developer marketing: you are what you measure. Successful developer marketing is built on data, and the ability to measure impact in real time is critical.

- **Revenue is the ultimate metric.** Everything marketing does should tie back to revenue growth, either directly or through leading indicators.
- **Define clear KPIs.** Every developer marketing organization should track awareness, conversion, expansion, and systems (ACES framework).
- **Build strong measurement systems.** Integrate analytics across all marketing and product touchpoints to ensure visibility into what works and what doesn't.
- **Leverage dashboards for decision making.** Real-time insights allow teams to identify bottlenecks and correct course before problems escalate.
- **Attribution is critical but imperfect.** While it's difficult to track every developer touchpoint, investing in attribution models provides valuable directional insight.
- **Data should drive continuous improvement.** Every campaign, content piece, and engagement should be evaluated for its impact, leading to constant iteration and optimization.

With a strong foundation in data-driven decision making, the next step is structuring your developer relations team to execute on these insights effectively. In the next chapter, we will dive into how to build a DevRel organization that not only drives engagement but also translates developer interest into long-term growth.

CHAPTER 4

Developer Advocacy

Developer advocacy (once referred to as developer evangelists, and these days sometimes referred to as DevRel) is the tip of the spear in terms of customer engagement. A developer advocate's mission is to **show developers a vision of their world with your product in it**. To do so, they should identify problems in our industry and provide solutions, assuring customers that using your product will help them work better, faster, and more efficiently.

THE TIP OF THE SPEAR

Developer advocates are responsible for teaching people the myriad possibilities that come from using your product or service. Ideally they have a showman's mind—they can take dull technical products and turn them into magical wonderlands. They can write prose and write code. And they love to shmooze, online and IRL. Developer advocates have the best job in the industry, albeit one that often struggles to garner the respect it deserves. Most startup founders and BigTech leaders have no idea how to manage them or recognize one with talent. Let's start by demystifying what they do.

WHAT DO DEVELOPER ADVOCATES DO?

I organize developer advocacy around four specific areas. That's not to say that any individual does or does not do all four. Commonly, some developer advocates specialize in one or two areas over others. That's OK, and it helps you build a well-rounded team (and it also helps you sift through the developer advocate job title to identify who is the best fit for your organization at any given time).

So view these core areas as functions you want to establish in your go-to-market motion:

1. capture and represent product feedback
2. build credible and authentic content that offers value to technical audiences
3. connect and build relationships with community leaders
4. attend and speak at events

Let's read a little bit about each of these areas first, and in the following chapters we will dive into each topic in more detail.

Capture and represent product feedback

The core definition of developer advocacy mandates that we spend time with prospective communities or customers to get them excited to try (and adopt) a product, and really good developer advocates have a strong idea of how well those prospective customers receive the product. Great developer advocates are expert observers and connectors: they earn the trust of engineering teams by crisply summarizing customer feedback, explicit and implicit—and then use their solid reputation and credible technical arguments to drive action within their organization.

In the process of building content and engaging with the community, developer advocates also see the full capabilities of the product "from left to right." An engineer on the team may be more deeply knowledgeable about a specific area of the product, but they also rarely have a need to pop up and build something with the entire surface area of the product. As a consequence, it's natural for the product to have inconsistencies in a scenario that involves using multiple functional areas simultaneously or in rapid succession. Developer advocates identify these "warts" quickly, either by building demos of common user scenarios or by meeting customers who have feedback to share.

Synthesizing this feedback and relaying it to the product team in a constructive manner on a regular basis is a core job requirement for developer advocacy. Companies like Stripe, Vercel, and OpenAI have elevated this priority to an art form with their developer experience engineers.

Build credible and authentic content that offers value to technical audiences

Some developer advocacy teams are also responsible for product documentation, which is advisable, particularly at early-stage companies. Your docs should represent the spine of your growth strategy. You may have the most beautiful website, but developers will quickly scan the homepage and search for "docs" or "developers" in the top-nav. To the chagrin of many traditional marketers, they'll bypass white papers and opportunities to sign up for a webinar and head straight to your docs. Your docs *must* be informative, entertaining, and comprehensive. If they're great, they can cover up paper cuts in your product. If they're excellent, your docs can turn a skeptical developer into a fan. You want your docs to spark the imagination of your developers and keep them coming back for more. It's not just API references and introductions to core concepts. It's also fun tutorials that fire up the creative impulses of your customers.

Simply put, get your docs right. We will talk a lot more about docs in a later chapter.

Beyond docs, developer advocacy teams should build fun and engaging content that reaches new customers, gets them excited to use a platform, and guides them through specific scenarios. Note the word *guide*: the prospective customer should not only feel a sense of accomplishment with the product, but understand how the product will apply to their projects or use case. Often this content reflects deep knowledge of the community or the types of developers that the product aims to recruit. Kathy Sierra does a great job discussing this concept—and many others—in her book *Badass: Making Users Awesome.*

Typically you want a good mix of first-party hosted content (product docs, company blogs, etc.) and third-party content (Twitch livecoding streams, videos on YouTube, nonsponsored articles on DZone, Smashing Magazine, and so on). Third-party content always includes liberal links to first-party content (your docs and tutorials). You want to entice and motivate people to learn more and give them the ability to do so by clicking through to detailed technical guidance. This is a big reason why it's so important that your docs are stellar: you drive developers to them through everything you do.

For example, when posting on social media, use animated GIFs of your product in action with links to tech docs for developers to explore themselves (this is different from social media advertising, which is pure marketing and where you'd use campaign landing pages).

Developer advocates shouldn't be the only ones creating content though. Even if you're a startup, it is a much better use of time and money for your top engineers to author quality content alongside your developer advocacy team and earn your way into top publications.

Good content is important. Your content must be technical and helpful, of course. But breaking through the din of content requires more.

Great content is a reflection of your personal brand. You can do all the SEO and organic-discovery tricks in the book. But the difference between consistently good and consistently effective content is how often people seek out your opinions and authority.

Thus, while all developer advocates build good content, great developer advocates build their reputation, and through their reputation, their content becomes sought-after.

Connect and build relationships with community leaders

You aim to focus on long-term, collaborative, and technically credible activities. In other words, things that will develop over time involve a good deal of mutually beneficial technical discussion and are rooted in code.

Much of what we used to think of as "community engagement" revolved around meetups. Of course, community development is a lot more than buying pizza and giving talks. Spending time with like-minded enthusiasts helped us stay abreast of the latest thinking from community and product leaders, as well as the latest use cases from developers.

Today communities exist everywhere. From private Slacks and Discords, to hashtags on Twitter, to large YouTube followings, to email lists (what's old is new again!). Identifying the communities most critical to your product is the first step.

You have to earn your way into a community. The way I've always done this is to join one and lurk for a while, learning the culture and common questions. I'll then author content to answer the most common questions. In those content pieces, I take the time to research the background behind the question. Why has a particular issue persisted, version over version, for a product? Often there's a good reason, with reasonable trade-offs. Providing that background is important. Later, when an opportunity organically arises, I'll jump in and answer questions, providing links to resources that provide more background on the answer.

Here are a few additional ideas:

- Partner with your internal engineering team and contribute to open-source projects of the community leaders you admire and with whom you would like to build relationships.
- Support meetups or start some of your own.
- Create working specs for future products or services and share them publicly for collaborative feedback. "Developing and designing in the open" has tremendous benefits for both product design and community development.

Be authentic friends to your community. Adam Grant wrote wonderfully about this in his book *Give and Take*.

As we've discussed, the fundamental frame of the developer advocacy role is to engage with communities and get people excited about using your product, service, or project. You should never ever do fly-by-night activities or marketing tactics with these folks: Don't ask them to tweet something for you, don't ask them for a quote in your press release, don't ask them to endorse your product in exchange for a fee. These shortsighted approaches are inauthentic and will do far more damage than good. Mary Thengvall wrote an excellent blog post on this topic as well as a book, *The Business Value of Developer Relations.*

Attend and speak at events

This tends to be the most glamorous part of the job, and I always intentionally put it last.

I've worked at companies big and small, and there's always a reckoning with management over the cost of events. Whether your management is free spending (lead acquisition at all costs) or errs on the side of frugality doesn't matter. At the end of the day, justifying the expense of sponsorship, travel and entertainment, and time out of the office is always hard.

The first thing I would say is to take stock of all the events you believe are worth speaking at. If you're a remote-first team with employees around the globe, you'll likely be able to take on more events, since the cost will probably be less. Depending on your circumstances, some combination of time, resources, and cost will factor into which events make the cut for you.

From there, ask yourself whether you want to be in the sponsorship game. If your marketing team elects to sponsor booths and maintain a physical presence at events, more power to them.

More important than booths for developer advocacy is the opportunity to speak. Crafting CFPs is an art form, and we will talk about that in more detail shortly. Submit CFPs liberally. There's nothing like working on a talk to really make sure you know your stuff!

But here's the important part: **Write the talk no matter what!** That's right, whether you win the CFP or not, write the talk!

And don't just write the talk.

Write the blog post or white paper to go with the talk. Build the docs, write the sample code. Host a landing page dedicated to the event. There's no point in getting on stage if you don't have resources to point people to as a follow-up so that they can do everything you did on stage and continue to learn and engage with your company.

And record a video of you giving the talk! (Don't post it yet, though . . . Some conferences only want original material. You can post it after your talk is done.)

Now when you speak at the conference, you'll have two assets, a blog post / white paper and a video, to point your audience to. That's a very powerful call to action for someone who was intrigued by your abstract and sat through your talk in its entirety.

MEASURING DEVELOPER ADVOCACY

Measuring your work is important. Let's face it: not every company understands the role of developer relations. I'm not going to belabor the point, but in lean times demonstrating your value to the organization has merit. At the same time, measuring what matters gives you room to experiment, improve, and scale your efforts.

Metrics that matter

Each of the four areas of developer advocacy—product feedback, content, community engagement, and events—can be measured. And just as there are best practices for the tactics themselves, there are some guiding principles and best practices for how we measure each tactic.

Whenever I look to define metrics, I start by asking myself what success looks like in each of the four core areas:

1. **Capturing and representing customer feedback**
   - Developer relations feedback is accepted and considered valid by the product team.
   - Developer relations feedback is prioritized by the product team.
   - Developer relations feedback is acted upon by the product team.

2. **Building great content**
   - Developer relations content reaches lots of new customers.
   - New customers touched by the content activate the product at a higher rate than the control.
   - New customers touched by the content consume more of or spend more money on the product than the control.
   - Existing customers return to our docs.
3. **Connecting with community leaders**
   - The number of first-time and repeat attendees to virtual meetups is growing.
   - Community leaders welcome developer relations contributions to their open-source projects.
   - Community leaders provide feedback on products or services.
4. **Attending and speaking at events**
   - For physical events, you can measure booth traffic and lead acquisition, as well as activity based on attendance at your talks.
   - For virtual events, apply classic TV metrics such as number of viewers, time spent watching, most popular section, and so on.

One of the things that attracted me to developer relations thirty years ago was that it was a great opportunity to exercise the creative aspects of my personality (I was a drama major and a screenwriter when I was younger) with my more mathematical and algorithmic side (I was also a computer science major).

You are what you choose to measure, as the axiom goes. And one of the things I would not want to do is subtract the creative aspects of the job. With that in mind, we want to minimize process, maximize insight, and retain creativity.

Measuring feedback

With customer feedback, if your developer relations team uses the same task management service as the engineering team (they should!), then you can run queries on their submissions and determine if those submissions meet your criteria for success:

- number of bug reports submitted and accepted
- number of customer-feature requests considered

Ultimately you're looking to answer two questions: Is high-quality feedback being contributed to the product team? Does the developer advocate have sufficient rapport with members of the product team to ensure that their feedback is considered seriously?

Measuring content

I measure content and event impact in very similar ways—and my approach requires knowledge about basic web-measurement techniques: URL query parameters.

What you're trying to do is append any link to your site (domains you control/own) with a tracking code, so you can see how many people arrived at your site as a result of a given activity, determine which channel is most effective at driving growth and adoption, and invest your time and resources in the highest-performing tactics.

It's important to note that this strategy does not associate visitors with any personally identifiable information—it merely allows you to see anonymous individuals' traffic and engagement.

Today, the best marketing people are quasi-data scientists who run queries to identify which routes to product sign-up and usage are the best. When developer relations does this, it opens up a whole world of nerdy growth hacking, given the loop between producing content and measuring efficacy is tightly contained within one person or team in the organization.

You can use any tool or parameter structure for your tracking codes. The key is to have flexibility, so that you can see instances of tactics, not just the tactic itself. In this example, we'll use the Google UTM format (via Google Campaign URL Builder). The important thing is to adopt a standard, consistent schema, so that you can run queries later to determine the efficacy of general tactics; specific pieces of content, publications, or events; and even specific team members.

As a refresher, Google UTM links consist of three primary fields, and while they are frequently used by marketing people, we can easily adapt it for developer relations' purposes.

For each of the three primary fields, I've listed a schema I suggest for developer relations:

- **utm_source**—the precise content that's referring traffic (where you're using the link).
  - These are specific, like the actual name of an event or session ("event-session-year"); piece of content ("title-of-blog-post-authorname"); publication ("partnername-blog"); podcast ("name-of-podcast"); organic social media ("companyname"); paid promotion on social media ("companyname-paid").
- **utm_medium**—the type of content/distribution channel that's referring traffic (what you're publishing or sharing the link via)
  - blog
  - email
  - event
  - website
  - YouTube
  - Twitter
  - LinkedIn
  - Reddit
- **utm_campaign**—the larger campaign or initiative
  - This includes things like new releases ("1-1-release"); major projects ("amazing-feature-launch"); or events ("aws-reinvent-2023").

Let's talk for a moment about how content flows to your site. Let's say you write an article about using GraphQL with PostgreSQL and you post it to the DEV community. Within the article, you link to your product documentation. You would append the following UTM parameters:

- utm_source: graphql-article-authorname
- utm_medium: blog
- utm_campaign: dev-community

These parameters allow you to filter visitors based on what led them to your site and, depending on your website and product-analytics tooling, actions they took on your properties. That way you can look at your signed-up users and see which inbound tracking codes may have led them to your site (in, say, the last ninety days). It's impossible to identify causality in a world where a customer may interact with you in multiple ways before deciding to sign up (so-called multitouch attribution). But you can identify correlation and take note of which tactics are most commonly present in your recent customer sign-ups (or any customer cohort you define).

One thing you may want to consider is having one or two people in your team manage these UTM parameters. You want to be consistent in how you use them so that you can analyze the aggregate data effectively.

Measuring community

In community engagement, the highest priority is authenticity. The second-highest priority is being helpful. I'm a firm believer that engaging with community leaders (and others in the communities of importance to you) cannot be driven by a quid pro quo.

You can't expect anything in return.

If you show up with an authentic desire to learn and help, you will do your job. If you try to associate the time you spend in the community with sales or other metrics, it can lead you away from an authentic desire to learn and help and instead down a path of self-centered desire to grow your business.

There are many ways in which developer advocates engage with the community. In a later chapter we will dive into influencer marketing in particular. We will see how developer influencers can amplify our marketing efforts and how we can measure the impact of working with them.

Measuring events

Events are slightly more complicated. Often, events in which you participate as a speaker or attendee are hosted by third parties.

If you're hosting a booth or other form of physical presence at the event, you'll probably measure booth traffic, leads captured, meetings booked, and opportunities created. (We will discuss this in detail in a later chapter.)

If you're giving a talk, you need to get creative. Earlier, I talked about turning an event talk into multiple pieces of content: blog posts, white papers, videos, live streams, whatever it takes. Reuse the effort you put into creating your talk.

Then, during your talk, reference your related content. For example, "I wrote a blog post on this topic if you'd like to read more."

I like to use a link shortener (such as Bitly, or a branded one like Dub.co) coupled with the aforementioned UTM parameters so that I can drive traffic to my website along with the correct attribution. In this case, utm_source would be title-of-talk-speakername, utm_medium would be event, and utm_campaign would be conference-name-2023.

The measurement won't be precise. Many people in the audience may be on their phones when they first check out your shortlink, and that won't necessarily follow them if they check it out later when they're at their desk. But you'll at least be able to see how many people were plugged in to your talk and sufficiently interested to visit your content.

Pulling it all together

Once you and your team append tracking codes to all your links inbound to your product or service, you can begin to run queries using your favorite analytics tool. Here are some questions I like to ask:

- How many new sign-ups is developer relations driving overall? What activities are driving the majority?
- Are Twitch live-coding streams more effective at driving traffic or netting new visitors than webinars?
- Which third-party sites are most effective at driving new users?
- Which types of content are most effective at driving new users?
- Is Sally better at events or content?

You'll definitely want to create a dashboard so that everyone on your team can quickly slice and dice this data to get insights on what is working. One of my core management principles is to eliminate all forms of information asymmetry in an organization. To that end, I'm also a big believer that all dashboards should be shared broadly in an organization.

Measuring developer advocates

So far we've spoken about measuring the output of developer advocacy itself. But is this a useful proxy for measuring the efficacy of a developer advocate as well?

It depends.

I believe metrics give you part of the picture. But beyond metrics, the biggest thing I look for in developer advocates is whether they're listening to customers in a way that shapes their work. Are they publishing content and looking to see how it's received? Are they adjusting their approach constantly to identify what works, or are they blindly following a preordained path?

The measurement tools I've described here are guidelines more than a checklist. Use these tools to help you formulate a go-to-market plan that is highly responsive to customer needs.

For the bulk of my thirty-plus years in developer relations and developer marketing, measuring content, events, and community activities has been extraordinarily difficult. Developer relations has always seemed like an ambiguous role, and I've certainly been part of organizations for whom developers were the third- or fourth-most important constituency. Even though I would strongly advise developer relations professionals who are job hunting to select organizations that prioritize developers, it's likely that no matter how much importance an organization places on developers, they'll need to justify their existence, so to speak.

A concerted effort around measuring what matters will enable you to focus your efforts on building and growing a community around your product and demonstrate quantifiable impact.

SUMMARY

Developer advocacy is the tip of the spear for developer engagement.

- **What do developer advocates do?** They inspire, teach, and connect with developers in authentic and meaningful ways.
  - ○ **Capture and represent product feedback about the developer experience.** Advocates gather unfiltered insights from developers and push them into product teams.
  - ○ **Build credible and authentic content.** Advocates should create valuable resources, not just product pitches.
  - ○ **Connect and build relationships.** Advocates engage deeply with communities and influencers to foster trust and credibility.
  - ○ **Attend and speak at events.** Being present in developer ecosystems is critical to advocacy success.
- **Measuring developer advocacy:** Metrics should focus on feedback, content impact, community engagement, and event effectiveness.
- **Telling the story of the product through demos:** Writing good demos is table stakes for developer marketing teams. A good demo tells a story and highlights the real-world impact of your product.

Over many years of hiring and coaching developer advocates, I've only rarely found an individual who excels at all four categories of activities. It's OK to specialize. Some people are exceptional community connectors who love to speak at events. Others are content factories who love to churn out blog posts and videos. Always look for people who can deliver great demos. Hopefully you'll be able to identify which category fits your personality best.

What matters most is that you are measuring output and experimenting to find the right mix for your business.

Now let's dive into what makes great content.

CHAPTER 5

Building Great Developer Content

Content marketing works.

It's the best bang for your buck in terms of developer marketing. If you build a reputation for producing excellent technical content for developers, you will largely solve your brand, awareness, and growth woes. People will seek out your opinion because you are technically deep, humble in how you teach, and prolific in understanding and addressing developer needs in real time.

THE DEVELOPER CONSIDERATION FUNNEL AND CONTENT

Developers arrive at your website in various stages of readiness to consider your product. Traditionally, we have referred to this as upper, middle, and lower funnel, and each stage requires different content to push the prospect further along the path to adoption.

- **Upper funnel:** These developers are conducting broad research, often without a specific problem or solution in mind. They might stumble across your content through a blog post shared on Hacker News, a tweet, or a recommendation in a community forum. They are generally looking to broaden their knowledge. They have a low propensity for converting into users, though they may sign up and file you away for later (a concept we will explore when we discuss sales enablement).
- **Middle funnel:** These developers have a specific problem and are researching solutions. They can be influenced by targeted content that defines the problem and explores solutions, including the history of solutions that may have partially addressed the problem in the past.
- **Bottom funnel:** These developers are ready to make a purchase decision and are actively evaluating products.

While this remains a good framework for content development and seems logical, the modern developer consideration framework is less a funnel and more a series of seemingly random steps toward building closer affinity to your brand. A customer may start by seeing a mention of you on Hacker News, then coming to your website, then visiting a subreddit where you are mentioned several weeks later, then finally coming up with a project idea for which your product could be valuable, and eventually signing up.

Think about how you bought your last car. You may have seen one like it parked outside. Then maybe you watched some YouTube reviews from unaffiliated creators. Then perhaps you visited the company's website. Then maybe you asked some friends (or an Uber driver!) who also owned that car. And finally, after weeks of consideration, you went back to the company website and configured a car before visiting a dealership to schedule a test drive.

All this is to say that it has never been more important to be everywhere at once. You need to produce a dizzying amount of content that meets developers where they are, given what they're in the mood to do (research, try a demo, read a white paper, etc.). Different types of content can improve results across the stages of the consideration funnel.

THE TYPES OF DEVELOPER CONTENT THAT WORK

Let's focus on the varieties of developer content you may be tempted to produce, and how best to use them. I would never tell you that something will never work. For example, many developer relations leaders believe webinars are a waste of time, but many a developer-focused company has built a very strong webinar-based growth engine.

The truth is, if you decide as an organization to put your energy behind and commit fully to any one of these types of content, you will probably find at least some modicum of success.

The best advice I can give is to measure everything and use the data to recognize when it's time to cycle off of one form of content and onto another. What got you here may not be what gets you to the next stage. You'll know it's time to move on when the performance velocity (e.g., leads, web traffic, click-throughs) starts to level off for two to three consecutive months. Holding on too long is often a mortal sin. Whereas, if you abandon a tactic too early, you can always come back to it with a fresh perspective and pick up where you left off. So when it comes down to it, skew toward embracing new perspectives and approaches. As I like to say, **value innovation over tradition.**

Here are the types of developer content that I like to produce:

1. blog posts
2. benchmarks and side-by-side comparisons
3. tutorials and how-to content
4. microsites
5. calculators, templates, and other lead-generation tools
6. programmatic SEO
7. video
8. infographics and interactive content
9. checklists and listicles
10. case studies, case study videos, and customer interviews
11. white papers
12. ebooks
13. courses
14. webinars
15. podcasts and streaming shows
16. swag

Let's dive into each of these.

First: Inside out vs. outside in

You'll have the opportunity to create two kinds of content. The first is what I call inside out. Inside-out content is about you and your products. This content is of interest to a very narrow portion of the population—effectively, the folks who are already in your camp. Inside-out content includes launch posts, changelogs, video tutorials, documentation, and other material related to your product.

Outside-in content takes matters of great interest to developers in your target market and provides historical context, summarization of the problem, discussion of solutions and alternatives, and ultimately information about what products or services you provide to address the matter.

Outside-in content will (hopefully) drive leads, while inside-out content will drive conversion and customer satisfaction. They're both great, but for content marketing I'm mainly going to focus on outside-in content. We will cover inside-out content in our chapter on documentation and in our subsequent chapter on product marketing.

Second: Be audacious

In his exceptional book *Audacious*, Mark Schaefer posits that while artificial intelligence can handle many routine (and rote) tasks, it takes human creativity—what he terms "audaciousness"—to stand out from the din of petabytes of AI-driven slop across the internet. He uses many examples to drive home the point, and I highly recommend reading his book as a companion to this one. Using the tactics described in this book alongside a genuinely audacious and creative marketing strategy can elevate any developer marketing game.

For example, Supabase is the master of memes. Their presence on social media transcends boring corporate speech and elevates their brand to one that is shared and discussed often in developer circles. The AI accounting company Digits used creative billboards and bus ads in San Francisco to drive attention and sharing by the extremely online crowd. Vercel delivers a brand that is almost luxurious, oozing quality from their website to their product. Their Next.js conference is one of the best developer conferences around today.

You cannot embrace audaciousness without substance, as it will come off as disingenuous and "trying too hard." The tactics we'll describe in this section will give you ideas for substantive content that developers will respect and love. But the strategy advocated by Schaefer in his book will turn these tactics into an authentic formula for driving awareness and growth. Further, the concept of "audaciousness" should be inexorably linked with how you execute your developer brand, which we will discuss later in this book.

Blog posts

Blog posts are amazing when they're written for developers. What I mean by this is that it's easy-to-churn-out content optimized for search engines. Just put keywords everywhere. But Google does not like this and will, in fact, penalize your post if it reads like clickbait.

Instead, Google prefers content that provides a unique perspective and educates and informs the developer. You could spend your days freaking out about what Google will or won't like. (We'll cover SEO in a moment.)

Let's try a different approach: Write for an audience, especially an audience you've made substantial efforts to understand fully, and try to teach the audience something new. Maybe illuminate a topic that has vexed or confounded them for years. Highlight things or ideas that they will appreciate.

In short: Help First.

At the same time, you can pepper your post with targeted keywords. But the first and most important consideration is to inform and entertain your audience. Do that, and the Google Juice will flow.

TIP: When writing blog posts, take care to improve your internal linking. In other words, link to and reference other blog posts. Go back to prior blog posts and modify them to link back to newer blog posts. Internal linking is a critical component of SEO health.

Revisit old blog posts

It's easy to leave old blog posts alone and not touch them. But as your business grows and your most-successful traffic and keywords come into better focus, you should go back to your previously published content and modify it to reflect your strengths. In addition, rather than constantly getting on the new-content treadmill and running until you're blue in the face, you'll be able to leverage prior work and save yourself hours, if not days, in content-generation time.

Last, as your business evolves, certain topics will wane in importance. You can prune low-performing blog posts that are no longer relevant and improve the overall SEO health of your domain in the process.

Benchmarks and side-by-side comparisons

Developers *love* benchmarks. Love them.

But be careful: developers do *not* love benchmarketing.

What do I mean by this? Your benchmarks must be truthful. They must come from a place of high integrity. In your benchmarks, explain how you win and how your competitors win, and provide context for why.

For example, suppose you're a database vendor and your competitor beats you in benchmarks when the amount of data being stored is low. You can explain that, yes, your competitor is better in this regard, and then use the opportunity to position them as a "great database for getting started," but when you need a serious database for serious workloads, developers should choose you. This is the approach we took at Timescale when we benchmarked TimescaleDB vs. ClickHouse.

Be truthful. But don't fail to provide context.

As for the benchmark post itself, the form it takes is irrelevant. You can publish it as a blog post, as a microsite, or as a contributed article to a third-party website. I've done all three and found the most luck with blog posts, but there's a great opportunity to build interactive explainers in microsites.

Timescale prides itself on exceptional benchmarks, and their benchmark posts are a true elevation of the art form.

Tutorials and how-to content

These are my favorite pieces of content to produce. Tutorials, how-to content, and samples can be fun and informative, and the call to action embedded in this content is easy: sign up to complete the tutorial.

But inherent in tutorials is a distinct trap: off-topic content or datasets. Let's say you have a product aimed at developers of highly scalable systems. These are developers building enterprise-grade applications. You wouldn't create a tutorial that uses a tiny dataset and solves a simple problem. The leap from a toy dataset to "this product can handle the workload I'm considering on the job" is pretty big.

Even if the topic of the tutorial is a little more fun than a boring corporate scenario, make sure the bones of the tutorial represent the types of applications your customers are building.

And here's a quick side word on vocabulary:

- **Tutorial:** an end-to-end explainer of how your product can be used in a specific scenario
- **Sample:** a full application that can be git-cloned, along with documentation on how to use it
- **How-to:** a short application that solves one tiny sliver of a problem

Templates and starter kits

Developers love a good starter kit. It enables them to solve a particular problem quickly with prebuilt, pretested code. Most starter kits also have natural communities of other users who have taken them and customized them for their needs. When you combine starter kits with discussions in your community Slack, Discord, or forum, you're building a phenomenal engine for developer adoption and advocacy.

Starter kits also have natural SEO benefits. If you take your more horizontal (generally applicable) product and build vertical-specific starter kits, you can reach developers in specific industries with content that addresses a core pain point of theirs.

If possible, open-source parts of the starter kits so developers can contribute improvements and tailor the solutions to their use cases.

As with solution pages, which we'll discuss later in the product marketing section, starter kits tailored for industry verticals should take care to adopt the terminology and customs of the industry in question.

For example, Timescale, a Postgres database for time-series and analytical data, may want to create an Internet of Things Starter Kit with a schema for device telemetry, automated alerts for anomalies, and prebuilt Grafana dashboards for visualization. Developers searching "best database for IoT sensor data" or "store and query machine telemetry" will naturally land on this page.

Microsites

One other thing I love to do is create games. I worked on a project for a causal-reasoning platform to identify root causes of errors in cloud-native infrastructure. We had a sample dataset that we could "replay" so that it looked like a live set of data points. Now, because they had a product that customers had to drop in to their infrastructure in order to see data, many of them were reluctant to experiment with the product in the early-exploration stage.

Instead we took the replayable dataset, built a demo microsite, and encouraged customers to sign up for the product and search for clues that would resolve the error represented by the dataset. The microsite was a huge hit, and 70 percent of their demo requests came from customers who had completed the game.

Palantir did this to great effect in their early days, and it's something that has always stuck with me.

Lead-generation tools

You're always looking for ways to give customers a chance to provide you with their contact information in exchange for information about you. These lead magnets are unique assets related to your core value proposition. They attract customers within your target market and entice them to identify themselves.

For example, a shortlink provider could offer a free UTM builder that enables people in a team to coordinate their UTM parameters and link tracking. This free tool would be targeted at marketing teams, just like the "parent" link-shortener product. This free tool would also encourage people to invite their teammates to collaborate. With this free tool, the company could build a list of potential target customers and reach them through emails, event and webinar invites, ebooks, and other tools to build a relationship and bring them closer.

A fast, high-end data-engineering product could build tools to generate fake data streams to test the database. An object-relational mapper could provide a downloadable PDF poster of its API reference. A hosted cloud service could provide free website speed testing.

Building free tools and giveaways that appeal to your target audience is a great way to grow your contact list so that you can use it in email marketing and even warm prospecting.

Programmatic SEO

Programmatic SEO is a strategy to automatically generate pages based on data or templates. It's one of my favorite tools to build, and each time I've done it, it worked really well.

The canonical example is Zapier, which automatically generates integrations pages that explain the benefits and scenarios of using tool A with tool B. This strategy works best for long-tail keywords: those that have high search intent but low overall search volume.

You implement programmatic SEO by combining structured data (e.g., locations, product specifications, or integrations) with dynamic content templates optimized for SEO. These pages target specific queries at scale, often resulting in significant organic traffic.

Programmatic SEO is particularly well-suited for developer-focused products because developers often rely on highly specific, niche search queries to solve problems, find integrations, or explore tools. By leveraging programmatic SEO, you can create tailored content at scale to meet those needs.

Some high-value use cases include the following:

- integrations pages demonstrating how to use multiple tools together
- language or framework-specific guides for using your product
- industry or scenario-specific pages
- error-resolution pages that explain, for example, "how to fix [error message] in ClickHouse"

To build these pages, follow these steps:

- Do your research and find long-tail keywords that your target developer audience searches for.
- Build a structured dataset such as a list of error codes or integrations products.
- Enrich your structured dataset with descriptive content, code samples, definitions, history context, or other information you believe your audience will find useful.
- Create a dynamic template to host your content and optimize it for SEO.
- Closely monitor the performance of your pages and adjust accordingly.

It is very important to follow best practices for creating these pages. Poorly constructed content can do more harm than good.

- **Ensure high-quality content:** Avoid "thin content" by adding unique value to each page, like examples, FAQs, or user stories.
- **Add CTAs:** Include contextually relevant calls to action, like "Try [Product] for Free" or "See How [Product] Works with [Framework]."
- **Leverage open-source:** Use community contributions (e.g., GitHub projects, examples) to enrich content.
- **Promote pages:** Share programmatic pages on forums, newsletters, and social platforms to drive traffic and backlinks.

Video

Producing video is some of the most fun and rewarding work most developer advocates do. Video is obviously far more immersive than long blog posts, and people are conditioned to watch and listen to video, especially for informative topics. Code-focused topics, where people are expected to copy/paste and work alongside you, is probably still best served through the written word (or perhaps a combination of the two).

If you're not familiar with the world of YouTube videos for developers, start watching and fall into your own YouTube hole. You'll notice a few things:

- Video where the talent is on screen (in a picture-in-picture window) and explaining things is far more interesting than just watching a screencast. And it will generate far more views too.
- Put production value into your video. Getting a good YouTube setup isn't actually that expensive these days, so invest in the camera, ring lights, microphone, backlighting, and software to produce great video content.

- Experiment with your video descriptions and thumbnails. You can't re-upload your video later without losing your view count and likes. But you can change your thumbnails and descriptions as much as you'd like. Blatantly copy successful videos and look for the formula, look, and feel that work best for you.
- The line between technical developer content and general content is blurry. Developers tend to have varied interests, so don't hesitate to copy the technical aspects of some of your favorite nondeveloper content.

Here's one other comment about video content, especially the topics you choose: A common mistake many companies make is to publish inside-out video content, about their own product or service. While this may be necessary (for example, you may want to embed video into your docs), this alone will likely not generate the view count you're looking for.

Instead look for content that drafts off a more successful product. For example, if you have a new feature in your JavaScript framework, maybe show how developers can use that feature to make it easier, to use Sequelize or another popular ORM. Think about how to worm your way as a guest star onto someone else's bigger stage.

One additional comment about video: I've seen organizations get paralyzed by concerns over maintaining the accuracy of videos as products improve. Yes, user interfaces may change, and features may be added over time. This isn't a reason to forego a major channel for how people learn today. Record videos and hide or delete stale ones as time goes on.

Infographics and interactive content

Infographics are awesome ways to highlight important concepts in your blog posts and videos.

Be sure to excerpt them and use them in other areas, including social media. Think about ways to make them interactive and embed them in microsites or your homepage. Turn your infographics into star attractions in the landing pages of your paid ad campaigns.

If you've done a ton of hard work (for example, running benchmarks), be sure to reuse that work in as many places as possible. Infographics can often be very easy ways to encapsulate tons of work into one bite-sized nugget.

After all, a picture is worth a thousand lines of code.

Checklists and listicles

People love checklists, and no matter what they say, the data clearly shows that people love listicles too. Arranging complex topics into an easy-to-follow narrative that doesn't require a significant time investment is always a winner ("7 JavaScript Tips from Power-Users").

Take your common keywords and think about ways you can build listicles around them.

Case studies and interviews

You want your customers to speak on your behalf about how awesome you are. Case studies are a pillar of every team's marketing mix.

We'll cover case studies in a lot more detail later, but I wanted to cover one aspect of case studies that developer advocates in particular are helpful in producing. I like to think about two different types of case studies:

- **What I call the A Side:** This is the glossy case study you're probably most familiar with. It's great for your website, with awesome graphics, logos, and screenshots. It's also awesome when turned into PDFs for your sales team.
- **And what I call the B Side:** This is a technical Q&A with a lead developer as your customer. I love to post it on the blog along with a link to the A Side case study.

One other thing I love is video case studies. If you're able to record your customer reiterating the points made in your case studies, you'll have an asset that can be reused in multiple places. The actual YouTube video may not get many views, but when the video is chopped down to fifteen-and thirty-second soundbites, they're awesome for social media. Video case studies can be produced at low cost (simply record a Zoom or Riverside interview) or at significant cost (send a video crew to interview a customer onsite). Either way, they're worth investing in and using, as people love to watch and engage with customer interviews in social media.

White papers

White papers are a special form of blog posts, but they tend to be more polished and formal. Often they are offered as PDF downloads. These days I prefer interactive microsites to PDF downloads. I feel like this improves SEO performance while providing a more immersive reading experience for developers.

Many marketing teams like to put white papers behind lead acquisition forms (a customer is required to provide contact information before downloading). I personally loathe having to obtain content by first providing my email address, but this tactic works for accumulating high-quality leads.

Ebooks

Ebooks are a packaged booklet of your best content. Take your high-performing blog posts and website content and reuse them in a glossy PDF (or physically printed and bound) for distribution to customers at events and meetings.

For years I thought ebooks were a waste of time, but having spoken to many salespeople and conference attendees, I've come to the conclusion that if you are talking to someone with the potential to be a high-quality lead, offering them a leave-behind book with tons of excellent technical content serves as a helpful reminder to follow up with you for more information about your product.

The other thing about ebooks is that you can use them to create lead magnets, which give customers another opportunity to engage with you. You already know about product sign-ups and demo requests. Maybe a customer just wants information or an opportunity to learn. Give them another way to raise their hand and let them download an artifact of some kind. Ebooks are tried-and-true lead magnets, but there are several others, including online courses (Segment did this very well in the early days).

Not every business will benefit from ebooks. If you are building a long-tail developer product, you will likely skip this tactic. But if your product is aimed at enterprise audiences, you may find it immensely helpful. It's worth experimenting.

Original research

Your successful product and your customer wins afford you a unique place in the industry as an expert. The knowledge you've gained in building your business can be "productized" as original research. This research is another fantastic lead magnet.

Here are some examples of great research:

- **Analysis of (anonymized) usage patterns:** If your user base is sufficiently large, this is great fodder for an infographic and long-form text content.
- **State-of-the-industry reports:** People will gladly fill out a survey about something that interests them. If you can get a sufficiently large number of survey submissions, you can then publish the results as a "report" that your customer base will love. For example, consider Timescale's annual *State of PostgreSQL* report.
- **Benchmarks:** We've discussed benchmarks about products before, but offering industry benchmarks that customers should reach (such as mean time to failure) and providing information about how customers can meet those metrics is something customers would gladly hand over their email to receive (which can lead to fruitful conversations).

One important note about this kind of content: it's not easily replicated by an LLM. The research and insight are yours, and it's original and unique. While AI has eliminated a raft of content—definitional posts, such as "What is Postgres?", or simplistic how-to content, such as "How to install Python"—it won't easily generate original research in the immediate future. Use your expertise!

These types of research projects can be time-consuming, but if the end product is aligned with your target customer's needs, then the effort will have been worth it in terms of qualified leads.

Courses

Another phenomenal lead magnet is an instructional course. In a course, you will teach prospects about something that applies to your entire industry. In the early days of Segment, they built a course that explained how to build a tracking plan and use customer data to inform outreach. Tinybird has a course called "Principles of Real-Time Analytics."

A course is also fantastic for SEO, and it gives customers an opportunity to sign up to learn. Remember, we always start from a place of Help First, and giving your prospects a chance to level up their careers with new knowledge is an excellent example.

Be sure to gate the content with an email form, and then provide the content for free. You'll get a good number of customers who have interest in a problem space your product or service addresses.

Webinars for developers

There's a belief among some people in developer relations that "developers will never attend a webinar." I think this statement is a bit overblown . . . Most developers will never attend something *called* a "webinar." While I use the term here, consider branding your live videos as "live-coding streams," "live workshops," and so on.

What's most important is that if your webinar is technical, offers great information from well-known sources, and provides an opportunity for developers to learn something new, they will, in fact, sign up to attend.

Needless to say, your first and most important task is to find something interesting to say. To Help First.

Remember my emphasis on outside in? Your topic should be something instantly appealing and interesting to developers. It should be less about you and more about a topic they are curious about. Try to get an industry expert or one of your best customers to join you as a guest. It will lend your webinar a sense of credibility. This will make it easier to promote and drive registration and attendance.

There are multiple ways to run webinars, and I won't belabor them here. I will describe for you what I love to do, as it's low friction and feels less "enterprisey" and more modern.

1. First I put up a landing page that describes the webinar; includes important information (date, time, speaker bios); and offers a form for people to sign up to be reminded.

2. I set up three nurture emails. The first is delivered immediately after sign-up. The second is a reminder twenty-four hours before the webinar that again includes the pertinent information as well as the link to join and an "add to calendar" link. And the third is a follow-up summary twenty-four hours after the webinar with links to resources, white papers, ebooks, videos, and anything else I may have referenced during the webinar itself.

3. I promote the webinar across my ad channels using my keywords. The call to action for these ads leads to the landing page. This is optional and I have found varying degrees of success here.

4. I put a banner on the top of my website encouraging people to click and sign up to attend.

5. I've experimented with Zoom Webinars (which I love), but I've come to really, really depend on Restream. I think Restream is fabulous. You are able to go live and then broadcast across all your social media accounts. By using Restream, I can both capture potential attendees' contact information before the event *and* appeal to those who may

be browsing social media and are inspired to simply join in. Restream also enables you to run a very professional-looking webinar.

6. On the day of the event, I modify the landing page to embed the live video. I then continue to promote the modified landing page on my ad channels.

7. After the event, I embed the recorded video and include links to all the same resources in my post-event nurture email.

8. Also, after the event I run retargeting campaigns (assuming I have sufficient audience size) for everyone who visited the landing page, using some of the key messages from the webinar itself.

I think these steps really give you a professional webinar, the ability to capture leads beforehand, and the serendipitous ability to capture audience during your stream.

Webinars for buyers

It's more common to do webinars for buyers, the economic decision makers for products or services in large companies. Buyers are concerned with things like cost reduction, resource efficiency, return on investment, and so forth. Whereas a webinar for a technical person might be something like "Optimizing Queries for Postgres," a buyer-level webinar might be titled "Reducing Cloud Costs Through Intelligent Database Optimization."

As with technical webinars, the hardest part of a buyer webinar is getting people to attend. Driving awareness of it is critical to its success, for obvious reasons. You might promote the technical webinar on Reddit or Twitter, or through your email list. With the buyer-level webinar, you might want to promote it through LinkedIn (organic and paid channels, which we will discuss later), and incorporate it as part of your outbound sales motions and through a higher-titled segment of your email list.

Buyer webinars may or may not involve code, but they must always tie back to business outcomes. A common mistake is treating these webinars like technical deep dives without linking features to value. Developers will forgive a purely technical webinar, but buyers need direct, tangible benefits. Every topic, every slide, every demo should explicitly answer the question "How does this make my company more competitive?"

For example, instead of a demo that simply showcases query performance improvements, frame it as "How optimizing queries led to a 30% reduction in cloud spend for ACME Corp." Customer case studies and testimonials work exceptionally well here. Real-world proof points always outperform theoretical benefits.

Most technical people will look at buyer webinars with skepticism. But they are nonetheless important. This is a great example of how fusing a traditional B2B SaaS approach and mindset with knowledge of a developer audience can be beneficial to your go-to-market motion.

Here are some tips for running a successful buyer webinar:

- **Solve a business problem, not a technical challenge.** Frame your topic around cost reduction, efficiency, security, or competitive advantage.
- **Use data to build credibility.** ROI metrics, cost savings, and real-world benchmarks will resonate more than feature specs.
- **Involve a customer or industry expert.** Buyers trust their peers more than vendors. A well-placed customer success story can turn curiosity into serious intent. Even better, a joint webinar with a customer can be very powerful.
- **Leverage sales for pre- and post-webinar outreach.** Your sales team should be following up with attendees immediately to continue the conversation.
- **Think beyond the webinar itself.** Record and repurpose key insights into blog posts, LinkedIn snippets, and follow-up email sequences to maximize the content's impact.

These refinements ensure the webinar is not only well-attended but also aligned with the business priorities of your target audience. Would you like additional guidance on how to integrate these webinars into a broader go-to-market strategy?

Podcasts and streaming shows

We all love podcasts, but having attempted (as a startup) to start a podcast, a streaming show, and a user group, I can tell you this: It is a lot of work.

On top of the demand-generation motion you already need to run to drive awareness of your product, you're also now running a demand-generation motion for your podcast. It's hard enough to break through noise with one thing, so why bother trying to do it with two things?

That said, if you are aiming to be the industry expert on an important area (read: one with a large enough audience to draw from), or are already a well-established technology company, launching a podcast to underscore your ostensibly neutral interest in making that important area successful could be a great tactic.

A more effective tactic is to find ways to be a guest on popular podcasts and streaming shows. Given we are in an era when even BigTech struggles with developer credibility, the advice may be doubly important for them. Working with popular content creators and influencers helps a lot. We will discuss this tactic in the next chapter.

Swag

Swag (originally an acronym for "stuff we all get") is an essential component of any marketing plan. Whether it's stickers, T-shirts, or booth giveaways, swag is a great opportunity to extend your brand and engage with developers at the most tactical level. Developers love to wear T-shirts—at one point in my life, my entire wardrobe consisted of corporate tees—and a cool, fun shirt goes a long way toward advertising the existence of your product or startup. Whenever I've run an event or meetup tour, I've created a special "concert T-shirt" exclusively for attendees.

Make the effort to select and design fun swag and the benefits will pay off in spades down the road.

CASE STUDIES THAT CONVERT

A great case study tells a compelling story about how your product solves a problem of wide applicability for a given customer. It's not just a dry recitation of features and benefits. It's a narrative that highlights the customer's challenge, the importance of solving that challenge, how your product meets and exceeds their needs, and the tangible impact your product has had on the business.

- **Start by choosing the right customer.** As part of your ideal customer profile definition (which we will discuss in a later chapter), you will have a good idea of the industries and customer types best suited for your product. Look for a large number of case studies that slot into these various industries, giving prospects an opportunity to look at someone "just like them" for inspiration.
- **Interview the customer and identify the story to be told.** I'll provide some interview questions and tips in a moment, but remember, this isn't a dry white paper or datasheet. You want to describe the pain point, the importance of solving it, the ways in which your product addresses it, and so on.
- **Record the interview.** The recording will obviously be of interest to the team internally, but it may also be incredibly helpful for social media assets later (with the customer's permission, of course). I like to use Riverside for a more professional video-recording experience.
  - The corollary to this is to never do these interviews over email. Do them live or via video conference! You'll get a lot more out of it and be able to guide the interview in the best possible direction.
- **Keep it focused.** Aim for 1,500 words maximum, and incorporate images, screenshots, tables and charts, and other visual assets.
- **Align to your positioning and messaging.** If your core positioning is about developer productivity, your case studies should underscore that message. If you're instead

focused on flexibility, then gear your case studies toward that message. Nothing happens in a vacuum. Get on message and stay on message.

Customer interviews are always fun, but for case studies, you are doing less customer discovery and a lot more cheerleading. With that in mind, it's OK to employ leading questions in these interviews, whereas in customer-discovery calls, you'd never do so out of fear of biasing your research.

(I created an appendix with my standard case study questionnaire along with an AI prompt to help you turn an interview transcript into a draft case study.)

Once your case study is completed and approved, consider these follow-up steps with your customer:

- Ask them to post a review on G2 and other customer-review sites.
- See if they'd like to join a webinar about their problem and solution.
- Embed references to your case study across your website, including in product pages and perhaps even in documentation.
- Turn each case study into a single slide for use in your sales team's first meeting deck.

THE ART OF THE PRODUCT DEMO

Perhaps nothing more exemplifies the skills of a developer advocate than their ability to turn a routine recitation of a product's features and benefits into full-on entertainment. We've all met people who can turn a story about meeting the pope into a laborious, tiring affair that has you scanning for the exits. We've also met people who can turn a story about chewing bubblegum into a hilarious, intoxicating experience that pulls you in and can entertain you for hours.

If your developer advocate can't, at minimum, do the latter, you've lost before you've even started.

Great developer advocates can deliver product demos as beautiful, engaging stories.

I'm going to teach you the secrets I've learned from delivering product demos on stage with countless BigTech execs, past and present. There are two tricks to a great product demo, whether you're doing it live on stage in front of tens or thousands of people, or in front of a camera for YouTube or your website:

- a captivating scenario that either inspires or amuses
- an engaging story with a start, middle, and end

But the preface to all of this is something very important that seems to be lost on the many keynotes I've seen of late from Google, Microsoft, Amazon, and Apple. The demo must be real. No faking. No videos. Do it live, on stage or in front of a camera, without a net. (Well, maybe a little bit of a net . . . I'll teach you that trick in a moment also.)

The scenario

A good demo scenario is a small slice of life that resonates immediately and deeply with your audience. When you first take the stage and describe your scenario—for example, "Today, I'm going to show you how development and operations teams work together to prepare for Black Friday . . ."—everyone in the audience should be able to relate to and appreciate what's going to happen next.

Remember, you aren't going to solve all their problems on that stage. Your job is to show them that you understand the kinds of challenges they face daily.

You can get ideas from customer scenarios (talk to your sales and customer-success teams) and engineers. Be sure to avoid contrived or overly idealized—or overly trivial—scenarios. Socialize your ideas with your product and engineering team, your customers, and members of the marketing and sales teams.

Is your scenario about a front-end developer who's racing against a deadline? Or is it a database developer trying to speed up performance in time for a huge rush on Black Friday? Maybe it's a back-end developer trying to launch a new online game.

In the end, you want to be memorable. So your scenario should either inspire or amuse:

- **Inspire:** how can your product help people achieve something extraordinary? For example, your database can handle as many transactions per second as Walmart and Amazon combined on a typical Black Friday. Inspirational scenarios are ideal for launch keynotes and customer presentations.
- **Amuse:** invite audience participation in something frivolous and lighthearted. For example, maybe you have a chatbot that hilariously mixes up coffee orders until you use your product to fix it. Amusing scenarios are fantastic for meetups and community events.

Think of the scenario as the stage on which you'll work your magic. Identify a scenario that many in your target audience will relate to (and be willing to pay to address), and start your demo by telling them about this scenario and what the hero is up against. Set the stage.

> **TIP:** Even your sales engineers can benefit from these kinds of tips. Build inspiring or amusing demo scenarios for each industry vertical and leave your customers with a memorable experience about your product or service.

The demo tells the story

Every good story has a *protagonist*—the hero. And every hero goes on a journey. In your case, the target user is your hero, and the problem they're trying to solve is the journey. **These—not your product—are the stars of the story.** You may feel tempted to jump into features and benefits, but you can't do that until you describe the "why" first.

The next thing every good story has is a *transformation*. In a novel or film, the most important part of the story isn't what the protagonist does to get from point A to point B, it's how the protagonist changes on the journey between point A and point B.

Luke Skywalker transforms from a simple farm boy with lofty dreams but filled with self-doubt to the hero who saves the galaxy and defeats the villain by learning to trust himself. We all love pew-pew-pew and lightsabers, but the difference between a mediocre movie and one that has stood the test of time for three generations is that we root for (and ultimately believe) Luke's transformation.

In a product demo, you will show how the hero's fate will change because of the products you are shipping. Focus on only two or three capabilities. Now is not the time to regurgitate your entire feature list. You've chosen a great scenario, so concentrate on a small number of feature areas that solve the problem.

The key in the transformation stage is to build slowly. Choose features that will garner applause from your target audience. Build your outline so that you progressively show more amazing features. Don't lead with the most amazing one.

One of my clients has a phenomenal product that identifies the root cause of infrastructure problems in cloud-native environments. Fortune 100 customers, including big banks, love them. They start their demos with a Jira ticket, indicating that the scenario will be about using the insight their product delivers, not merely identifying a problem.

As you're showing each feature, tell the hero's story. Explain how their fate changes with each new feature you show.

With the aforementioned client, the demo takes them from a Jira ticket that raises a problem and assigns an owner, toward a journey starting with the types of problems that can be identified, the integration between their tool and systems of record that already exist in an organization, and the analytics that show how much a customer's systems have improved since the introduction of their product.

The finale

And finally you reveal the aha moment: what success looks like. Faster deployment. More resilient databases. Scalable servers. Better cross-organizational collaboration.

Demonstrate the fully functional scenario.

You took the hero from a position of self-doubt and, thanks to your product, put them in a position of confident triumph.

Recap what you showed, taking customers briefly from the start of the scenario through the transformation and then what customers will be able to do once the finale has concluded. The recap is a great way to underscore the product messaging and relate it to the scenario and story.

Mitigating mistakes and errors during live demos

As I mentioned, keynote demos should be done live. It depresses me whenever I see an obviously canned demo. But there are things you can do to protect yourself against the demo gods:

1. **Rehearse:** The best actors in the world put months of rehearsal into their craft. Nobody shows up on stage or set ready to tackle their nerves and perform. You have to work at it. I can still remember word-for-word my entire demo on stage with Bill Gates from thirty years ago. That's how much I rehearsed that thing.
2. **Have a "shadow" backstage:** One year I did a demo on stage with former Microsoft CEO Steve Ballmer and had someone on my team shadow me backstage. We practiced every day for several hours for two weeks leading up to the keynote. He echoed every one of my mouse movements and keyboard entries. Upon hearing my code word, *peanut butter*, backstage, he knew to instantly switch the KVM to the computer he was shadowing me with.

3. **Have canned data, just in case:** If your demo requires live internet access, assume the connection will be too slow or will drop at some point. Be ready with canned data so that you can still show off the features of your product.

4. **Have a backup (and one-liners) ready:** Developers in the audience will understand if you attempted a live demo and it didn't go well. Be ready to accept your fate with humility and a little humor, and have a backup machine or scenario ready to go.

A FINAL WORD ON CONTENT REPURPOSING

No content is an island. When you put a ton of energy into building a piece of content, you need to think about all the ways you will reuse it.

Turn your blog post into a series of infographics for social media. Turn your tutorials into an interactive landing page that guides customers through a scenario and immerses them in the value of your product. Turn your content into webinars or guest stints on podcasts. Don't forget to take your best blog posts and convert them into conference talks and submit CFPs.

All your content needs to be repurposed multiple times. The rule of thumb I ask my teams to follow is that every piece of content needs to be reused at least three ways.

Here's a checklist of formats to help you repurpose a given piece of content:

- ☐ an infographic
- ☐ a series of quick tips and tricks
- ☐ a Twitter thread
- ☐ short and long videos for social media
- ☐ an ad campaign to support particularly high-value content (maybe work with your growth manager)

These parallel pieces take time to develop, but you want them ready to go at the same time as your main piece of content, so you can use them to amplify it. Using AI to help you repurpose content is totally fair game. Feeding an LLM a completed blog post and asking it to generate a shortened version, a set of tweets, a LinkedIn post, and so forth can save a considerable amount of time.

CHAPTER 6

Distributing Developer Content

Once you've built great developer content, you need to prepare and distribute it so that it's read broadly, indexed by search engines, and prepared for AI tools and large language models (LLMs). Since the early days of the web, people have both struggled and mastered the art of distribution. It's not easy, and it often requires a ton of legwork and hustle. There are no magic bullets. Often the answer is to try as many tactics as you can so that the gains add up and produce the momentum you're looking for.

Moreover, by diversifying the avenues through which you attract new users, you're protecting yourself against outcomes out of your control. Google could change their algorithm and tank your SEO traffic. A new LLM could appear and disrupt AI-driven traffic. A community site could fall out of favor with developers. A social network could be bought by thin-skinned billionaires and overrun with toxicity. There are many things you can't control, so ensure that you're hedging with *all* these tactics.

Let's start by looking at the act of producing the content itself.

PRODUCING CONTENT EFFECTIVELY

Content marketers can really accelerate your content-development process. The content marketer is responsible for identifying the best content to create, working closely with the creator on planning and editing, ensuring brand consistency and tone, and publishing and amplifying the content.

To ghostwrite, GPT-write, or produce in-house?

You have lots of options for generating content. You can, of course, have your favorite LLM generate outlines and portions of your content for you, editing and clarifying for consistency and tone. You can layer in additional material and depth, and you can generally create passable content.

You can also contract subject-matter experts to write it for you (with or without their byline included on your blog). I've had mixed results with this. In many cases, I've regretted doing so because the time necessary to edit, review, and prepare something for publication is often the bulk of the effort involved in producing content, and someone outside the company rarely has the context necessary to build content that will resonate with our audience. Your mileage may vary, however.

Producing it in-house, via developer advocates and engineering, is the tried-and-true method and often results in high-quality and consistently on-brand results. The problem, of course, is the opportunity cost. If you're going to pull engineering time to write a blog post, you need to be sure that the blog post is going to perform up to expectations. Pairing a developer advocate with an engineer to write the content is the best course of action.

Good marketing leaders are always building relationships across the organization. A great marketing leader also gets to know engineering leadership at all levels. Make sure you are frequently communicating with your counterparts in engineering; ensure that they know your goals (which are, to be clear, everyone in the organization's goals: revenue and customer success); and convince them to participate in your marketing efforts. In my experience, most engineers are more than willing to raise their own profile and would be delighted to participate in marketing if the time commitment is minimized.

Identifying great content

The content marketer has to be plugged into many aspects of the marketing team and company:

- The growth manager will have a good idea of which keywords to target for SEO content. They'll also know the historical performance of content and can guide decisions about format, goals, metrics, and so on.
- The product marketing manager will have a good idea of which topics will be useful for future product launches or for the sales team to use as part of its engagement model.
- Developer advocates are closely monitoring industry trends and developments, as well as engaging with the developer community to learn about their pain points and interests. This is done through regular interactions on forums, social media, and other online platforms, as well as through attending industry events and conferences.
- Engineers have deep knowledge of what their fellow engineers will want to read and watch, and what they're interested in learning.
- Your exec team will have a good idea of the kinds of strategic content that will help progress toward companywide goals.

Additionally, conducting surveys and gathering feedback from developers can provide valuable insights into the types of content that will be most relevant and valuable to them. By staying closely attuned to the needs and interests of the developer community, you can create content that resonates with your audience, helps to solve real problems, and addresses common challenges.

Think of it as a *Rashomon* exercise, where everyone has a different viewpoint on the problem. The right answer lies somewhere at the nexus of it all.

Periodically—every two weeks or once a month—the content marketer should gather all stakeholders for a content brainstorming session. During this session, everyone should bring their input and propose content. I liken this to a television show's writer's room, where all the writers get together and pitch story or character ideas. Once the session ends, you will have a good first stab at topics and ideas for content.

The next step is to work closely with stakeholders to identify the content pieces of greatest value and highest potential impact. Finally, the content marketer will also work with growth marketing to set realistic short-term and long-term expectations for the performance of the content.

Planning and editing content

The content marketer works very closely with the developer advocate (or other content author) on the materials. If you're part of that team, here's what the collaborative process might look like:

- Determine the best format for the content. Are you building a blog post, a benchmark, a how-to guide?
- Get a commitment on a timeline for completing the content, and ensure that everyone is sticking to it.
- Start workshopping titles and key phrases to include, in close coordination with the growth manager.
- Throughout the process, develop a clear understanding of the kinds of charts, graphs, and other design needs for the content piece. Make sure these requests are teed up to your design team or contractor so that they can be completed on time.
- Work closely with the author to ensure proper grammar is used, whether it's a written piece or a video piece.
- Look for opportunities to punctuate the content with social proof: customer evidence, usage statistics, industry trends, and so on.

- As the content takes shape, think about ways it can be amplified. For example, is there an influencer or podcaster who would really love it? Maybe reach out to them and get their thoughts on the topic, and perhaps even ask them if you can quote them and include them in the final piece.
- Identify the UTM parameters and shortlinks to be used during content amplification. (We will talk more about this later.)

By staying involved in the process, the content marketer can anticipate needs and ensure that the content really sings when it is published. Nearly all these tasks are much more difficult to complete at the tail end of a project.

Brand and messaging consistency and tone

Marketing managers can ensure brand consistency and tone in content by implementing several strategies:

- **Create a brand guide** that outlines the brand's tone, voice, and messaging. This guide should be shared with all team members and regularly updated to reflect any changes to the brand.
- **Establish a content-approval process that** involves reviewing all content before it is published. This process allows for any inconsistencies or deviations from the brand tone to be identified and addressed.
- **Provide regular training and support** to team members to ensure they have a strong understanding of the brand and its tone. This can include workshops, webinars, and one-on-one mentoring sessions.
- **Establish a consistent branding strategy** across all channels and platforms. This includes ensuring all content, visuals, and messaging aligns with the brand and its tone.

Publishing content

This is more of a mechanical step, and while it may seem like admin work, having one person on your team in charge of loading content and hitting "publish" ensures that you will do so without missing key steps like tagging categories, having a consistent YouTube video description, ensuring proper use of UTM parameters and shortlinks, and so on.

It's OK to publish your content in multiple places, but to avoid SEO penalties and duplicate-content issues, set up a canonical URL (a tag that tells search engines which version of the content is the original and should be prioritized in search rankings). Always point the canonical URL to the version hosted on your website to ensure you get proper attribution and search authority. That said, the guiding principle remains: meet developers where they already are.

Hyping your content

If a piece of content drops on the web and nobody hears about it, did you really write it? You need to think about the marketing plan for your content. Preload your community with information about it.

What topic are you exploring? Pose some general questions to the community and ask for their feedback.

As your content takes shape, tease its delivery to your community. Ask if anyone wants to review it, then take them up on the offer. They'll be invaluable pillars of support when it comes time to amplify the content, which we will discuss in a moment.

As your publication date nears, let your community know to watch out for it and let them know all channels are open for their feedback. This invites them to provide their input, and in the process increase the buzz around your piece.

Amplifying content

Marketing managers can amplify content by utilizing a combination of tactics and strategies to reach a wider audience and drive awareness and conversions among software developers.

The most effective route to amplifying content is to use existing online sites and relevant newsletters with high reach. You can try buying placement in key newsletters and submitting your content for inclusion in their publication. It's often a great way to drive awareness among your target audience. In addition, build a strong relationship with the author(s) of the newsletters you've chosen. They are often looking for both organic (nonpaid) and paid content.

Another effective way to amplify content is to leverage social media platforms such as Twitter, LinkedIn, and Facebook. Use the parallel pieces you developed as key elements of your amplification strategy. Post an infographic along with commentary excerpted from the main content piece. Post the videos and encourage people to check out the main piece. And so on.

By sharing relevant and engaging content on these platforms, marketing managers can reach a large audience of software developers and generate interest in their products or services. It's also important to engage with the audience on social media by responding to comments and questions and encouraging them to share the content with their own followers.

Next is my favorite way to amplify content: by leveraging the power of influencer marketing. By building relationships and partnering with influential software developers who have a large following on social media or within the software development community, marketing managers can reach a wider audience and generate more awareness and conversions. Influencers can promote the content to their followers and give it credibility, which can drive conversions.

Don't forget to post your content internally and encourage your team to like, share, and comment. My teams have won numerous awards and caused content to trend solely as a result of internal amplification. Just be sure to tell your team to customize their posts and comments in their own voice, with their own sentiment. You don't want seventy-five posts that look exactly alike from the same company. Unless you work for Meta. (I kid, but only slightly.)

Last, don't forget to keep resharing. We live in a short-attention-span economy. The reason someone never read your piece is that maybe they didn't see it. Maintain an always-on amplification strategy so that your content is constantly in the public eye. It's OK to promote old content!

Reporting progress

The content marketer will also monitor the performance of content and keep all stakeholders apprised of views, conversions, and other key metrics.

I usually ask content marketers to post monthly reports about content performance and key learnings so that they're always top of mind for people as they're thinking about what's next.

AN SEO ENGINE THAT WORKS

Building a reliable SEO engine is one of the most effective ways to drive long-term, sustainable growth in developer marketing. Developers are self-educating buyers, and they often turn to search engines to solve specific problems, evaluate tools, and learn best practices. Even as LLMs consume more market share, especially for the most practical developer searches, SEO will become even more important as developers turn to search engines as fallback research tools for which they will carry forward their expectations of immediate results. By developing an SEO strategy tailored to developer audiences, you can ensure that your product becomes part of their discovery journey.

TIP: Publishing being what it is, this book was written in early 2025. By the time it is published, who knows what effect LLMs will have had on the entire SEO industry. We are already seeing tectonic shifts in the ways consumers use search engines over LLMs such as ChatGPT. For now it appears that SEO and optimizing for LLMs has enough overlap that it's worth doing both. If the process diverges in the future, it will be worth considering the effort involved for the benefit obtained.

Here's how to create an SEO engine that works.

Understanding developer search behavior

Developers search for solutions to problems. We've talked before about maintaining a deep understanding of and empathy for the problems developers face, and being available to help. Later in this book, we will see how that attitude informs all our positioning and messaging.

Offer historical context

When building content, don't be afraid to provide context into the problem: historical context (what causes the problem to exist in the first place); technical context (what are some approaches to solving the problem); product context (what are some products that have attempted to solve the problem); and finally your solution.

Direct competitive comparisons

Developers are also looking for comparison material. Maybe they are at the middle or bottom of the consideration funnel and understand their problem and are researching the various alternatives available to them. Content that directly compares your product to your competitors' will be particularly helpful in SEO—in my experience, especially when you're going up against a big competitor like Microsoft or Google. They typically won't bother to write their own version of a comparison doc, and as a result, you will find yourself owning the comparison keyword.

Best practices

Best practices are always top of mind for developers. Think about your problem area and write content that gives them a list of tips, tricks, resources, and learnings from experts who have lived and breathed the space for a long time.

Troubleshooting

Finally, developers always encounter problems and search for solutions. Building troubleshooting content that is common in your space is always a good idea for SEO.

Build a keyword strategy

Start by listing the relevant keywords for your product, industry, and technologies (especially open-source ones). The most effective keyword strategies I've seen have come out of the research done while defining the ideal customer profile (we will discuss this in a later chapter). The ICP is a description of the best customer for your product, and knowing what alternatives and problems your customer searches for is immensely valuable in general, and especially for creating your list of keywords. From there, use your favorite SEO tool (I love Ahrefs) to identify two types of keywords:

- High-volume but low-competition keywords. This will be the basis for your foundational SEO content.
- Long-tail keywords that target niche developer queries.

For example, consider the high-volume "API design best practices" vs. the more niche "REST API error handling for Express back-end applications."

Do your keyword research

While ICP-led keywords are important, there is still more research you can do. Developers search for information across multiple channels, including Google, YouTube, GitHub, and other key platforms. Unlike traditional B2B marketing, developer keyword strategies must balance technical depth, problem-solving intent, and ecosystem positioning.

Start by identifying developer search trends. After all, developers don't search the same way that business decision makers or knowledge workers do. They aren't looking for vague business benefits—they're searching for concrete solutions or documentation for a problem they currently experience.

I like to **start with GitHub trends**:

- Use GitHub Star History to identify trending open-source projects and technologies.
- Monitor repositories and frameworks adjacent to your product to uncover emerging keywords and discussions.
- Look for fast-growing projects and analyze their README files, issues, and discussions for commonly used terminology.

From there, **analyze your competitors' traffic using Similarweb**. Look at referring domains, top-performing blog posts, and highest-traffic pages to find keyword opportunities. Identify content gaps. What are competitors ranking for that you are not?

Now you want to dive into **keyword research using tools like Ahrefs**. Look up your competitors and analyze their highest-ranking pages. Identify long-tail developer queries ("how to connect Postgres to Next.js" as opposed to "Postgres database") and find question-based searches that are ranking.

Semrush is often considered interchangeably with Ahrefs, but **Semrush provides great value in identifying overall search trends** across the broader industry. You can use SERP feature analysis in Semrush to see which keywords trigger featured snippets, knowledge panels, or "People also ask" results in Google search results. Search results that show these SERP features often get clicked on far more frequently than normal search results, or even ads!

Beyond Google, you also want to **optimize for YouTube**. Use tools that analyze search volume on YouTube and get insight into how developers consume video content. Make sure your keywords are used in your titles, descriptions, tags, and captions.

Another good source of keyword data is **Reddit threads**. Look for problem-based keywords and questions ("How do I find the root cause of a slow query in a microservice?"). In particular, examine how developers describe issues in their own words. A lot of times, we marketing professionals get too focused on our own world and forget that developers often search for things on their own terms.

Structure your keyword strategy

Once you've collected keywords from all these sources, structure them into content pillars. I organize my content pillars in the following categories:

- **Core product keywords:** These are high-intent keywords that lead directly to sign-ups, things like "serverless Postgres pricing" or "deploy a managed database on AWS."
- **How-to keywords:** These are keywords that help developers solve problems, such as "how to call Supabase from Next.js."
- **Comparison keywords:** These keywords focus on where you are being compared to alternative products or solutions, such as "Postgres vs. MongoDB analytics."
- **Developer pain-point keywords:** These are issue-based searches that should lead directly to content answered by your documentation or blog content. For example, "Why is my database slow?" should lead to a blog post on query optimization.

A developer keyword strategy is not just about high search volume. It's about understanding developer intent, pain points, and real-world usage scenarios to make your content discoverable and useful across multiple platforms and to developers at their highest point of need.

Create high-quality content with topical authority

Google is constantly evolving its algorithm. Long gone are the days of sprinkling your keywords across your site and being done with it. Now you need to write content that demonstrates **topical authority**. Achieving topical authority is the process of becoming the definitive expert on a specific subject or problem domain, from the perspective of users and the Google algorithm. That's important if you want to stand out in a crowded space.

You achieve topical authority by writing well-organized, information-dense content that is interconnected throughout your site. Google rewards sites that demonstrate not just one authoritative piece, but several internally linked pieces that add up to topical depth.

Developers are discerning readers who look for and fully consume accurate and detailed information. Coupled with the high performance of your website achieved through technical SEO-optimization strategies out of scope for this book, topical authority drives organic traffic and engagement there.

To build topical authority, follow these steps:

1. **Choose a focused niche** that aligns with your product's unique value proposition, highlights the common pain points your customers encounter, and gives you the high-volume, low-competition keywords you're looking for. For example, the Postgres-as-a-service startup Neon may focus on "Postgres optimization tips," while Docker might focus on "containerization best practices."

2. **Assess your existing content** and identify strengths, weaknesses, and opportunities. Look at your competitors and see what topics they're covering that you aren't. Look across your problem domain and identify important sub-topics that you're not covering yet.

3. **Identify pillar topics** around which you will cluster content. For example, Neon may elect to focus on "Postgres optimization" and build supporting content that covers indexing strategies, troubleshooting slow queries, and more. By demonstrating their mastery of the complexity

of Postgres optimization, they can make a case that they're the best option for hosted Postgres. Make sure these pieces of content refer to one another so that the Google algorithm views them as related and your site as comprehensive.

4. **Always focus on quality.** Developers insist on it.

5. **Go over the top with thought-leadership content.** Have your founders or technical leaders publish insightful articles and blog posts that illuminate the topic. Webinars, benchmarks, and "future direction of the industry" posts are all fair game.

6. **Make sure you write compelling headlines** and use H1 and H2 tags in your posts that leverage your keywords.

Once your content is published, follow best practices for socializing it within communities, social media, and open-source discussion groups to raise its profile and drive backlinks.

For example, Vercel dominates web performance and deployment topics with actionable content, tools, and community showcases. Few companies do SEO better.

> **TIP:** Backlink agencies are rarely helpful for developer products. Because of the technical nature of the products we work on, the best-performing backlinks will be from other, equally technical products. Backlink agencies rarely have the ability to secure backlinks from these other sites. On the other hand, building partnerships, writing joint blog posts, securing joint webinars, and similar strategies have a much greater chance of success.

Create long-tail content that solves specific problems

SEO agencies tend to focus on keywords with high volume. It is important to build pillar content with strong topical authority that addresses these keywords. However, it is equally important to address long-tail keywords with low volume but very high intent.

As an example, let's say you're building an advanced causal analysis tool for microservices applications. You will build thought leadership and pillar content about the importance of causal analysis, the cost in time and money of poor quality in your microservices applications, and the need to employ causal artificial intelligence in your observability stack. This will capture developers who are in the market for causal analysis and more advanced observability tools and are in the midst of evaluating such solutions.

But there's another kind of developer: the person who has a problem now that causal analysis can help them solve. Maybe they've encountered an error message or a log entry that vexes them. Maybe their application exhibits strange behavior for which they cannot identify the root cause. To meet these developers where they are, you can employ programmatic SEO and generate landing pages for every Kubernetes error message that your causal analysis tool could address. Now, when a developer is searching for a specific error message, your page will appear in the search results and your product can be positioned effectively as a solution.

These long-tail keywords may not generate much traffic at all. Maybe on the order of tens of developers will search for these terms every month or perhaps even every quarter. But the ones who are searching for these keywords have an immediate problem that your product can address. You have a much higher chance of converting a developer with an immediate need than a developer who is window shopping or merely browsing.

This is the fundamental difference between SEO for a consumer or B2B product and SEO for a developer product.

Measure, learn, and iterate

Use your favorite SEO tool to measure a few things:

- **Total clicks:** You can see this from Google Search Console. It's a raw performance metric, but it tells you how well your site is growing in attracting visitors from search.
- **Organic traffic:** This is the raw amount of organic traffic you're getting—a metric readily available in Google Analytics 4 (GA4).
- **Referring domains:** Also called backlinks, these are still an important part of Google's algorithm. The best way to get them is to build great content that developers are compelled to share and link to.
- **Engagement rate:** This is easy to measure now in GA4 and tells you how many engagements (clicks, conversions, etc.) you're getting on each page.
- **Landing page performance:** Having a list of all the pages on your website and which ones result in conversion is a great way to evaluate your blog for performance.
- **Keyword rankings:** This information is best obtained from SEO tools like Semrush and Ahrefs. How many keywords are you currently ranking for? This number needs to be constantly going up.

And, of course, make sure your web development team stays on top of all technical SEO metrics.

MARKETING IN THE AGE OF LLMS

Artificial intelligence tools and large language models (LLMs) have changed the landscape of search. Google's core search business is in jeopardy as a consequence. After all, why search for the answer by clicking through to various sites if you can simply ask an LLM a question and get the answer? And the answers being generated by LLMs like ChatGPT are getting more accurate over time.

How do you get inserted into an LLM's answer? Let's dive into it.

How do LLMs accumulate their information?

Large language models are trained on a mixture of text data that covers a wide variety of topics including public internet content (articles, blogs, forums, etc.); books and academic papers; open-source codebases; public datasets; and user-generated content on social media, forums, and similar sites.

The model learns language patterns, structures, and associates during a pretraining phase. The text is broken down into tokens (every LLM does this differently), and the model predicts the next token in a sequence. Through this process, the model learns the grammar, syntax, and context of the content.

After this initial pretraining step, the model is optimized (tuned) for specific problem domains. General models, like GPT-4o, serve the broader public, while numerous LLMs are being built and trained across specific problem domains, like legal, medical, coding, and so on.

The model is then optimized through a series of steps, some of which help omit biases and introduce safety barriers.

Some platforms continuously integrate real-time content feeds built from periodically crawling the internet.

LLMs deliver answers either by using their training data or by searching the web, when necessary. For example, asking an LLM to help you write a case study using a set of provided facts and quotes will result in it most likely using its training data to write your first draft. However, were you to ask an LLM about pricing information for a product, then it would likely crawl the web for the latest information, synthesize it, and put it into context using its training data.

Some things never change

In this regard, you still need to build great content with significant topical authority. That won't change. All the steps you take to build SEO quality content will still apply.

Quality content still wins.

Focus on writing comprehensive, in-depth pieces on topics that you want to be known for. Demonstrate detailed expertise in your topic area. Write content that humans actually enjoy reading, with proper section headings, line breaks, approachable language, and quotability.

Keywords may not matter to LLMs, but the concept behind them still does. Keywords indicate areas of interest. Be sure that you are fleshing out knowledge for various areas of interest.

Some things are forever different

With iOS 18.1, all mobile platforms now summarize information in notifications, messages, and emails. This will have a profound impact on the readability of newsletters and email marketing. Make sure you experiment with crisp, clear, and shorter content that can be summarized accurately by both iOS and Android.

Integrate with LLMs

Some LLMs, like OpenAI's GPT, allow businesses to integrate their proprietary data directly into the AI's knowledge. Use APIs to fine-tune LLMs with your specific data, making it easier for users to access your expertise when interacting with the model.

In addition, community efforts, such as llmstxt.org, have sprung up to standardize the way websites can make their content LLM-readable. Per the proposal,

> We propose that those interested in providing LLM-friendly content add a /llms.txt file to their site. This is

a markdown file that provides brief background information and guidance, along with links to markdown
files (which can also link to external sites) providing
more detailed information. This can be used, for instance, in order to provide information necessary for
coders to use a library, or as part of research to learn
about a person or organization and so forth.

While much-deserved attention has been placed on LLMs scrap-
ing and reusing intellectual property without permission, not enough
has been done to prepare websites (such as documentation sites for
developer products) to make their content more digestible by and explicitly prepared for LLMs.

Using tools like Profound, you can monitor your website for AI
crawler activity and identify the content that is most frequently being
used in real time by LLMs. This can help you optimize the pages that
already garner attention from LLMs.

Expect this to be an area of significant progress in the immediate
future.

Using the Model Context Protocol

The Model Context Protocol (MCP) is an open protocol that enables seamless integration between LLM applications and external
services. By establishing a standardized means of communication
for accessing documentation, APIs, and external data sources, MCP
eliminates common pitfalls like hallucinated responses, outdated information, and unreliable AI-driven suggestions. MCP servers can
also enable AI tools to directly change or alter external systems on
behalf of the user.

At its core, MCP provides a structured way for LLMs to retrieve
context from trusted sources before generating responses. Instead of
relying solely on pretrained knowledge (which may be stale or incomplete), an LLM using MCP can dynamically pull real-time information
from external services that have implemented an MCP-compatible
interface.

Let's say you were using an AI code-assistance tool like Cursor or Lovable and wanted to use an external product, such as Supabase. Using the Supabase MCP server, the AI tool could unambiguously obtain the latest information from the Supabase documentation, connect directly to Supabase, alter schemas, write functions, and aid the developer. In the case of Cursor, this would include code autocompletion in a manner that reflects the best practices described in the Supabase docs, while in Lovable's case it could mean implementation of a complete Supabase backend, again reflecting the best practices described in the Supabase docs.

MCP represents a critical component for ensuring that AI tools base their output in grounded truth and can further be used to automate results on behalf of the user. Now, MCP doesn't aid in organic content discovery. However, it does ensure that when LLMs surface your product or service as part of their answers, the information they convey is accurate. It is still important to follow good SEO principles around creating topical authority.

Your site implementation also matters

AI crawlers, like those used by ChatGPT and other large language models, are limited in their ability to process JavaScript. Unlike Google's search crawler, which can render JavaScript to access dynamic content, AI crawlers primarily index static HTML. This means that websites relying heavily on JavaScript, such as React-based websites, for content rendering may appear blank or incomplete to AI crawlers, reducing their chances of being included in AI-generated answers or recommendations.

To ensure your website's content is accessible to these crawlers, you need to prioritize server-rendered HTML. This approach makes your content visible to both traditional search engines and AI crawlers, improving your discoverability in the evolving landscape of AI-driven search and information retrieval.

- **Adopt server-side rendering (SSR):** Use frameworks like Next.js (for React) or Nuxt.js (for Vue) to generate and deliver prerendered HTML for your web pages. This ensures all content is visible without requiring JavaScript execution.
- **Leverage static site generation (SSG):** Build your site's HTML during deployment using tools like Gatsby or Hugo. This approach works well for content-heavy sites that don't need frequent updates.
- **Implement incremental static regeneration (ISR):** For dynamic content, use ISR to pregenerate static HTML that refreshes periodically, ensuring your site remains up-to-date without compromising performance.
- **Test your website:** Disable JavaScript in your browser and use your favorite web-testing tools to ensure critical content is visible when JavaScript isn't rendered.
- **Prioritize core content:** Identify and server-render the most important content you want AI crawlers to index, such as product pages, documentation, and FAQs.

In addition to increasing your website's visibility to AI crawlers, you'll also future-proof it against AI changes and probably end up with a much faster site, which will help you with your technical SEO and rankings. Win-win for all involved.

Dial up your community engagement

As we discussed, LLMs are heavily influenced by open-source and community-driven content. ChatGPT, for example, leverages content found in Reddit. Make sure you are engaging with your community and socializing content across various community channels.

- **Share** your expertise and join conversations on social media, including Reddit, LinkedIn, and Twitter, each of which has content agreements in place with various LLMs.
- **Contribute** high-quality answers to forums such as Stack Overflow, Hacker News, and Quora.

- **Engage** with contributors and maintainers of open-source projects.
- **Encourage** (and maybe even incentivize) your users to share their experiences with your product, write reviews, and participate in the aforementioned social media and community sites.

To date, LLMs (and search engines) cannot penetrate conversations hosted on Slack or Discord. For this reason, you may also want to think about ways of taking high-value questions and answers on these community platforms and reposting them in places that are both search engine and LLM readable.

BUILDING A CONTENT STRATEGY

So where should you focus your content efforts? Here are six tips for building your content strategy:

Tip 1: Measure your work

First, it is very important to measure everything you do and double down on what's working and kill what isn't. Let's say you write a series of blog posts or record a series of YouTube videos. Two or three posts into what you'd planned as an eight-post series, you realize you are not getting views, conversion, or whatever your core metric happens to be. Don't be afraid to just stop and focus on something else. After all, if no one is reading, then no one is really expecting you to continue! As they say in the screenwriting world, "Kill your darlings."

Conversely, if one of your posts really seems to resonate, then double down on it! Try turning it into a video, then cut up the video and use it on social media. Turn your full post into a series of posts on LinkedIn. Then start thinking about follow-on posts, and use the traffic to your original post to guide people to your next set of posts.

We'll talk in a moment about how to be a little more intelligent when choosing topics, but the truth is, sometimes one of your posts does really well for no particular reason. Only through rapid experimentation can you land on something great.

Tip 2: Don't skimp on quality

If you seek to build your brand as a knowledgeable engineering organization capable of solving the most complex problems developers face, then your content needs to reflect the sober, serious nature of your work. Don't be afraid to be wonky; don't be afraid to show developers your reasoning. They will appreciate the opportunity to see how your team thinks and will often find it a sign of an organization that is thoughtful.

Even if you are building quick-hit listicles, make sure you put the effort into quality. In many of my teams, writing a strong blog post often took three to five weeks, at minimum. Developers know quality and hard work when they see it. Don't cut corners.

Tip 3: Don't sleep on SEO

Every founder of a developer-focused company wants content that rockets to the top of Hacker News and stays there. But viral content is a massive sugar rush. You are reaching a lot of developers, the overwhelming majority of whom probably do not have a pressing need to try your product now. Thus, while this viral content is critical for driving brand recognition and conversation about your company, it likely won't lead to meaningful conversion toward paying users.

That's why I spend as much, if not more, time focused on long-lead SEO content. This content answers questions developers are searching for at their greatest point of need. It may not be content that drives a high number of page views, but it will be content that drives the most conversion in your portfolio.

Don't get addicted to candy. Eat your veggies too!

Tip 4: Remember your audience

We live in a very crowded media environment. Information is both free and copious. Cutting through the noise means providing value. Use your inherent domain expertise to teach others. Developers in particular are highly discerning content consumers.

Remember my mantra above all: Help First.

Tip 5: Form matters

Think about the shape of your posts. Some businesses call for long-form essays, while others tend to perform better with quick-hit pieces full of images, diagrams, and animated GIFs.

If you're recording videos, are they polished presentations, vérité-style demos, or interviews? Are you aiming for brand perfection (beautiful style) or grassroots appeal (person in basement with ring lights)?

Is your social media going to be direct and corporate or fun and lighthearted?

As you learn your audience and analyze the performance of your content, you will land on what is most appropriate for you. People you speak with might tell you what worked for them, but only through experimentation and analysis will you be able to identify what works for you.

Tip 6: Use my framework for developer content strategy

It's tempting to dive into creating content, but before you do, take a moment to think about what you're trying to achieve. Every business is different, and only through experimentation will you find your sweet spot. That said, it's important to start with a well-informed hypothesis and evolve as the data tells you to evolve.

I think about content across two axes:

Credibility vs. Capability		
	Capability: content that explains your product or its features	**Credibility:** content that leverages your company or team's expertise and builds your brand accordingly
Virality: content with a very high initial burst of traffic	• Launch posts and content • Identify a problem one of your features solves and write a post about the history of that problem	• Benchmarks • "How we built it," where you focus on a thorny engineering problem you solved (these can sometimes go viral if the problem is interesting enough) • Guest stints on podcasts or YouTube channels
Vitality: SEO content that drives a steady stream of organic inbound traffic over time	• Side-by-side comparisons of your features vs. a competitor's • How to solve X using your product (where X is a long-standing pain point) • How to use your product with a more popular product to solve a problem • Product documentation • Videos, if embedded in high-traffic sites	• Benchmarks also drive long-tail SEO traffic • Deep dive into a typically confusing or complicated industry topic • Listicles about things interesting to the industry (e.g., "13 tools for optimizing . . .", "Top 5 VS Code extensions") • Case studies, if written in a way that is optimized for SEO

The left edge of the table is labeled vertically: **Virality vs. Vitality**

- **Virality vs. Vitality:** Do you want your post to drive an initial boom of traffic, or do you want your post to steadily bring in new traffic (in other words, SEO)?
- **Credibility vs. Capability:** Do you want your post to be about your expertise and therefore raise your credibility among developers? Or do you want your post to be about how you solved a particularly difficult problem in our industry with your product?

Over time you will cover content across all these dimensions, but it's helpful to start somewhere to guide your efforts.

There are some proven types of content within these axes.

Tip 7: Virality isn't automatic

You may be thinking, *Hey, I wrote one of those posts, but it got no traction!* The thing is, you need to work on virality. Get friends with high existing social proof to post for you on Hacker News and Reddit, then share with their followers on Twitter. Rally people you know to read your article and upvote it (be careful not to have people swarm all at once).

If you build it, it's not guaranteed they will come. You need to work on distribution to juice your initial viral burst.

SOCIAL MEDIA AS CONTENT

The social landscape changes dramatically. At the time of this writing, Twitter is near death after renaming itself, overrun by toxicity and a lack of moderation. LinkedIn is decaying, overrun by toxic engagement bait. Threads, Bluesky, and Mastodon all have their own problems, and relatively low audience size.

Ultimately the social media world will shake out and the second-generation winners will emerge.

But the key to social media isn't simply posting. It's growth *through engagement*. You must engage with your audience. Yes, certainly thank people who @-mention you, and reply to those who post direct questions. But even more than that, it's to seek out conversations related to topics of interest to you and engage with them as they happen.

This kind of earnest, humble engagement (all centered around Help First) drives followers, which creates an audience for your content.

SUMMARY

Creating great content is only half the battle. Getting it in front of developers is the real challenge.

- **Developers don't go looking for content, they stumble upon it.** Your job is to meet them where they are and insert your content into their workflows.
- **Don't be afraid of AI.** We're not writing the next great Pulitzer Prize–winning novel here. We're trying to sell software. Don't be ashamed about using AI to help you move faster.
- **SEO is still the foundation.** If your content isn't searchable and discoverable, it might as well not exist.
- **Be present in developer communities.** Reddit, Hacker News, Discord, Stack Overflow, and Twitter are essential distribution channels.
- **Email is underrated.** A great newsletter keeps your audience engaged and drives repeat visits.
- **Syndication is a growth hack.** Publish your content on Dev.to, Medium, Hashnode, and other platforms while keeping canonical URLs in check.
- **Cross-promotion compounds impact.** Reference other blog posts, embed videos, and create multiformat content to keep developers in your ecosystem.
- **YouTube is the second-largest search engine.** Short, highly practical videos drive engagement and bring developers into your world.
- **Developer documentation is content too.** Many developers land on your site through docs first. Make sure your docs guide users to next steps.
- **The best content has a long shelf life.** Evergreen technical posts and tutorials generate value long after publication.
- **Measure what works.** Track where your best traffic comes from and double down on those channels.

Content marketing is the engine of your entire developer marketing and developer relations engine. Take the time to understand your market and build the content that your customers are seeking out.

With a good foundation of content, you can begin engaging with your community. Let's dive in.

CHAPTER 7

Building Community and Engaging with Influencers

A developer community isn't something you can force, buy, or manufacture on demand. True communities are earned, not built. They take time, consistency, and commitment. You don't create a thriving community by simply setting up a forum or launching a Slack group. You earn it by contributing value, engaging authentically, and showing up day after day. And yes, you need to throw in a little love too.

There are three pillars I adhere to when thinking about a community strategy:

- **Long-term:** I am in it for the long haul. I want to build something that lasts and endures, not simply something that serves my purpose for now. If I'm participating in an existing community, my intent is to contribute thoughtfully for an extended period of time.
- **Authentic:** I always do things that are natural to the community. I don't parachute in, ask people to click on a link, and leave.
- **Technically credible:** I lead with technology and ask highly technical people to post frequently.

Today we are all participants, in one fashion or another, in a community of some kind. Whether it's an online group about a favorite sports team or hobby, a support group for a life moment, a group of friends who get together to play board games, or something else entirely, we humans crave interaction and belonging. When we look for communities, we are looking for three things:

- **Our tribe:** people who have a passion or interest in common and want to learn more about the topic
- **Support:** a healthy, encouraging environment where we feel safe to ask questions and be vulnerable
- **Recognition:** being called out for excellent contributions to the community's health and vibrancy

These same principles apply to developer communities. This chapter will break down how to approach developer community building with these values in mind and how to genuinely earn a community's trust and loyalty. In a later chapter, we will talk about segmentation and the ideal customer profile. Identifying segments with prebuilt communities, and making the effort to contribute meaningfully to those communities, will make your entire go-to-market engine faster and more effective.

THE POWER OF COMMUNITY

At first glance, community may seem like a nice-to-have benefit or a means to deflect support inquiries. But if you look at the most successful developer-focused businesses of the last decade (Vercel, Stripe, Supabase, and so on), the defining characteristic they all share isn't just great technology. It's the strength, depth, and engagement of the developer communities that have grown around them.

Community is your ultimate moat. Technology is rarely the true competitive advantage. It can be copied, reverse-engineered, and improved upon. Features that once set you apart are eventually commoditized. What remains defensible is trust and engagement. What you seek is a self-sustaining network of developers who rely on your product, advocate for it, and contribute to its growth.

A strong developer community is a network-effect moat: the more developers who use and invest in your ecosystem, the harder it becomes for competitors to displace you. A new tool might claim to be "better" or "faster," but if developers have already built workflows, extensions, integrations, and mental models around your product, they are far less likely to switch. Community becomes your stickiness.

Moreover, the most successful developer companies don't just rely on traditional marketing or sales motions. They leverage their community as a core-growth loop:

- **Communities drive awareness** of products and features and accelerate feature adoption.
- **Communities lower acquisition costs** as prospective customers seek out their advice before making a purchase decision.
- **Communities help support your product** and reduce your support burden.
- **Communities guide your product direction** by providing instant and passionate feedback—if you choose to listen. (Many companies neglect customer feedback at their own peril.)

Authenticity and trust are the most valuable currencies in developer-focused companies. Communities are instant barometers of authenticity and trust.

OPEN-SOURCE COMMUNITIES

Open-source companies don't worry about competition copying their software, because the product itself is not the moat. Rather, the community is. A competitor can fork your code, but they can't fork your brand trust, your developer relationships, or your contributor ecosystem.

- **Developers contribute to the projects they believe in.** The larger your engaged contributor base, the harder it is for a competitor to siphon away momentum.
- **Ecosystem effects reinforce the original project.** Popular open-source projects spawn third-party tools, plug-ins, integrations, and content, further entrenching your position.
- **The trust factor:** Open-source signals transparency, which is invaluable for developer adoption. Developers trust tools they can inspect and modify more than proprietary black boxes.

For developer-first businesses, open-source is not just a distribution model, it's a movement. And when nurtured correctly, it is the strongest and most defensible competitive advantage you can build.

HELP FIRST + INTEGRITY

The mantra of Help First is rooted in a philosophy of selfless leadership. You give to others what you do best, with no expectations or strings attached. Over time, a community appreciates your efforts. That appreciation translates to brand equity in our world of developer products.

Inherent in this selfless act of giving is integrity, which is the currency of developer marketing. If you have it, you continue to build on it. If you lose it, you've lost the game. As everyone knows, a reputation of integrity is built painstakingly over time—and can be lost in an instant.

So in all my discussion about earning a community, I start with integrity. This translates into many things as you build your market-requirements document, go-to-market plan, and sales-enablement plans. Here are some examples of how integrity manifests itself in how you run developer marketing:

- You treat your people respectfully, allowing them to explore their ideas, fail, and learn. As a leader, you act with integrity at all times, which sets a similar expectation across the organization. How you treat your people is how they treat your customers.

- When you publish content, it is honest and truthful. No fake numbers, no fake testimonials, etc.
- Benchmarking, not benchmarketing. Explain honestly where you succeed and where you fail against competitors. Developers are already going to find this out eventually. Play the long game and earn their trust.

ONLINE COMMUNITIES: WHERE TO HOST YOUR COMMUNITY

This is perhaps the least-interesting component of a community, yet the one that most people fixate on. In a way, it's easy to see why. After all, shipping a website or a community Slack/Discord is something you can check off as accomplished. But community development is something that is ongoing, forever.

As for where to host your community, make a decision quickly and don't belabor it, as the true magic of a community isn't the software, but the vibe. Here are my thoughts (based on hard-won experience) on types of online communities you can launch for your product:

- **Slack or Discord:** Both these chatlike tools are inherently popular nowadays for developer communities. They have a real-time feel, and they make it easy to "police" behavior. Tools are available for managing a Slack community and for automating messages and other interactions that make it seem more vibrant. The big drawback of the Slack/Discord option is that Google doesn't index the content. And, in the case of Slack, you have to pay—depending on the size of your community, a sometimes substantial amount!—to keep an archive of questions.
- **Forums:** These enable you to host conversations about your community and product online. They lack the real-time chatlike feel of Slack or Discord, but on the flip side, the content can be indexed and searched by Google. Discourse is my favorite forum. It's easy to customize and use.

IN-PERSON COMMUNITIES: THE ART OF THE MEETUP

In the beginning, there were "user groups." Over time, these morphed into "meetups." And most recently, meetups have become profitable enterprises for community leaders. You used to be able to reach out to a meetup organizer, offer to pay for pizza, bring some stickers and T-shirts, and get a few minutes to talk about a topic of interest to you.

Back then, as now, we never did product pitches. We focused on solving a problem of interest to the user group and, oh by the way, we would show our product in the process.

Lately meetups have begun accepting sponsorship fees for vendors to secure these speaking slots. What used to be community-driven and fun is now a mini-event exercise. Capitalism!

Nevertheless, people who attend meetups are sacrificing their evening to hang out with like-minded enthusiasts. They are there because they *want* to be, not because their employer told them to go or they are otherwise compelled to attend. This is their tribe.

When you attend a meetup, whether as a sponsored guest or just an attendee, keep in mind that you are effectively walking into someone else's living room. Be an earnest, humble participant. Introduce yourself to others. Listen more than you speak. And regardless of whether you represent Google or an unknown (yet) startup, earn your stripes.

Before I ever consider sponsoring a meetup or requesting a speaking slot, I like to attend at least twice. After attending and introducing myself to various people as well as the organizer, I reach out and see if they're interested in speakers. If you're with a BigTech company, offering to host a meetup is almost always welcome.

But the bottom line with meetups is to do the work to really appreciate the social mores and constraints of the environment you're walking into before you start asking for things.

INFLUENCER MARKETING FOR DEVELOPERS

Some of the most popular ways that people choose to learn today are podcasts and YouTube. Creators around the world build exceptional content that teaches and helps grow the types of developers with whom you want to drive awareness of your products. These creators cultivate (often as major contributing factors to their livelihood) large communities of technical users that probably matter to you.

First let's dive into how to identify and qualify creators, then let's explore two ways of engaging with them: earned media and sponsorships.

Identifying creators

As part of your marketing strategy, catalog (list out) all the people who are building and creating content around your subject area. Building this list will enable you to prioritize people based on audience size and sponsorship costs, as well as general applicability to your product or service. So start with this list and spend a good chunk of time with your developer advocates and your engineers, understanding who *they* listen to and go to for information.

In addition, during every customer interaction, be it someone at a tradeshow, a prospect on a sales call, or a customer you have already won, always ask where they go to learn and get more information about the industry. Ask them who they trust for an opinion on a new technology or area. Ask them what they subscribe to: podcasts, newsletters, YouTube channels, and so forth. In particular, take note of content to which they have a paid subscription.

These are great ways to identify where other like-minded customers congregate and what media they consume. But this is just the start of our research.

Researching and qualifying creators

For the next phase of your research, take the time to listen to these podcasts. Do the tone a podcast takes and the audience it speaks to match the tone you'd like to take and the audience you'd like to reach? Are the products that they talk about in the same price category (or the same general category) as your own? Does the creator seem open-minded about trying new products, or are they legacy-minded and not a good fit for a forward-thinking company? Would you want to be a guest on their podcast?

You will then be able to whittle your list down to a group of creators you would like to work with and could potentially benefit from.

Now you can begin to craft outreach. Remember that everything you do should be for long-term benefit, authentic, and technically credible. So when you reach out to a creator, you want to build a relationship. Don't run ahead and try to close the deal. Perhaps start with an opening remark about why you're interested in this creator's work. Maybe it was a podcast that you heard that resonated with you. It could be a YouTube video where you enjoyed their style of demoing products. Regardless, what you are looking for is an opportunity to connect naturally and authentically with this creator.

Here's an example of an email I sent to a creator who built PostgreSQL content:

> Hi XXXXXX,
>
> I just watched your video on YYYYY. I wanted to send you an email thanking you for the explanation. I have been learning SQL for my role here at ZZZZZZ and yours was the crispest definition I could find.
>
> If you're interested in having guests on your videos, I know my Founder & CEO would love the chance to talk with you about what we're building.
>
> Thanks,
>
> –P

As you can see, the email is earnest, it demonstrates that I actually watched the channel, and it involves a clear request. The subsequent conversation resulted in the creator filming a demo video about a product I was working on at the time.

Working with creators

The key when working with creators is to respect their integrity. They represent their personal brand, and expecting them to write only good things about you is unrealistic. The more authentic they are, including describing the warts in your product, the more their customers will trust them. No product is perfect, and no product is perfect for everyone. Enabling creators to use their own voice to make content about your product will help you stand out.

You should also be careful not to pressure creators on timelines or quality. They have their own process and their own goals. Respect them both.

Sometimes creators will ask for compensation for videos, or you may want to offer it ahead of time. You don't need to go overboard here. If you're a small startup, somewhere around $500 to $1,000 is sufficient for a creator with fewer than one hundred thousand subscribers. But even if you offer to pay, make it clear that the creator has full artistic license to record the video they want, without interference from you. You will always be there to answer questions, of course. But the final video and voice is theirs and theirs alone.

Sponsoring creators

Podcast and YouTube sponsorships are great ways to drive awareness of your product if you have the budget for them. I have found that a concerted podcast effort as a component of a larger developer campaign can be very effective in amplifying my message across a large group of developers.

Remember, when you are building a sponsorship for something like a podcast, it has to fit into the broader context of any campaigns that you're running. For example, if you're running a campaign that emphasizes how to secure web applications and how your product addresses that issue, you should be searching for podcasts and creators who specialize in helping harden web applications. Your creator's interests, your audience's interests, and your own interests need to be fully aligned and consistent with the campaign you are running.

Unlike earned media, you have control over sponsored content and mentions (within reason, of course). Make sure your sponsored content matches the consistent themes of your marketing campaigns, thus amplifying your core message across as many channels as possible.

Measuring influencer marketing

Providing creators with personalized affiliate links and coupon codes is a tried-and-true method for gauging whether leads or sign-ups are being referred from content. I like to use shortlinks (Bitly, Dub.co, BL.INK, etc.) with specific UTM parameters and give them to the creator to include in their videos and descriptions.

If your product supports it, you can also generate special coupon codes or affiliate links that can be used within it that will help you identify where leads came from.

> **TIP:** I love using shortlinks in marketing activities, but remember that many developers will simply enter a company URL in an incognito window. In this case you'll just need to track when videos go live and see if there's an uptick in site visitors and sign-ups. It's not perfect, but as I've discussed before, attribution is not an exact science. Usually getting directional indicators is sufficient.

You can also use the YouTube Data API to run queries every day and obtain information about mentions of your product, the number of views generated by videos that mention you, and how those numbers have grown. The YouTube Data API is free with generous daily limits, and you can generate a Python script in seconds with ChatGPT or your favorite LLM.

COMMUNITY ENGAGEMENT

You have many tactics for building a strong, vibrant community. These aren't mutually exclusive, and often you'll want to layer in all these efforts.

Build more than your own community.

By all means, launch a Slack/Discord or forum. This will be where your new and existing users, people who are already aware of you, can get their questions answered. But to use a community to drive awareness, you must be present in other communities where developers already congregate. Identify the communities most relevant to your business and actively participate in them. Offer help, ask questions, and be genuinely kind and good members of each community.

Identify the key technical influencers.

These folks write technical blogs about your product area or are highly regarded open-source contributors. Get to know them. Find out how you can help them.

Community participation comes in many flavors.

Sometimes it's answering questions in online forums. Other times it's contributing to an open-source project or volunteering at a meetup or event. Think about all the ways you can help, and then jump in and do the work with a Help First mindset.

Be authentic and technically credible.

Don't do things that aren't natural to the community. Your primary interactions there should be technical in nature, not marketing. For example, don't ask people to tweet your product announcements. Simply share announcements in your forums and trust that your most active users will share on your behalf.

Always think long term.

Don't do community activities in the hope of getting a quick gain: a tweet, a quote for a press release, or something transactional. Instead do them with an eye toward the long-term health of the community in which you've chosen to participate.

CULTIVATING YOUR BEST FANS

Often you'll develop active, vocal fans in your community, folks who are quick to lend a hand to others who have questions. They are passionate about your product and your mission. And they enjoy the work, even though it's nowhere near their day job.

Think about ways you can reward them. Providing them with access to prerelease products is table stakes. T-shirts are always a good idea, as are other low-key swag items. But also consider getting this kind of community member one-on-one face time with your CEO. Include them when you're soliciting input and feedback on new services and products. If you get extra conference passes as part of a sponsorship, ask them if they'd like to join you.

Simple acts of kindness and recognition often do wonders for the relationship.

In the early days of Microsoft's developer relations strategy (in the early 1990s, to be exact), they created the Microsoft Most Valuable Professional (MVP) program. The MVP program has always had exceptionally rigorous selection and qualification criteria. Thus it is an honor within the Microsoft developer community to be awarded admission into the program. At the same time, Microsoft has worked hard to provide fantastic perks for its MVPs, from access to senior executives, to an annual summit/retreat, to free software, to early access to new builds. Microsoft MVPs support the company, and the company supports them.

One thing I'd advise is to not jump ahead and brand a program if you're an early-stage startup. The Heroes and MVP-style programs are great once you're established. The exception is rewarding open-source contributors with recognition, swag, and opportunities to meet your exec team.

CODES OF CONDUCT

Communities need to be healthy. That means no hate speech, bullying, or disrespectful behavior. You're running a business, not a social experiment. Encourage people to keep things professional.

Every community should have a clear code of conduct with a well-defined and -publicized escalation path. There are several open-source codes of conduct to choose from. Pick one, customize it for your needs, and make sure everyone in your community knows that they are expected to abide by it. For example, when they sign up for your community, provide them with a welcome message and inform them about the rules that you've set forth.

This goes for your own team as well. In the past, I have demoted and even fired team leads who were disrespectful in the community. Developer advocates should be held to a higher standard when it comes to how they engage online, even in forums unrelated to work.

DON'T FORGET LOVE! 😊

There's a lot of acerbic nonsense in the world today. Choose love. Choose to act with kindness and empathy. Even if a competitor annoys you, take the high road and be good. Choose to build a community where all community members are celebrated.

SUMMARY

Communities are powerful moats around your product. They can provide valuable direct feedback to your product and engineering team. They can help welcome and onboard new users. They can help existing users share their best practices. And they can show up for one another when times are tough.

- **Developer communities form organically. but you can nurture them.** Support forums, Discords, Slack groups, and GitHub issues are all great starting points.
- **The best developer communities are useful.** If your community doesn't help developers solve real problems, they won't stick around.
- **Content and community go hand in hand.** A great blog or YouTube channel can naturally grow into a full-fledged community.
- **Champion your power users.** Recognize and amplify community members who advocate for your product.
- **Events are still valuable.** Meetups, hackathons, and conferences build relationships that digital channels can't replicate.
- **Engagement matters more than numbers.** A small but highly engaged community is infinitely more valuable than a large but silent one.

Now that you have your content and community engines working, you can maximize your presence at events. Let's see how developer events—perhaps the most glamorous part of the job (and the biggest time- and expense-sink)—can level up your marketing program.

CHAPTER 8

Developer Events

Events are the final component in the developer advocacy mix. They are certainly the most time-consuming and the most expensive. The first question to ask yourself is whether events are even worth it as part of your marketing mix. Because of the costs involved, you should make the investment intentionally.

That said, there are many types of events you can participate in. We covered meetups in the previous chapter. In this chapter we will cover the following kinds of events:

- third-party events (hosted by others)
- first-party conferences (hosted by you)
- first-party road tours
- first-party sales and customer breakfasts or dinners
- business roundtable events
- virtual events

ARE EVENTS A WORTHWHILE INVESTMENT?

To answer this question, you need to clarify your objectives. What are you trying to get out of events? Typically we elect to do them for one or more of the following reasons:

- to generate leads
- to build brand awareness
- to strengthen community relationships
- to engage with existing customers
- to launch or promote new features or products

The reason could differ from event to event. For example, you may elect to sponsor a small regional roundtable because you want to strengthen community relationships with the organizer. You may want to attend a major conference and invest in a large booth in a premium location to build brand awareness. And you may want to attend a sales event with many buyers in attendance in order to generate leads.

Your goals will help you determine metrics for measuring the efficacy of the event, and you can use that information to decide whether to attend similar ones or the same one next year. But always start with evaluating your goals up front for each event.

THIRD-PARTY EVENTS

Typically, the ways you can participate in an event fall into three non-mutually exclusive buckets:

- sponsoring it in some manner
- submitting a talk proposal
- attending and networking

It is possible to sponsor the event but not attend. I've done this for a few very small events for a small amount of money in order to support an influencer or community of interest. But most of the time, if you sponsor, you will attend. And many times if you sponsor, you will get a free sponsored talk as part of the deal—and you should negotiate for this every time!

Attending third-party conferences involves several considerations:

- choosing the right events
- evaluating sponsorship costs
- submitting calls for papers (CFPs)
- sponsored talks
- pre-event outreach
- networking with attendees
- booth layout, structure, and giveaways
- booth attendee training and behavior
- post-event follow-up
- post-event marketing
- ancillary activities during the event

Choosing the right events

The first question on your mind should be *Which events should I attend?* I always tell my teams, "Events don't pop up out of nowhere. You usually get at least six to nine months before the event to consider it." Events take time, effort, and most of all advance planning to run well, so organizers will announce their conference well ahead of time. If you're running a developer business, you're already plugged into your community. Start listening for conferences people are considering attending.

Your list should consist of conferences where there's a large concentration of decision makers for your product in your target market. If you're running a database company, this could be both database conferences and industry conferences where attendees are selecting a database for their project—for example an oil and gas trade show. The key is to make sure that, regardless of the nature of the industry, the attendees are in a position to make a technology decision. This is the first and most important analysis for you to make.

Once you have your list of events, start prioritizing them based on a few factors. First, will leads from this conference have a high propensity to convert? In other words, will you be speaking with people who are capable of making an adoption or trial decision about your product? Second, is the conference located in a city where it will be feasible to send employees? And finally, what is the cost to sponsor the event, and is that within your budget?

Evaluating sponsorship costs

Events are expensive. And I'm going to be perfectly honest with you: they rarely generate an immediate ROI. You do an event for three reasons:

- to acquire leads and book meetings with prospects
- to meet with existing customers and drive expansion conversations, or introduce them to other potential customers as living testimonials for your product
- to build awareness of your brand within the developer community

The last bullet is nearly impossible to measure, so I usually discount it as a goal. I focus on the other objectives.

If you sponsor an event and you've determined that the attendees are, in fact, the kind of people who would be interested in your product and able to make a technical adoption or evaluation decision, then you can work toward calculating your goals.

Usually I take 5% of the total attendees and establish to the team that we will book that many meetings. So, a 10,000-person conference? Book 500 meetings. That's a tall order for most teams, but if you work backwards from the data, you'll see why:

- 10,000 attendees, some percentage of whom will not be your target customer
- 500 meetings booked (5% of total attendees)
- 400 meetings flake out on you, but 20% do attend
- 100 meetings held, but only 10% are qualified opportunities
- 10 qualified opportunities

> 5% of total attendees = meetings-booked goal

Obviously, these numbers are overly pessimistic to illustrate a point. You need to work your tail off to turn a sponsorship fee for a conference into results.

There are many ways to do that.

Submitting calls for papers

Submitting a talk via a CFP is nearly always worth it.

First off, working closely with your developer advocacy and engineering teams to pull together a roster of speakers and talks is a lot of fun and brings the teams closer. You should do this no matter what, as the ideas you come up with for talks are generally excellent ideas for content. In fact, even if you don't win the CFP, you should **write the talk and build the content anyway**!

And as I've written several times, content repurposing is critical. Take your conference talks and turn them into blog posts, and vice versa. Record your talks and put them up on your YouTube channel.

Beyond preparation for CFPs being really good team hygiene, conference organizers are always looking for new companies and new voices to fill out their roster. Beyond including the requisite Google or Microsoft speaker to legitimize the event, organizers love to be seen as forward-thinking industry leaders. Thus, your chances as a startup to secure a speaking slot are actually pretty high, provided your content topic is high quality.

Which gets me to content topics: never, ever, ever do product pitches.

No one wants to be sold to. Instead, remember my mantra, Help First: teach developers something new. Use the talk to establish yourself and your brand as knowledgeable experts. People will check out your company if it is known for solving hard problems!

Writing CFPs is an art form in and of itself. Your goal is to convince the talk-selection committee that not only is your subject matter interesting, unique, and relevant to the conference audience, but you are the single best person to talk about it. Here are some tips:

- **Use an attention-grabbing title.** Make sure it is clear, concise, and intriguing. "Scaling PostgreSQL Beyond 1 Million Writes per Second" is a lot more interesting than "Scaling Your Database."
- **Write a compelling abstract.** Summarize your talk with your unique angle. Focus on the "why" as much as the "what."
- **Speak to the audience.** It shouldn't have to be said, but if you're speaking to database engineers, your talk should appeal to database engineers.
- **Solve a real problem (with customer proof).** We never do product pitches, of course. But highlighting a customer who has done something amazing using your product is always fair game.
- **Your biography should be credible.** Highlight your relevant experience (relevant to the talk, that is). It's OK to have boilerplate bios, we all do. But before you submit yours, tailor it to the audience and the talk you're giving.

If I were to summarize my thoughts on CFPs, it would boil down to this: don't submit product pitches; repurpose your talk content everywhere you can; and even if you don't win your CFP, build the content anyway!

Developer advocates are perhaps best known for their attendance on the conference circuit. But if you pay close attention to session reviews and conference chatter, many technical-engineering attendees have grown weary of developer advocates who give talks.

"They're just product pitches," goes the refrain.

In that vein, work with your engineering team to present. If engineers are shy about presenting information, developer advocates can coach and train them. I've always maintained that public speaking skills are a great determinant of future career progression. Everyone should work on this all the time.

Sponsored talks

Usually your sponsorship will include a booth, a lead scanner, some additional benefits, special passes, and potentially a sponsor talk.

One word of caution about sponsored talks: they are usually placed at the back end of the conference, such as a Friday afternoon, when most attendees are gone, or in the early evening, when everyone is tired and heading home. It may still be worth it, but in all likelihood you're not going to be able to buy your way into the keynote.

The calculations you'll need to make in evaluating sponsorship opportunities will vary on a case-by-case basis. There are no hard-and-fast rules, there is no formula, and the only thing you can do is make educated guesses about whether the sponsorship is of value to you. Maybe the sponsored talk is what tips it in favor of doing the event.

Whenever I do a sponsored talk, I like to bring a customer to do a presentation for me. If a customer is speaking instead of me doing a product pitch, there's a greater likelihood that people will want to attend the talk, and a greater likelihood that people will want to learn more about the technologies mentioned. The customer may speak about my product for just five minutes out of a thirty-minute talk. But those five minutes are a tacit endorsement, and that's always going to be much better than a half-hour product pitch that's poorly attended.

If you go the customer-talk route for your sponsorship and the customer is willing to do a case study, make sure that case study is part of your social media promotion of the talk. Mention it everywhere you can. Take pictures of the customer on stage, take pictures of the customer slide—especially where they mention you—and link to the customer's case study so people can follow up and learn more.

Turn the sponsored talk into something that is extremely valuable to you—and worthwhile for attendees!—even if it's in the worst-possible time slot in the conference.

Pre-event outreach

A few weeks before the event, you and your sales team should huddle and sift through your existing customer lists. Identify the people most likely to attend. Maybe they're local, maybe they've attended in the past. Build a plan for personalized outreach from the sales team to each of these customers. You want to let the customer know a few things:

- **Existing customers:** *Come meet us at the booth and get a special thank-you T-shirt!* This is a good opportunity to check in with the customer, make them feel welcome, and see if there are expansion opportunities on the horizon.
- **Existing pipeline:** *Let's meet at the show so we can show you our new features in action!* Maybe grab coffee or dinner, and continue to progress the relationship.
- **Cold or closed/lost:** *Here's an update on what we shipped since we last spoke!* Ask if they're attending the show and would like to meet there to discuss more.

And so on. The goal is to use your customer list to book productive meetings for your sales team and executives who are attending the show.

Network with attendees

Attending the conference and networking there is another great way to make friends in your target customer's community. Arrange coffee conversations with people you know will be there. Post on social media that you'll be attending and want to meet folks. Have hallway conversations. Ask speakers questions after their talks.

Not everyone in your company is suited for this kind of extroverted approach. Identify and send your most gregarious developers to the event. Give them a budget for picking up bar tabs and buying lunch or dinner for small groups of attendees.

Make sure they write up a trip report afterward with as much detail about their observations as possible.

Booth layout, structure, and activities

Sponsoring the conference usually means getting a booth or table in the event's exhibits hall and getting a mention during the keynote, including perhaps your logo on each slide deck at the event. It could also include a sponsored talk. I have been known to sponsor a talk but decline the booth because I don't have sufficient staff available, but I know that being present at the conference is still important to the brand. You have to make the calculation yourself about whether the give-and-gets are meaningful to you.

OK, so you're attending an event and have chosen to sponsor and obtain a booth. Now you need to maximize your presence and ensure that the event delivers a high ROI.

Booth logistics

Several weeks before the event, you will need to get your booth logistics in order. Follow your event organizer's instructions to ensure that your booth's graphics, signage, and any A/V needs are met. Get your brand/design team together and start formulating ideas that are consistent with your brand identity.

Take a step back and think about the average attendee walking by the show floor. What questions will be top of mind? What kinds of talks are typically given at this event, and what kind of ideas will they typically spark? Your graphics and signage should be consistent with your brand and positioning, yes. But they shouldn't be complete copycats of your positioning statement. Adjust your messaging for your audience and make your booth stand out in a way that attracts passersby.

I did some work for Causely, a causal-reasoning platform for autonomous service reliability, when they exhibited at an AI conference. In order to appeal to passersby on the show floor, they went with the following booth messaging: The Brain for Agentic Service Reliability. Similarly, at Tinybird, a data engineering platform for real-time analytics, we exhibited at Kafka and Confluent shows with booth verbiage that read Kafka to APIs in Minutes.

Ensuring that your booth messaging aligns to the conversations most likely to be top of mind at the event will translate to better booth traffic and results.

Booth demo

You will also want to start planning your booth demo a few weeks early. What kind of demo scenario and associated dataset do you need that will make attendees feel like you get them and their industry? Do you need more than one demo, depending on which vertical industry or use case a typical customer at the show will have? If you attend an oil and gas conference and are showing a demo about web analytics, you've failed. Knock out multiple birds with one stone: this is a great opportunity to merge your solution-focused content needs with your event needs. We'll talk more about booth demos in a moment.

Identify staff

Make sure it's not just developer advocates attending. Pull in folks from sales and customer success. Everyone will benefit from meeting with real, live customers. Do not under any circumstances choose unqualified booth staff based solely on their looks. This is an unwelcome, unappreciated, and highly dated tactic that no company should ever engage in.

Booth giveaway

This is different from swag. Offer sweepstakes of some kind for attendees who watch a demo. If they complete a demo, they get a raffle ticket. Hold the draw at the end of the conference (or, for a large conference like AWS re:Invent, hold a draw every afternoon). Take lots of pictures for social media of the crowd around your booth. Interview customers on video about what stood out to them at the show, about your product, about products they saw elsewhere. For the price of a Nintendo Switch, you will educate many more customers about your product and generate excitement that can be used across your marketing channels.

Buy swag

I hate T-shirts because of the bulk and the expense of shipping. Socks are played out. Fidget spinners are so 2017. Figure out what kind of giveaway you want. In recent years, there has been a trend, which I love, of giving away a business card with a redemption code for your swag store or the option of donating five dollars to a charity. This idea saves costs, is better for the environment, and makes customers feel good.

Build your comms plan

Identify journalists and key influencers who will be at the event, and make sure you've reached out and secured time to chat.

Social media promotion

Make sure you have a social media plan in place. It could be anything from posting hourly with key observations at the event, to posting daily with a picture of the team at the booth and a reminder of where attendees can find you. Don't forget to use the event hashtag.

Have the people attending the event send you a constant stream of photos for your social media account. They don't need to be perfect or professional. Behind-the-scenes photos of your team, "action shots" of your team interacting with customers, and photos of your booth and giveaways are all fair game for social media.

One thing to be aware of: lead-capture devices always fail. Always. So while you want to teach your team how to use the lead-capture devices provided by the event organizers, also train your team on a backup process. Maybe it's "Take a pic of people's badges with your cell phone," or "Here's a bunch of notepads to get names and email addresses."

Booth attendee training and behavior

Everyone who attends will have a job to do. Do not let people just stand around twiddling their thumbs.

The first and most important role is **The Sweepers**. These are your most outgoing folks. They're going to wait in the pathway farther out from your booth and talk to attendees as they go by. "How's the show going for you? Would you like to hear about our new galaxy-class database?" Their job is to understand who the customer is and what's top of mind, and then bring them to the booth.

The next role is **The Demo-er**. This is the person who is going to listen to the customer's pain points and then subtly adjust the demo talking points to address them as they go through it. This person is always technical.

The last role is **The Finisher**. This person listens to the demo alongside the customer and once the demo is finished, engages the customer in a conversation about what they're looking for and how your company can help. The Finisher is also responsible for capturing the lead and then taking notes about the level of interest. They should try to book the meeting with the customer on the spot. Remember, your goal is to generate meetings and turn them into opportunities after the event. The Finisher role is almost always a sales development representative (SDR) or account executive (AE).

One other important job to assign is **The Spy**. This should be someone technical on your team, and they should be responsible for visiting all your competitors' booths (as well as booths from companies closely related to your space). You'll want them to take pictures of booths, get demos, and take notes on key positioning and messaging points.

In addition, there are some baseline rules everyone should follow:

- No phones, social media scrolling, checking email, TikTok, whatever. This is time to focus on the customer. Don't have a customer to talk to? Go find one.
- No gum, no coffee, no food. Only water.
- Breath mints.
- Nothing is someone else's job. If you see something that needs to be done, do it. This includes booth setup and teardown. One of the most impressive things I've ever seen is a former CEO of mine (of a public company) who came to check on a booth before a show and had no issues whatsoever helping clean up trash and carry boxes.
- Treat everyone with respect. Events can sometimes get harried and emotions can run high. Stay cool and respect your coworkers and customers.

Every day, at the end of the show, the team should get together and go over some key questions:

- Are our demos working well?
- Do people react well to the messaging?
- Is the collateral effective?

Make adjustments and move quickly.

The art of the booth demo

Earlier we walked through best practices for building a demo in general. You may want to make a few tweaks for a demo in a booth on a crowded show floor.

Trade show floors are chaotic and loud. Prospects may come by your booth because they're intrigued by your signage or because they've already heard of your company. You want to make sure that you give them a great first experience with your company and your product. The best way to do this is with your product.

Above and beyond my earlier tips for creating great product demos, here are some best practices for building a booth demo:

- **Use a prerecorded demo on the main screen.** Take your product demo with the most expansive and inclusive scenario and screen-record it using a professional screen-recording tool. My favorite is Screen Studio. Use appropriate (not too much) zooming in and out to highlight specific features or areas of the product. Run this on the screen everyone sees as they go by. Don't forget to add subtitles so that "gawkers" on the periphery of your booth can follow along (and for accessibility reasons also). One helpful tip: if it's easy and if the show organizers permit it, regroup every evening and tweak the demo to reflect the questions you're hearing from customers.

- **Provide a QR code to a landing page with a lead-generation form.** Typically your biggest crowd will gather during periods when breakout sessions are not currently happening. This means everyone at the conference will be on the show floor, wandering by. Your booth staff may be busy with customers when a prospect comes by. Have a QR code printed out and framed, or placed as a sticker in a prominent part of your booth, visible to passersby. Include a message that says, "Don't feel like waiting? Scan the code and we'll arrange a private demo just for you." Now you can follow up during the show or when you're back in the office.
- **Plan for WiFi to go out.** If your demos require internet access, have all of them available as recordings that you can play offline. Yes, live demos are the best. Customers can ask questions, and you can veer off the path and answer questions. But if WiFi goes down, you want to have a plan. And customers will understand. After all, WiFi is down for them too!
- **Have multiple demo machines prepared.** Unfortunately, sometimes laptops and iPads get stolen. Sometimes laptops don't work with booth screens and equipment provided by the conference. Have contingency plans.

The "Know Before You Go" guide

Whoever is responsible for the event (your events marketing manager, perhaps) should write a detailed background document ("Know Before You Go") about the event (your goal there, your core message, the activities you've planned around the event, etc.) and related logistics (the location of your booth; what your swag looks like; the hotel where your people are staying; flight arrival and departure information; public transportation; contact information for everyone, including emergency contacts; nearby restaurants; etc.).

Leave no stone unturned and make the guide as detailed as

possible. Marketing people often forget that most people in an organization never travel for business and need extra hand-holding.

In addition, you should hold a preshow meeting where all attendees from your company can hear firsthand from marketing the goals for the show, details about what the show will entail, and core messages; see demos in action; and be able to ask questions.

Postevent follow-up

You also need to plan your efforts after the event:

- **Plan your post-event nurture.** You've accumulated email addresses. What email will you send after the event, what call to action will be included, and who will the email be from? You should have this ready to send two to three days after the event concludes.
- **Run a retrospective.** Get everyone on a Zoom or in a room and walk through everything you'd like to Start Doing, Keep Doing, and Stop Doing. Summarize this information while the event is fresh in everyone's memory.
- **Write the trip report.** Solicit input from all attendees and codify your observations of customers, community, the event itself. Include the results of the retro as well. Be sure to answer the question of whether you'd do the event again.

Several weeks later, you should be able to gauge the ROI of the event and append it to the trip report, answering the following questions:

- How many scans did we get at the booth?
- How many meetings were booked?
- How many meetings turned into opportunities?

You can then look at the total potential pipeline from opportunities and compare it to the sponsorship cost.

Keep track of and memorialize all your data. Ensure that future decisions about events are made based on past experience.

Hopefully you accumulated some great content, photos, and videos during the event. Use these in the following weeks across your social media platforms to continue driving quality engagement with customers and prospects.

FIRST-PARTY CONFERENCES

So you want to do a developer conference? Congratulations! This means you have reached critical mass in terms of customers and community, and you're ready to put on a big show.

A developer conference is an all-company affair and a major milestone, no matter how big or small your company is. Everyone in the company or group will align around this conference. The product and engineering team will have new features and launches ready to go. Product marketing—we'll talk more about that later—is suited up and ready to deliver the biggest, most powerful launch the industry has ever seen. The marketing organization is ready to drive sign-ups and registrations for the conference. Your partner marketing organization is ready to work the phones and get people to cosponsor, to drive the perception that you are an industry leader. Developer advocates are busy building talks and coaching engineering on their own docs. Even your HR team can get involved. You can run pre-event workshops for special groups and turn the conference into a recruiting wave.

I've run several first-party developer conferences in my life, ranging from two-hundred-person to twenty-thousand-person events. I've run launch events featuring the CEOs of BigTech. And I've turned ordinary product launches into industry conferences.

Let me tell you my secret:

Whatever can go wrong will go wrong.

Be resilient

If you're in charge of running a first-party developer conference, you need to be resilient and you need to be the kind of leader that teaches resilience to everyone who depends on you. Because random things will go wrong at random times. And your ability to handle those issues and pivot to positivity will make or break your conference. And your customers will be able to tell. Always.

With one conference I ran, the website wasn't ready on the day we announced the event. We regrouped and delayed launching-event sign-up and registration by two days. With another conference, the registration check-in computers went down a half hour before the keynote. We scrambled and checked in people by hand. With another, my team was called in two weeks early to help fill the remaining four hundred seats by engaging with our community. (We did it, but that was an experience never to replicate!)

First-party conferences are difficult, and it's important that the entire team (especially the executive team) be prepared. Make it your job to lead them through the storm. Careers are made with these kinds of events.

Components of a great conference

When I think of a first-party conference, I break it down to a bunch of functional areas. For each one I recruit and/or assign a leader, and I run a weekly meeting to get reports on their progress. And I report progress, nonprogress, mistakes, and the harsh truth to my executive management.

Most important, I treat each functional area as part of a team. I can tell you war stories about massive problems that were solved by a senior comms or legal person in the room, simply because their frame of mind was different than everyone else's. Diversity matters. Embrace it.

Let's talk about some of the functional areas I find most valuable:

- the keynote and core message
- the breakout sessions
- case studies, customer evidence, customer video testimonials
- VIP experience with priority registration, seating, and private lunches for top customers
- partners, including a potential partner pavilion with booths and the opportunity to do lightning talks or smaller breakout sessions
- diversity and inclusion event the night before
- event venue and logistics coordination
- event website, registration, on-site check-in and badge pickup
- attendee party

And this doesn't even include the contractors and vendors who run the actual logistics of the on-site event itself. Unless you are in a large BigTech organization, my recommendation is to outsource this to a third party.

I ask every leader to create a project document for their functional area. And we use the project document to formulate the plan, the schedule of deliverables, the budget, and any other necessary request.

Typically this project will be driven by the senior marketing leader on the team. It can be tempting to ask the events manager to run the whole show, but your key message is the core thing you're trying to get across.

Let's dive into a handful of the functional areas for more detail.

Building a great event keynote

These are the moments marketing people live for. We've all dreamed about being Steve Jobs unveiling the iPhone for the first time. (Don't lie, you have too!) At minimum, every marketer on the planet has watched that YouTube video maybe a hundred times in their career.

There are, of course, many lessons to be learned from a "Stevenote." Here is my advice for building a great event keynote:

- **Your CEO or senior-most leader needs to be the keynote speaker.** If they're not comfortable on stage, you need to get a speaker trainer on board to get them to an elite level. I've only worked for two CEOs who were naturals on stage. All the rest have been stilted but have committed to getting better. Mark Zuckerberg still has a strange, forced stage presence, but it is light-years better than when he first started.

- **Keep it short and sweet.** Ideally, the keynote is thirty to forty-five minutes. Do not take your cue from the overly long, ridiculous BigTech keynotes. They suffer from "VP syndrome," where every VP in the company needs to feel validation by having a slide in the keynote. No keynote should ever be longer than forty-five minutes.

- **This is the time for vision.** Lay out the company's vision and why it's important to the world; the challenges to achieving that vision; why those challenges matter to customers (and the world); and what you're announcing today that will address those challenges. Then you can dive into the features and top-level benefits. Save the details for breakout sessions.

- **Include a demo.** See the section on the art of the product demo from earlier. I have had great success selecting experienced demo presenters as well as early-career-stage employees. Figure out who is able to step up, and get them prepared. I've seen it time and again: careers are made during keynote demos. Mine was.

- **Include a customer video.** Pick your best customer (or maybe your top two or three) and record a high-production-value video testimonial from them.

- **Include a partner section.** Highlight the ecosystem you're building around your product, if applicable. Include testimonials—either quotes, videos, or on-stage appearance—from your top partner or partners. You are trying to signal that you're building an industry movement that developers need to be a part of.

- **Kick off the whole thing with a sizzle reel.** The old Microsoft keynotes always had a funny video starring Bill Gates or Steve Ballmer. At Twitter, we had a high-production-value video that highlighted more than two hundred of our top customers in rapid fire (using App Store icons) set to high-energy music. Get the audience warmed up before the "voice of God" introduces your keynote speaker.
- **Aim for demographic diversity.** Keynote talk participants should be inclusive and representative.

As the marketing leader, the most difficult part of writing the keynote will be weighing input from all stakeholders. You should have a strong opinion, but you should hold this opinion loosely. Be open to feedback and consider everyone's suggestions. Approximately two weeks before the event, book quality time with your CEO or senior-most leader and go through the whole program, from the keynote to the breakout sessions. Iron out inconsistencies and accommodate differences of opinion from various stakeholders.

At this point the decision has been made about the main storyline. Do your best not to reopen the can of worms. Instead, focus on getting everyone prepared and on board with the final production.

I write all this knowing full well that CEOs often change slides at the last minute. My finest hour came at Microsoft when the CEO changed the entire talk the night before. At Twitter, the CEO sent an email two days before the event saying he didn't want slides, just a logo, and that he'd write his talking points himself. We didn't learn about the talking points until we were all in the green room before the show started. Fortunately, the talking points were innocuous and general enough that it didn't affect the messaging of the show.

Stay resilient.

Best practices for breakout sessions

All your breakout sessions need to call back to the vision laid out in the keynote. Leave your breakout sessions to focus on practical technical content. Here are my guidelines for breakout sessions:

- Your product and engineering team should be the presenters.
- Opt for slides plus live coding. (My best breakout sessions had no slides, just Notepad with my name and email address, followed by jumping into coding. They were also the most fun!) No recorded demos.
- Make sure the talks are outside-in: they focus on customer pain points and how you will address them with the product.

Case studies and video testimonials

We've talked already about building great case studies and case-study videos. For keynotes, the case-study video needs to be very high production value. As in, send a video crew out to meet and record the customer and have a professional editing team cut your video for you.

Ordinary case-study videos can be done via Zoom or Riverside. Keynote case-study videos demand a higher bar.

FIRST-PARTY ROAD TOUR

The road show is a smaller version of a first-party conference. As a company, you are taking your show on the road and meeting your customers where they are. You will first identify a list of cities, and from there, you'll run an event-logistics program very similar to your conference's. There may be some elements you choose to omit (for example, a partner experience) and other things you choose to add.

My advice is that if you're going to run a conference or road show, make sure that your demand-generation engine for your main product is totally dialed in. If you're not confident in your demand gen, where your demand gen comes from, and which levers are most effective in driving it, you will have a very difficult time with a road show.

Road shows require highly targeted regional demand generation. It's one thing to fill a thousand-person venue with attendees from around the world. It's quite another to fill two hundred seats in Berlin or London or New York. Unless you have a major brand like Google or Microsoft behind you, as a startup it's a huge lift to run two demand-gen actions simultaneously.

For local events, you can expect close to 50 percent drop-off from registration to actual attendance. The performance will be even worse in cities like London and New York. And it will be considerably worse if you select a less-expensive venue that is far away from a major public transportation line.

Much of the keynote and breakout session from above will apply to a road show. However, here's one word of advice: when your team is in town for a road show event, book them solid for customer visits and meetings so they can experience a customer's "day in the life." Schedule appearances and speaking slots at local meetups. This is a great opportunity to combine event activities with customer research and community development.

FIRST-PARTY CUSTOMER DINNERS AND BREAKFASTS

The goal here is to run an intimate event with ten to twelve customers where you can have and lead a discussion about an important industry topic. (As we've discussed many times, you do not want to do a product pitch at one of these events.) Ideally you'll have a customer willing to lead a conversation about this important topic.

For example, you may want a customer to come in and lead a conversation among other VPs of data engineering about the future of data pipelines in an AI-driven world. That's a topic that other data engineers would find very interesting. Maybe they have thoughts they'd like to share. Maybe they just want to listen to other people. Regardless, it's an interesting topic that is orthogonal (somewhat related) to your business.

In finding these people and recruiting them to attend your event, you are identifying people who fit your ideal customer profile. (We will discuss the ICP in a later chapter.)

Your customer will lead these ten to twelve prospects in a discussion. Your senior sales leader and possibly your CEO (if you're a startup) will be there to listen to and facilitate conversation. Maybe you'll chime in at certain times. But the goal is to further the dialogue, not to interject yourself into it just yet. Have a series of questions ready to prompt discussion in case the conversation wanes at any time.

After the event, follow up with the attendees. Typically you'll send them a gift. For example, if you hold the event at a restaurant, consider sending them a copy of the restaurant's cookbook. After the attendee receives the gift, a member of your sales team can follow up and book a meeting to discuss whether your product or service is germane to that attendee's business.

These events work. However, the sales team needs to buy in to make them work, and your outbound team needs to be incentivized to drive the proper attendees. Everyone needs to agree on the profile of the customer you want to attend. If everyone agrees, then you need to have a very crisp way of identifying whether an individual fits that profile before you invite them.

I once ran one of these events and somehow someone from a Fortune 10 company was in attendance. Everyone else in the room was from a company of five hundred to five thousand people. The individual from the biggest company monopolized the conversation with topics that were beyond the scale of anyone else in the room. It was an important lesson learned that every single person in attendance must fit the profile.

BUSINESS ROUNDTABLE EVENTS

These events are typically run by third parties. They curate an audience of decision-maker titles (e.g., CTOs) and then recruit sponsors to pay to meet these decision makers. The events I've run involved first writing a brief on my company, its products and services, and the kinds of problems we help solve. When you write your brief, tailor it to the audience being curated. What is top of mind for CTOs, or VPs of Engineering, or data engineers, or whoever is in attendance?

From there, the attendees sign up to meet with you. Depending on your sponsorship package, you can receive a number of requests for meetings.

These meetings are conducted by your account executives, and they determine whether the lead is qualified.

In my experience, the logos at these events are tantalizing, but ultimately the results fall short of expectations. Most AEs deprioritize this kind of work in favor of their own prospecting (or prospecting off product-qualified leads, which we will discuss in a later chapter). So, getting buy-in from sales is crucial. But even with buy-in, the likelihood of all your meetings turning into opportunities is low, so the time and money spent to accumulate five opportunities out of ten leads is disproportionate compared to results you would typically get were that time and money spent elsewhere.

VIRTUAL EVENTS

The quality and execution of virtual events necessarily improved during the pandemic, and we're still reaping the benefits today. For relatively little cost, and with no travel expenses, you can get better (and certainly more quantifiable) results with virtual events. Customers don't have to leave the office (or home) to get a ton of information and knowledge that they would otherwise have received only by schlepping to a faraway conference city. The information is also available on demand, meaning they can schedule time to interact with it over a few weeks.

For vendors, a virtual event is a great opportunity to build long-lasting content that reaches more potential users. You miss out on networking, but you gain good enough results at a much lower cost.

If you're watching your CAC carefully, consider investing in a handful of virtual events to test the waters and perfect your engagement and follow-up technique.

SUMMARY

No topic elicits more frustration from senior executives than events. They're costly—not just in terms of money, but also time and bandwidth. But if done properly, events can be a consistent vector for growth.

- **Events serve multiple objectives.** They drive awareness, educate developers, and build relationships that lead to long-term engagement.
- **Developers attend events for value, not hype.** They want actionable insights, real-world case studies, and technical depth, not marketing fluff.
- **Choose the right event format.** Conferences, meetups, hackathons, and webinars each serve different purposes and require different strategies.
- **Your event presence should be well integrated.** Your booth, talks, workshops, and networking all need to be aligned to maximize impact.
- **Speaking at events builds credibility.** A well-crafted talk positions you as a thought leader and draws interest to your product.
- **Sponsoring events is not a silver bullet.** Event sponsorships require thoughtful execution. Just putting your logo on a banner won't drive results.
- **Virtual events require more effort than you'd think.** Without physical presence, you need to be deliberate about engagement, participation, and follow-ups.
- **Developer events must be measured and analyzed** like any other marketing investment to justify the cost and optimize future efforts.

To maximize the value of events in your developer marketing-and-relations strategy, focus on quality over quantity by investing in a few high-impact events rather than spreading your budget thin. Ensure your team is fully prepared to engage attendees with a strong booth presence, compelling demos, and well-trained staff who can effectively communicate your product's value. Finally, remember that the true ROI of events often comes from postevent follow-ups. Be sure to have a clear plan to nurture leads, re-engage attendees, and turn event interactions into meaningful long-term relationships. If you want to run an events program, commit to doing it right.

CHAPTER 9

Building Awareness Through Marketing

Developer marketing is all about building programs that amplify your messaging and content to reach your desired audience. This chapter will cover several tactics for driving awareness, including understanding different types of developers and how their jobs are evolving, distribution channels for reaching developers, community programs for effective nurturing, and the essential marketing-content assets you'll need.

Think of awareness as two things:

- making more developers in your target market aware that you or your product exists
- keeping your existence top of mind with those who know of you, but have not yet committed to using your product

Driving awareness rarely involves just one or two things. It's the summation of many small pieces of work across content, community, and events. Your mission is to span the digital and physical world with consistent, accurate messaging so that developers see you everywhere and ascribe to you a sense of inevitability.

It's a marathon, not a sprint. Adopt an experimenter's mindset. Measure everything.

THE TWO KEYS TO GROWTH

You could spend a lot of time chasing the flavor of the month ("TikTok!", "Stack Overflow!", or the one that gives me PTSD . . . "We need to be on top of DB-Engines' rankings!")

The answer is really simple:

- Know your customer so well that you know where they hang out to exchange ideas and learn. It could be multiple places, depending on the type of developer. It could be Slacks, Discords, or forums. Or it could be certain podcasts or YouTube channels. Or it could be newsletters. But every person on the planet finds places to learn.
- Know what is special and unique about your company and product that your customers will love.

Now you can hang out in those places (remember our community tips) and build content for your potential customers that highlights the things that make you unique. Build content that inspires, teaches, and, as I always say, helps. Share the content in organic and natural ways within those places, and always be responsive and helpful.

TYPES OF DEVELOPERS

The term *software developer* is a catch-all for many different types of specialists. As you build marketing programs, it's important to know your target audience. Let's cover some of them here, followed by a list of communities, newsletters, and podcasts where each type of developer goes to learn more.

- front-end developers
- back-end developers
- database engineers
- data engineers
- data scientists
- DevOps engineers
- site-reliability engineers
- platform engineers
- security engineers
- AI and machine-learning engineers

In general, AI makes development incredibly fast. Developers can use LLMs as well as tools like Cursor, Lovable, and others to turn text-based descriptions of an application's functionality into code. What used to take weeks to build might now take hours. At the same time, LLMs can't (yet) know when to refactor and reorganize code. So a developer's experience and knowledge of fundamental computer science concepts still matters in order to build maintainable, efficient code. LLMs can't (yet) identify performance bottlenecks or root causes of infrastructure errors, so the experience of SREs and DevOps engineers still matters.

So while it's true that AI is improving rapidly, human intervention is still necessary.

Front-end developers

Front-end developers focus on creating the visual aspects and interactivity of web and mobile applications. They are responsible for ensuring a seamless user experience, optimizing performance, and maintaining consistency across various devices and screen sizes. Common frameworks and tools they use include React, Vue, Angular, and CSS preprocessors like Sass, which streamline code structure and enable efficient UI development.

Front-end developers are overwhelmed by noise. There are countless frameworks, libraries, and tools, many of which are open-source and free. That makes it difficult for anyone new to break through with messaging that rises above the din. They also have extremely high design sensibilities, meaning your product needs to be polished from the onset, and your marketing (including website) needs to match. Front-end developers will not tolerate (consciously or subconsciously) any impedance mismatches in design across the website, documentation, products, or materials.

Communities	Newsletters	Podcasts
• CodePen Community • CSS-Tricks Forums • Frontend Masters Community • Dev.to (Frontend Tag) • Reddit: r/web_design	• Frontend Focus • CSS Weekly • Smashing Newsletter • Bytes	• Syntax.fm • ShopTalk Show • Frontend Happy Hour

Back-end developers

Back-end developers handle server-side logic, database management, and application scalability. They build and maintain the core systems that power applications, focusing on security and data handling and ensuring efficient responses to front-end requests. Frameworks commonly used in back-end development include Node.js, Django, Ruby on Rails, and Spring Boot, each of which provides a structured environment for developing and deploying server-side applications.

Back-end developers value reliability, scalability, and functionality. Marketing messages need to focus on technical merits and specific-use cases. Documentation and benchmarks are of paramount importance.

Communities	Newsletters	Podcasts
• Reddit: r/backend • Dev.to (Back-End Tag)	• Programming Digest • The Overflow • JavaScript Weekly	• Coding Blocks • Software Engineering Daily • Backstage Podcast

Database engineers

Database engineers are responsible for designing, optimizing, and managing database systems. Their work ensures that data is stored, retrieved, and processed efficiently, providing a reliable backbone for applications. Common frameworks and tools in database engineering include MySQL, PostgreSQL, MongoDB, and NoSQL solutions, each selected based on the specific requirements of the application and its data complexity.

Database engineers embody high technical rigor and are deeply analytical about new software. They will scrutinize performance, compatibility, and reliability, and will take the time to test any scalability claims. All benchmarks must be truthful and carefully position opposite competitors. Database engineers have historically been reluctant to change, and the venerability of PostgreSQL is a testament to that. Many new startups embrace and build upon Postgres, instead of attempting to replace it, for this exact reason.

Communities	Newsletters	Podcasts
• Reddit: r/database • Database Administrators Stack Exchange • DBA Forums by Oracle	• Database Weekly • Postgres Weekly • SQLServerCentral	• *Data Engineering Podcast* • *Postgres.fm* • *The SQL Server Radio Show*

Data engineers

Data engineers manage data pipelines, ensuring data is available, clean, and ready for analysis. They work to integrate disparate data sources and handle large volumes of data, making it accessible for analytics and machine-learning applications. Common frameworks and tools include Apache Spark, Kafka, and Airflow, which enable efficient data streaming and ETL (extract, transform, load) processes.

As the demand for real-time data processing grows, data engineers are increasingly working with cloud-native data solutions and machine-learning infrastructure. AI is also transforming data engineering by automating parts of the ETL process, improving data quality, and predicting data flow issues before they occur. Data engineers are now expected to understand machine-learning workflows and work closely with data scientists, blending traditional data engineering with AI to support more complex, real-time data needs.

By the nature of their work, data engineers want proof of how a product integrates into an already-complex workflow. Existing data pipelines are often brittle, and data engineers will express skepticism about replacing them. As a consequence, data engineers have a fragmented tools landscape, which means you are better off positioning yourself as solving a particular aspect of the problem rather than the entirety of the problem.

Communities	Newsletters	Podcasts
• Data Engineering Subreddit: r/dataengineering • DataTalks.Club • Kaggle Discussions	• Data Engineering Weekly • Analytics Vidhya Newsletter • Data Elixir	• *Data Engineering Podcast* • *The Data Stack Show* • *Be Data Lit*

Data scientists

Data scientists analyze and interpret complex data to drive decision making, create predictive models, and extract actionable insights. They work with frameworks like TensorFlow, scikit-learn, and PyTorch, as well as programming languages like Python and R, to build and deploy machine-learning models.

AI is both a tool and a focus for data scientists, as they use machine-learning models to make predictions and generate insights. However, as AI tools like AutoML become more advanced, they automate portions of model building and tuning, reducing the need for hands-on configuration. This allows data scientists to focus more on business implications, feature engineering, and interpreting model results. As AI tools evolve, data scientists are now expected to balance technical skills with strategic thinking to align data initiatives with business goals.

Data scientists straddle the boundary between people who write code for a living and people who do knowledge-worker-style work. The work product of data scientists is often consumed directly by nontechnical people. They use a number of specialized tools and generally believe "if it works, don't fix it." They tend to be more research focused, or at least statistically oriented.

Communities	Newsletters	Podcasts
• Kaggle Discussions • Reddit: r/datascience • Data Science Stack Exchange	• Data Science Weekly • The Gradient • Towards Data Science	• *Data Skeptic* • *SuperDataScience* • *Not So Standard Deviations*

DevOps engineers

DevOps engineers focus on continuous integration and continuous delivery (CI/CD), infrastructure automation, and monitoring to streamline the software-development lifecycle. Their role bridges development and operations, ensuring that code moves seamlessly from development to production environments. Popular tools and frameworks in DevOps include Jenkins, Docker, Kubernetes, and Terraform, each enabling automated deployment, containerization, and infrastructure as code (IaC).

AI is evolving the DevOps role by introducing predictive monitoring, automated scaling, and advanced IaC tools. AI-driven monitoring can proactively detect and resolve issues before they impact users, while predictive scaling adjusts resources based on anticipated demand, reducing costs and improving efficiency. DevOps engineers are now working with more intelligent monitoring and automation tools, requiring them to understand how AI can enhance operational resilience and cost-effectiveness in cloud environments.

As a group, DevOps engineers oversee a wide range of processes and tools, and this may vary wildly from company to company. It's difficult to position a product as addressing the comprehensive needs of all DevOps engineers. Like all developers, DevOps engineers place a premium on peer recommendations. But DevOps engineers will at times respond well to technically detailed case studies.

Communities	Newsletters	Podcasts
• DevOps Subreddit: r/ devops • DevOps.com Forums • Cloud Native Computing Foundation Slack	• DevOps Weekly • Monitoring Weekly	• *Arrested DevOps* • *DevOps Paradox* • *Kubernetes Podcast*

Site-reliability engineers

Site-reliability engineers (SREs) ensure the reliability, availability, and performance of systems and applications, bridging the gap between development and operations. They focus on incident response, capacity planning, and system automation, often using tools like Prometheus, Grafana, and Kubernetes.

AI is significantly impacting SREs by enhancing predictive maintenance, anomaly detection, and automated incident response. AI-driven monitoring tools can predict potential failures based on historical data, allowing SREs to proactively address issues before they impact users. Additionally, automated remediation tools powered by AI can handle common incidents, freeing up SREs to focus on more complex tasks. This evolution means that SREs must understand how to integrate AI-based monitoring and incident-response solutions into their workflows.

The internet as we know it depends on SREs. They prioritize uptime and incident response, and all marketing must quickly and clearly highlight how a product helps achieve these goals. SREs are risk averse and value stability of the infrastructure under their charge above all.

Communities	Newsletters	Podcasts
• SRE Subreddit: r/ SiteReliability • Stack Exchange: Server Fault • SRE Community Slack	• SRE Weekly • Uptime Newsletter	• *Gremlin Chaos Cast* • *SRE Podcast*

Platform engineers

Platform engineers design, build, and maintain the internal platforms that enable other engineers to develop, deploy, and manage applications effectively. They create scalable infrastructure and streamline developer workflows, often using tools like Terraform, Kubernetes, Docker, and Jenkins.

AI is transforming platform engineering by introducing smarter automation for infrastructure provisioning and resource allocation. AI-driven infrastructure-as-code tools can automatically adjust resources based on application demand, improving efficiency and reducing costs. Moreover, AI-enhanced security-and-compliance checks enable platform engineers to ensure their environments adhere to best practices in real time. As AI becomes integrated into their work, platform engineers are expected to leverage these tools to create more efficient, secure, and cost-effective platforms.

Platform engineers work across all subprofessions of developers and look for tools and systems that integrate well with others, without sacrificing long-term customization options. In your communications with them, focus on extensibility.

Communities	Newsletters	Podcasts
• Platform Engineering Slack • Cloud Native Computing Foundation Slack	• Platform Weekly • Kubernetes Weekly	• *Platform Engineering Podcast* • *Cloud Native Podcast* • *Cloud Native Now Podcast*

Security engineers

Security engineers protect systems, networks, and data from cyber-threats by developing security protocols, monitoring systems for vulnerabilities, and conducting regular security audits. They often use tools like Splunk, Wireshark, and Nessus for threat detection and incident response.

AI is transforming security engineering with tools that offer predictive threat detection, real-time anomaly monitoring, and automated incident response. AI-powered security platforms can proactively identify vulnerabilities and prioritize risks, allowing security engineers to focus on more complex and targeted threats. As AI evolves in cybersecurity, security engineers must learn to work with these tools to enhance detection capabilities and automate repetitive tasks, making their roles both more efficient and more strategically focused.

Necessarily, security engineers are paranoid. They will demand rigorous proof of any product's claims and will respond well to case studies from companies they perceive as having a larger security concern than theirs. Financial services industry case studies, for example, will hold a lot of weight. They also rely heavily on third-party audits and certifications.

Communities	Newsletters	Podcasts
• Reddit: r/netsec • OWASP Slack • Packet Storm forums	• Security Weekly • Cybersecurity Headlines • BleepingComputer	• *Security Now* • *Darknet Diaries* • *CyberWire*

AI and machine-learning engineers

AI and machine-learning engineers focus on designing, building, and deploying machine-learning models to solve complex problems like image recognition, natural-language processing, and recommendation engines. They work with libraries and frameworks like TensorFlow, Keras, and PyTorch, as well as cloud-based AI services, for large-scale model training and deployment.

AI tools and cloud-based platforms are reducing the barriers to entry in this field by providing pretrained models, AutoML services, and managed machine-learning infrastructure. As a result, AI engineers can now focus more on model customization and optimization rather than from-scratch model development. This shift allows AI and machine-learning engineers to spend more time refining models and interpreting results rather than handling underlying infrastructure, making the role more accessible and adaptable to business needs.

AI and ML engineers are the opposite of "AI hype." They are discerning and knowledgeable and can cut through the facade of any AI-related marketing. Be direct and honest, and if your product is truly innovative, be bold enough to stand by the claim with evidence.

Communities	Newsletters	Podcasts

• Hugging Face Forums
• Reddit: r/
  MachineLearning
• Weights & Biases Slack
	• Import AI
	• The Batch by deep-
	  learning.ai
	• AI Breakfast
		• *The TWIML AI Podcast*
		• *Gradient Dissent*
		• *Practical AI*

TYPES OF PRODUCTS

In addition to the type of customer you're targeting, you must also consider the type of product you're building. If your product has broad appeal, you can employ broad-reach awareness tactics. But if your product has niche appeal, you need to be more selective. It's the difference between net fishing and spearfishing.

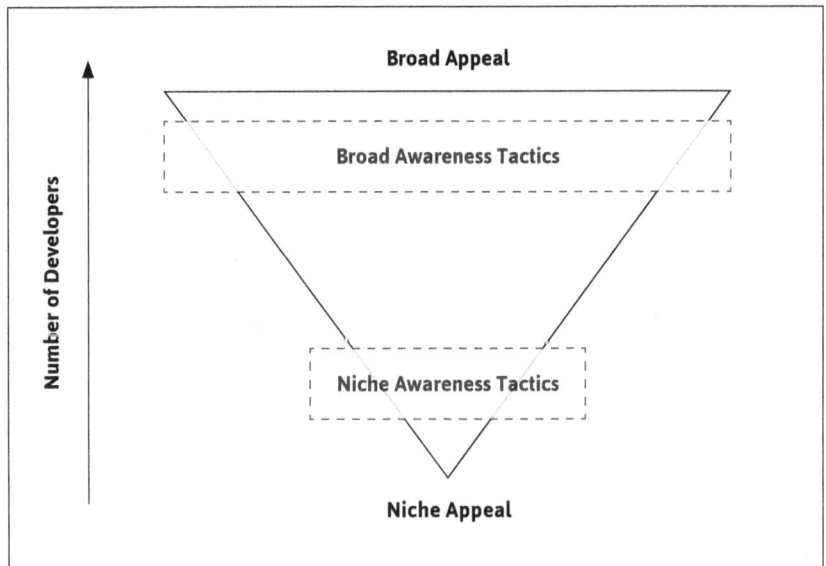

I've worked with founders who fail to grasp the difference. They have highly technical products intended for discerning audiences, but they want to see growth akin to that of products aimed at front-end developers.

That's not how it works.

The combination of your audience and your product will tell you what your total possible reach is. And now you need to use all the tactics at your disposal to maximize that reach.

Of course, broad-based markets are also inundated with noise and competition, while niche markets tend to be more focused. As a practical example of how this makes a difference, I'm not sure you'd ever need to run advertising for a broad-reach product that is steadily growing its following in a broad market. But you may well need advertising to reach developers in a niche market who have much fewer communities and newsletters feeding them information.

Your understanding of this concept will dictate much of your marketing strategy, to say nothing of your product and pricing strategies.

PAID ACQUISITION

Developers are traditionally skeptical of advertising. Being the most technically savvy of all consumers, developers will often turn on ad blockers, either in the browser or at the router level. They are more likely to adopt a privacy-centric approach to their daily lives on the internet. And they are more likely to be turned off by overly pushy sales and marketing tactics.

So when adopting a paid-acquisition strategy with developers, you need to be intentional with your approach, with clear goals and an eye toward continual optimization and improvement.

Do developers click on ads?

The glib answer is this: if your ads are good, on topic, and add clear value, yes, they will click on your ad. But of course there's more to it than that, and it all comes back to my central thesis of this book: Help First.

Your ads can't be overly polished or presumptuous. Instead focus on the problem, and attract developers to it. If they agree that they share the problem being described in the ad, then they will click through to the landing page, where you can talk more about the problem and how you solve it.

First, what are your goals?

Before you invest in paid acquisition, define what success looks like for you. Are you aiming to drive sign-ups for a free trial? Build awareness of your product in a crowded market? Increase traffic to a specific piece of content or landing page?

Establishing clear goals ensures your campaigns are aligned with broader business objectives. Here are just a few examples:

- If you're launching a new feature, your goal might be to generate a specific number of trial sign-ups or demo requests.
- If you're entering a new market, your goal might be to drive impressions and clicks from a specific geographic region or industry.
- For product-led growth (PLG) products, your goal could be driving traffic to a free-tier sign-up page, with a secondary focus on activating those users post-sign-up.
- Maybe your product is entering an existing, crowded market and you simply want to drive awareness, so your goals would focus on impressions.

There are myriad reasons why you would want to run paid advertising, and you need to be crystal clear about your goal. Mixing goals, or having two goals, or not being sure of your goals—all of these are recipes for overspending and being dissatisfied with the results.

Structuring a paid acquisition campaign

As I've mentioned many times, developers do not like overt marketing approaches typical in other industries. Your best bet is to focus on the problem faced by developers you're targeting. This will help you get their attention in a crowded marketplace.

Paid ads can take many forms:

- Google AdWords (bidding on keywords)
- LinkedIn, Facebook, or other display ads
- Video ads on any of the main social networks
- YouTube ads, to generate followers

Many of us are conditioned to ignore these ads when they show up. A Google search result is buried between anywhere from zero to five ads of varying degrees of annoyance. In a world where everyone is trying to sell you something, be the contrarian who is willing to empathize with a pain or problem.

Using intent and volume to guide keyword discovery

Through your research into your company's segmentation, positioning, and messaging, you've gained a very strong understanding of the problems currently faced by developers you're targeting. Buried within this knowledge should be an equally strong understanding of what developers do when they face a problem. What sites do they visit? What communities do they consult? Which influencers do they turn to? And what do they search for when attempting to solve the problem?

This is the beginning of your keyword research.

Keywords generally have two traits:

- **Volume:** How many times a day is this keyword searched?
- **Intent:** Does this keyword convey that someone is actively looking for a solution?

If we plot these two traits out, this is how we can use those keywords effectively:

	High Intent	Low Intent
High Volume	**Primary Conversion Keywords** • These should be the core focus of your SEO and paid search efforts. • These keywords drive direct sign-ups, downloads, or purchases. • Best used in product pages, landing pages, and comparison pages. Examples: "Best-managed Postgres pricing" "Deploy Firebase alternative" "Fastest serverless database"	**Brand Awareness & Top-of-Funnel Content** • These keywords bring in large traffic numbers but may have lower conversion rates. • Best used in high-ranking blog posts, YouTube videos, and documentation. • Use them to capture early-stage developers and establish authority. Examples: "What is a graph database?" "Postgres tutorial for beginners" "Serverless vs. traditional databases"
Low Volume	**Targeted Long-Tail Conversions** • These keywords attract highly qualified traffic even if search volume is low. • Great for technical use cases, industry-specific solutions, and deep integrations. • Best used in technical blogs, case studies, API documentation, and "vs." content that compares your product to a competitor's. Examples: "Postgres vector search for AI models" "Self-hosted Firebase alternative for GDPR compliance"	**Niche Thought Leadership & Experimentation** • These keywords are useful for innovation and early market trends. • Best used in dev community discussions, experimental blog posts, and emerging-tech articles. • Can be useful for getting ahead of new trends and capturing early adopters. Examples: "How to use Postgres with WebAssembly" "Best serverless databases for AI inference"

Ultimately, you want to . . .

- prioritize high-intent, high-volume keywords for direct conversions and product-focused pages.
- use low-intent, low-volume keywords for educational content, brand awareness, and community engagement.
- leverage high-intent, low-volume keywords to target niche audiences and capture specialized developer needs.
- experiment with low-intent, low-volume keywords to establish thought leadership and stay ahead of industry trends.

Let's take these two keywords as examples:

- **vector database:** This keyword, while niche for the general population, is rather generic for developers. It's a category of databases with a high volume of searches (again, relatively speaking).
- **storing vector embeddings postgres:** This keyword is much narrower and indicates someone is looking to solve a specific problem with their PostgreSQL database.

Now, if I was Pinecone (a vector database as a service), I'd consider defensively bidding on the first keyword. But if I were Timescale (a PostgreSQL database with scalability and performance superpowers, including the ability to store vector embeddings), the first keyword is too generic, and I will be bidding on a lot of traffic that may not be interested in what I have to offer.

This first keyword is high volume and low intent. Because of the volume, it will cost more to bid, though you may get more clickthroughs. And because of the low intent, it will attract developers who are mostly browsing vs. looking to solve a specific problem.

In contrast, the second keyword is very specific. People using that keyword clearly know and understand Postgres and what it's capable of, and they are looking for a solution for storing vector embeddings. This is an ideal keyword for both Pinecone and Timescale.

This second keyword is low volume and high intent. As you can guess, the low volume will indicate lower cost (and lower traffic!). But the high intent will mean that the people who do click through will be more likely to want to do business.

Lower cost, more qualified traffic, higher likelihood to convert. Guess which one you want to aim for?

The ad is just the start

If someone engages (clicks, taps, etc.) with your ad, they will land on a page that you host (the landing page). Don't send people to your homepage. Instead, lean into your ad creative and build landing pages that delve into the problem described in the creative and how your product or service solves this problem.

All of this follows your customer research into segmentation, positioning, and messaging (which we will discuss in the next chapter). But your campaigns don't necessarily need to follow your messaging exactly. Instead, align to your omnichannel campaign.

Let's look again at the low-volume, high-intent keyword we designed earlier: **storing vector embeddings postgres.**

If you were Pinecone, your landing page from this search would center around how to store vector embeddings and why a specialized database is the best decision you can make. In contrast, if you were Timescale, you'd explain why using the database you already know and love is the best choice.

The keyword focuses on the problem that a developer has. The ad creative emphasizes the problem and entices developers to click through. The landing page describes how you approach and solve the problem. If all three of these things line up well and are in line with the customer's expectations, then you'll end up with a conversion.

Beyond Google

As I'm writing this, after years of search dominance (and the arrogance that goes with it), Google is finally losing its grip on the market as ChatGPT, Perplexity, and others muscle in on their territory. Until the AI search tools arrive at the monetization (ad) trough, it's important to diversify.

One other ad network I've tried is LinkedIn. Now, my results have been fair to middling. LinkedIn is terrible for intent-based advertising. After all, nobody goes to LinkedIn with a problem and searches for a solution.

Rather, I used LinkedIn to target specific users with ads. We will talk more about this later, when we discuss account-based marketing (ABM), but the gist is that you can build an "audience" in LinkedIn composed of . . .

- companies
- regions
- titles
- other LinkedIn attributes

As long as the audience is more than three hundred people, you can serve them ads. LinkedIn "single image ads" (as the name implies) and "thought leader ads" (long posts that ordinary people and/or your employees post, which you then amplify) tend to work best.

In addition to creating the audience characteristics and text for the ad, you'll need to create any digital assets required for your paid campaign: images, videos, audio, and so on.

Setting up ad spend and budgets

My advice is to run targeted experiments with a handful of keywords or audiences and examine them weekly to see which keywords to add, drop, and modify based on the data. The mechanics of paid ads are out of scope for this book, but there is plenty of knowledge on the topic for you to study.

Monitoring and optimizing ads

Paid acquisition is not a "set it and forget it" strategy. Regular monitoring and iteration are crucial to maximizing performance. Here are key optimization tactics:

- **Ad copy testing:** Run A/B tests on headlines, descriptions, and CTAs to identify what drives the most clicks and conversions.
- **Audience targeting:** Refine your targeting based on performance data. For example, if one geographic region outperforms others, shift more budget there.
- **Keyword refinement:** Analyze search-query reports to find new high-performing keywords or exclude underperforming ones.
- **Landing-page optimization:** Ensure your landing pages align with the ad messaging and provide a seamless user experience. High bounce rates indicate a mismatch between the ad and the landing-page content.
- **Retargeting campaigns:** Use retargeting ads to re-engage users who visited your site but didn't convert. Retargeting is especially effective for developers who may need more time to evaluate your product.

Set up analytics dashboards to track metrics like . . .

- cost per click (CPC) and cost per acquisition (CPA).
- click-through rate (CTR) for ad effectiveness.
- conversion rate for landing pages.

Adjust your strategy monthly or even weekly to ensure you're allocating budget effectively and staying ahead of trends.

OMNICHANNEL CAMPAIGNS

Because developers are inherently skeptical about marketing, you often have to meet them where they are, creating various campaigns to reach them in these places. These campaigns could be delivered via various channels:

- a product launch
- a pile of SEO content, and the blog posts, sample code, and documentation that goes with it
- a webinar
- an ebook
- a social media push
- a paid ad campaign targeted at a specific problem
- a push with your outbound sales team
- and so on . . .

It's important to think of these channels holistically and maximize your presence across all these touchpoints. To do so, organize your campaigns around central themes (or problems developers face) and build materials in total alignment with them. Now everyone in your company and your marketing team will be singing from the same sheet. This "omnichannel" approach ensures that your customers see consistent messaging and focus from you.

I wrote earlier about a sense of *inevitability*. What I mean is that if developers start seeing you everywhere, they will perceive you as being bigger, more pervasive, and more prominent than perhaps you are (or, if you're already part of a BigTech company, they will see you as being *present and supportive* in the community).

Whenever I speak to founders who have experienced significant growth, it's because they have fully embraced the "everywhere, all at once" mindset. In practice this means three things:

1. You maximize SEO and show up in search results for the most important related topics.

2. You have a community presence (online and in person) where you are helping solve problems (Help First!), never bashing the competition, and promoting a positive attitude about the industry and products, whether or not they are your own.
3. You have an event presence, with or without sponsorships. You give out T-shirts, meet with other speakers, and use guerilla marketing tactics like putting your stickers on things.

None of those ideas should come as a surprise. We've been discussing them throughout this book. Fundamentally, inevitability comes when you lean into every tactic all at once.

BE STRATEGIC WITH CONTENT-DISTRIBUTION CHANNELS

In the heyday of social media, it was fairly easy to find a developer audience on LinkedIn, Twitter, Facebook, and so forth. However, as social media has fragmented and become a place rife with hatred, misogyny, and altogether sarcastic and difficult people, it is difficult to engage through these channels while maintaining your brand tone and consistency.

We've talked already about the importance of content reuse. Why keep reinventing things? If you've invested in high-quality content, simply reuse it and slice and dice the material into smaller chunks:

*   social media posts
*   infographics
*   short videos of you highlighting a point made in a blog post
*   demo videos

With your primary and reused content ready, you can consider these other potential channels to find your audience and grow your reach:

- **Newsletters:** If there are newsletters that cater to your audience (such as Postgres Weekly), consider reaching out to the newsletter owner and letting them know about cool new blog posts that you've published. You may also investigate sponsorship of these newsletters. In my experience, sponsoring a newsletter yields much better results than any other form of advertising or sponsorship.

- **Podcasts:** We've already discussed how to reach out to key podcasters and other influencers. You may also consider podcast sponsorships, especially if you're able to pair it with a promo code and track redemption.

- **Events:** In the chapter on events, we talked about CFPs. Another thing to consider is attending events and networking with speakers.

- **Developer forums and Q&A sites:** Platforms like Stack Overflow and Reddit are great for engaging with developers, but you have to be careful. Don't spam. Provide thoughtful answers and avoid being overly promotional. Subreddits like r/programming or r/devops can be goldmines if you approach them correctly.

- **GitHub and open-source projects:** Developers live on GitHub. You can publish open-source tools, contribute to relevant projects, or even sponsor popular repositories to build credibility. Open-source is a long game, but it works.

- **Specialized developer platforms:** Hacker News is great for launching new features or blog posts, but it's hit-or-miss. Product Hunt is better for targeting early adopters, just make sure you're launching something meaningful.

- **Community platforms and groups:** Many developers hang out on Discord or Slack communities tied to their technology of choice. Find these groups and join the conversation. Sponsoring a channel is also an option, but authentic participation works better.

- **Technical blogs and aggregators:** Platforms like DZone and Dev.to are solid places to syndicate your content. Developers love tutorials, how-tos, and problem-solving posts.

- **Video content:** YouTube tutorials and product walk-throughs are underrated. Twitch is also great for live-coding sessions or Q&A streams. Developers appreciate seeing your product in action.
- **Hackathons and competitions:** Sponsor a hackathon or run your own. Give developers a chance to play with your product and showcase their creativity. Bonus points if you offer prizes or other incentives.
- **Localized communities:** Don't ignore regional developer groups or meetups. Engage with these communities to build awareness in specific geographic areas.

EMAIL MARKETING

Once you have a developer's contact information, you need to work to keep them aware of your product. As we've discussed, it's fairly common for a developer to sign up for a product in the event they need it in the future. You should think about email marketing as an attempt to remain top of mind with the same quality of content that got them to your site in the first place. As always, avoid puffery and unsubstantiated claims. But do lean into new technical content you've published, opportunities to learn through live-coding streams or webinars, and product launches that may be of interest to them.

The key to effective email marketing has always been better personalization. As we discussed earlier, make sure your marketing tools have enough information from web and product analytics that you can segment your email list into various cohorts. Gathering quality intent signals from customers as they interact with your website and use your product will help you build more actionable emails. The more relevant your message is to the recipient, the better your chances of engagement. Here are some of the many ways to segment your email list for developer marketing:

- **By industry, company size, or other firmographic metric:** Using Clearbit or a similar tool, you can take your customer list and build hobbyist, small business, medium business, scale-up startup, and enterprise cohorts. This may be useful if you want to send out an announcement about a new pricing tier. You can avoid sending it to recipients to whom the tier doesn't apply. Or maybe you now have a new industry certification that could be applicable to a subsegment of your list.
- **By user behavior:** Target users based on their usage of your product.
  - ○ **Onboarding:** Users who recently signed up and are continuing to use the product could receive different emails from those who have already abandoned the product.
  - ○ **Feature usage:** Users who are using a particular feature could receive additional information, or information about adjacent features.
  - ○ **Engagement levels:** You could choose to reward power users, or send resurrection emails to those who have already abandoned the product.
  - ○ **Paid users, or level of payment:** You might want to send pricing offers or trial-conversion messages to different levels of paid usage.
- **By developer role:** I've talked about the different types of developers. Maybe you want to send role-specific information about your product.
- **By geography or location:** You could opt to send information about new localization languages, meetups or events, or region-specific features (such as support for a new standard or a certification that has been achieved).

Effective segmentation will help you deliver personalized communications that your developers will be more likely to read and act upon.

TIP: Consider using AI to personalize your email content. Intent signals give you clues to who your customer is, and whether they resemble other customers who have successfully upgraded (look-alikes). The AI personalization industry is evolving rapidly. Consult my blog, StrategicNerds.com, for frequent product reviews and recommendations.

YOUR MONTHLY NEWSLETTER

I'm a big fan of sending out a monthly communication to your installed base or your email list. This gives you an opportunity to recap all the announcements and launches that you've done over the last month, highlight any blog posts or other content that you've created, give people an update on future events or other kinds of activities where they can meet you in the real world, and generally keep your brand top of mind with people who may have signed up and become inactive over time.

There are a couple of approaches I've seen that have worked.

The first is a changelog point of view. This is usually done in plain text with very little HTML or other kind of formatting, the email is direct and to the point—all things that developers love. The email also renders very well on mobile devices, where most people will read their email.

The other thing I've tried and really loved is something I call the "monthly consumption report." The above-the-fold of this newsletter contains a summary of a user's month's consumption of the product: how much data they are storing, how much compute they have used, and so on. Below the fold, after the monthly consumption report, is content: upcoming events, and blog posts and launches they may have missed.

The monthly consumption report provides a fair value exchange to the developer. They're getting information from you that they really find useful, while also being updated on information pertaining to the product and company. If you can pull it off, it's a great way to structure a newsletter.

ENGAGING DEVELOPERS VIA OPEN-SOURCE

The open-source model is fantastic for contributors as well as maintainers. Contributors are people who, well, contribute to the open-source project. Maintainers, as you can imagine, maintain the project and keep it running smoothly. They also make sure that the community around the project is vibrant and dignified. It can sometimes be a thankless job.

If you are maintaining an open-source project as part of your product or service, you have an opportunity to recognize and reward everyone who supports it and perhaps turn them into a commercial business partner or customer.

If you are following or contributing to open-source projects that are not your own, you can use tools like Common Room to monitor the GitHub actions and activity related to the project. This should give you visibility into other developers who care about it. Those other developers could be fantastic potential prospects for your product or service. After all, you already have something very important in common.

Maintainers of open-source projects can also include messages inside command-line utilities that direct customers to sign up for newsletters or visit a changelog on your website. Just because someone uses an open-source version of your product doesn't mean they don't want to be apprised of how you're progressing. But always make this communication opt-in, and avoid collecting data that could violate someone's privacy rights.

SUMMARY

Developer marketing starts with awareness. If developers don't know your product exists, nothing else matters. Here are some tactics to ensure your product is visible in the places where developers naturally spend their time:

- **Awareness is about meeting developers where they already are.** That could be on search engines, in communities, on social media, and at events.

- **SEO is still critical despite the rise of AI.** Developers rely on Google, Stack Overflow, and GitHub to solve problems. Your content needs to be optimized for search.
- **Programmatic SEO is a powerful tool.** Generating thousands of landing pages targeting specific developer queries can accelerate organic traffic.
- **Leveraging existing developer communities is key.** Don't build your own if you don't have to. Instead tap into Reddit, Discord, Slack, and forums.
- **Social media works differently for developers.** They engage with technical content on Twitter, LinkedIn, YouTube, and Hacker News, but rarely on Facebook.
- **Influencer marketing can work in developer marketing.** Developers trust other developers. It's important to partner with respected figures in your space who boost your credibility.
- **Piggybacking on existing platforms accelerates reach.** Being featured on GitHub's trending projects, Product Hunt, or newsletters can drive a surge in adoption.
- **Partnerships can amplify awareness.** Comarketing with complementary developer tools expands your reach with minimal effort.
- **Measuring awareness is tricky but essential.** Track website traffic, social engagement, community discussions, and direct mentions to gauge visibility and improve efforts.

Driving awareness is the whole ball game. Without awareness of your products, services, and team's credibility, no one will hear about your company. Always start by understanding your customer. We'll talk later about building your ideal customer profile (ICP), but it's also important to understand the communities and tribes to which your target audience belongs. From there you can build a strategy that places content and your in-house expertise in prominent places where your desired customer will engage with it and move to the next phase in their journey to being your customer.

CHAPTER 10

Building a Strong Developer Brand

A brand is a lot more than a logo or tagline. Brands create deep connections with your audience by establishing trust, credibility, and a sense of belonging. Stripe, Modal, and Supabase all have strong developer brands. Despite being very different from one another tonally, they all adhere to the same practices to build their brand constructively.

THE SEVEN PRIMAL ELEMENTS OF DEVELOPER BRANDS

In his book *Primalbranding*, Patrick Hanlon gives us a formula for building an exceptional brand. Here are his seven primal elements:

1. **The Creation Myth:** The origin story that reflects a brand's values and mission. For developers, this often involves solving a personal pain point or addressing a gap in the ecosystems that the founders faced when trying to build another product.

Stripe founders Patrick and John Collison often tell the story of being personally frustrated when trying to accept payments online for content and goods.

To establish your creation myth, share your journey authentically in blog posts, videos, and community talks. Highlight *why* you created the product to begin with, and align that story with traditional values that developers trust: efficiency, simplicity, and transparency.

2. **The Creed:** A belief system or guiding principle that the brand stands for. For developer brands, this often (though not always) comes back to openness and empowerment.

Supabase's mission is to build the best developer platform in the world. They do this by building an open-source product on top of one of the most successful open-source projects of all time: Postgres.

Be sure to define your core philosophy and bake it into every interaction with your audience.

3. **Icons:** Symbols, logos, or visuals that make your brand instantly recognizable. For developers, this could mean evoking a traditional developer aesthetic of terminal windows or code.

Modal has a minimalist aesthetic that builds on the visual of a green cursor, shaped as several cubes together, on a terminal window. These cubes represent the containers for their serverless cloud infrastructure.

Ensure your design language reflects your technical audience's values for clarity and focus.

4. **Rituals:** Behaviors and traditions that create community. Developer brands can create rituals through regular product updates, community events, or contributions to open-source.

Stripe's Increment magazine fosters a ritual of deep learning and exploration within the developer community.

Build rituals into your brand through webinars, regular GitHub updates, or community meetups that developers can count on.

5. **Sacred Words:** Unique terms or jargon that establish belonging and identity within the brand community. Technical language that speaks directly to their audience without condescension can be very empowering to developers.

Supabase uses terms like *edge functions* and *self-hosting*, that signal its deep alignment with developer culture.

Your feature and product naming should resonate with developers' technical sensibilities while reinforcing your expertise.

6. **The Pagans:** A clear definition of what you are not. Developers respect brands that take a stand, whether it's against closed systems, poor documentation, or slow performance.

Modal differentiates itself from traditional cloud platforms by being unapologetically modern, serverless, and developer-first.

Communicate your differentiators by highlighting what you're disrupting or improving in the industry.

7. **The Leader:** The face or voice of your brand, often a founder, advocate, or influential community member. For developers, this could be a technically credible founder or a charismatic developer advocate.

Jeff Barr has been the face of Amazon Web Services since its founding.

Identify a leader who embodies your brand values, and ensure they are active in developer communities through blogs, interviews, and social media.

AUTHENTICITY AND TECHNICAL CREDIBILITY

As we discussed when talking about building communities, you must always maintain a high level of technical credibility when communicating with developers. And this communication has to be rooted in authenticity. When reaching out to an influential member of the community, find common ground through technical competency and commend them on their mastery of it.

To maintain authenticity, avoid overly polished or marketing-heavy content. When I worked at Amazon Web Services, Andy Jassy used to tell me all the time, "No marketing puffery." Developers prefer raw, honest communication that gets to the point. For example, Timescale's blog posts are always direct and full of technical detail.

Modal's product documentation is exemplary. It's rooted in both comprehensive reference material as well as practical guidance on how to solve the most common tasks one would use Modal for. Their documentation gives the developer a confidence boost when using the product. It also gives them the confidence to get started, because the practical guidance is there to help them through the initial setup and deployment phases.

Technical credibility should shine through your documentation, product-design language, and even marketing content. Demonstrate a deep understanding of the *problem* you're trying to solve. This is even more important than explaining your solution. We will talk about this in detail when we discuss building quality developer documentation.

DEVELOP A STRONG DEVELOPER COMMUNITY

We discussed the power of a strong developer community in an earlier chapter. Don't just establish an online community and engage frequently—imbue it with a power of place. Use the community to provide special events: highlight top contributors to the community, host Ask Me Anything (AMA) sessions, and provide early access to features to customers via the community. Consider letting your community know about key launches before publishing your blog post or press release.

One other strategy I have always tried to do: build an "event in a box" kit that allows your most passionate customers to host brown-bag discussions at their companies. Give them the slide decks, demo scripts, and even a way to order T-shirts and stickers, so that they can be happy and successful with their event.

BRANDS ARE CONSISTENT AND BUILT OVER TIME

Consistency builds trust. Developers should know what you are and what to expect with every interaction. This gives them a sense of calm when working with you. All your content, from documentation to newsletters, should reinforce your values and voice. Your datasheets and slide decks should use the same language as your website. Your fonts should be consistent. Your logos and iconography should be consistent.

Your tone should also be consistent. Speak to your developers as your technical peers. No marketing puffery anywhere, no pushy sales motions. Take an honest, curious, and consultative approach to your customers.

Brands also do not happen overnight. Invest in yours as you go. Every customer touchpoint is an opportunity to reinforce your brand promise. If your brand is all about technical depth and accuracy, then even your sales breakfast and dinner events should lean into technical depth: the speaker should be deeply technical, the swag should be nerdy and whimsical, the landing page and emails should connote technical proficiency and fealty, and so on.

FEATURE-LEVEL BRANDING

At some point you will help your product team name features. I discuss naming exercises and processes in a later chapter on product launches. At this point, however, I want to cover how names should be used within your marketing collateral and how those names can support your broader branding efforts.

To start, I divide features into two categories:

- **Capital Letter Features:** These are features that you will explicitly name and put branding and marketing energy behind. These features will appear in your marketing collateral and documentation in upper case, with the first letter of each word capitalized.
- **Regular features:** These are normal features that will never be capitalized in text and that you will refer to in a generic sense.

Your approach to feature branding should be intentional and aligned with your broader company positioning. Some features deserve significant marketing investment, while others are simply part of the core product experience and should remain in the background. By categorizing them into Capital Letter Features and regular features, you create a clear hierarchy that guides how you communicate them in marketing, sales, and documentation. At the end of the day, you're trying to avoid marketing bloat where every feature is of the same importance.

Capital Letter Features are of strategic importance. They help underscore your product and brand identity because they are memorable and jump off the page when read. Regular features fade into the background and support the meaning of content that surrounds it.

Typically, developer companies will enable users to create accounts, and within those accounts they can create Projects or Workspaces. The concept of a Project (or Workspace) in this instance is important and deliberately called out. In Supabase, a Database Advisor checks your database for performance and security problems. It's a sufficiently important and distinct feature that Supabase has elected to call it out as a Capital Letter Feature.

In contrast, the Supabase documentation mentions query optimization, which, as the name suggests, helps you get better performance from your queries. While this feature is certainly important, it's better used as a functional description than a minibrand. Regular features may be essential, but they are framed as enhancements (or table-stakes requirements) rather than differentiating factors.

Ultimately, you will make the call on which features should be Capital Letter Features and which ones should be regular features. You should use Capital Letter Features when a feature is . . .

- a key part of your differentiation
  (e.g., Neon Branching).
- a new or disruptive capability
  (e.g., Timescale Continuous Aggregates).
- meant to drive expansion revenue
  (e.g., Stripe Radar for fraud prevention).
- part of a broader industry trend
  (e.g., Supabase Edge Functions following the serverless movement).

And you should use regular features when a feature is . . .

- an expected part of the product
  (e.g., a CLI tool).
- not a competitive differentiator
  (e.g., a query-optimization update).
- primarily an internal or developer-productivity tool.
- in conflict with your positioning.

TIP: As you make these decisions, consider creating an internal glossary as part of your brand materials so that your internal stakeholders, and perhaps even partners and customers, can all stay on the same page.

MEASURING YOUR BRAND EFFICACY

Ultimately you're trying to measure the degree to which your brand is trusted by developers. Developer trust is the tip of the spear when it comes to whether they're going to accept a brand and recommend it within their communities. For this reason, I've always believed that the most reliable indicator of brand health is Net Promoter Score. Your best bet is to ask survey questions of your users in-product or in-community (e.g., Slack, Discord, forums, etc.) to gauge their affinity to your brand and their willingness to recommend it to a colleague.

CRISIS MANAGEMENT: WHAT TO DO WHEN THINGS GO WRONG

Outages, viruses, billing errors, oh my! When things go wrong with developer-focused products, they affect not only your customer, but your customer's customers, and perhaps even more. In the early days of AWS, a single outage could take down half the internet. Even today, a simple DNS error can have catastrophic effects on global commerce. A botched rollout of a patch or update can bring down airlines, hotels, and e-commerce globally.

Developers have outsized importance in the world, and with it, outsized consequences of their mistakes.

You need to be prepared today for things to go wrong with your product tomorrow. Sunny days are always the best days to buy an umbrella.

In addition, every crisis is an opportunity to build trust and credibility. And trust and credibility are the foundation of a strong developer brand.

Incident management

The first thing to iron out is your incident-management process. Let's say an incident is detected by a site-reliability engineer in production. What should she do next? Whom should she alert? Most engineering teams have pager-duty responsibilities defined. But if an outage has consequences, shouldn't others be notified also?

Here's a checklist I created for an incident-management process at a past company:

1. Tell customers that something is amiss and promise regular and frequent updates. And then deliver on that promise.
2. Page engineers on duty.
3. Start a Slack channel ("incident-*dateofincident-description*").
4. Invite SREs, engineers, marketing, legal, comms, and exec team.
5. Describe the incident in as much detail as necessary.
6. Attach a SEV number to the incident (e.g., "SEV1," "SEV2," etc.) The SEV number indicates the seriousness of the incident. SEV1 is a critical issue affecting a significant number of users in a production environment. SEV2 is a major issue affecting a subset of users in a production environment. SEV3 is a moderate incident causing errors or minor problems for a small number of users.

Work cross-organizationally

This is the kickoff of a cross-organizational process. As part of this industry, we in marketing have our own process we need to follow:

- Someone on the marketing team must have on-call responsibilities for a SEV1 issue.
- The marketing team member who is on call should have the account credentials for all social media accounts and the ability to post to the blog. Make sure you account for vacation coverage. In a larger organization with a dedicated social media team, the marketing manager should have a way to reach the social media manager.
- Outline a process for each SEV number. For example, for a SEV1, we should post a simple message to social media. Usually Twitter is sufficient. ("We are experiencing

technical difficulties. We are investigating and will report back soon with our findings.")

- Decide whether all automatic and scheduled social media posts should be paused depending on the SEV number.
- Notify the Slack channel of actions taken. ("I've posted to Twitter. I've paused all other social media posts across all channels.")

From there, monitor the group for findings and resolutions. If necessary, post updates to social media.

This handles the initial crisis. Now you need to deal with the consequences.

Communicating directly and succinctly

Outline a plan with your customer success team for when and how to share the resolution and postmortems with customers. Depending on the SEV number, you may want to publish a postmortem blog post and/or notify customers with billing remediation instructions. Your enterprise customers may have reliability guarantees in their contracts that customer success may need help messaging appropriately.

In all communication, remember these important tips:

- **Remain calm and matter-of-fact.** At all times, adopt a tone that reassures customers that you know of the problem and are finding a resolution. This also applies to any meetings that marketing may attend. No one benefits from marketing panicking. Engineers are working toward a resolution. Offer the gift of your serenity. If you are concerned with the speed of the resolution or the lack of seriousness with which the problem is being addressed, take it up privately with your exec team.
- **Be truthful.** Don't attempt to cover up the issue or, perhaps even worse, obfuscate it with florid marketing or business language. As with all developer-focused communications, be direct and honest.

- **Support postmortems.** Mistakes are opportunities to learn and build trust. Publishing a detailed postmortem of the problem helps other engineers (and your customers) find confidence that you have learned from your mistake and taken steps to prevent it from happening again. Developers may be exacting and demanding, but they're also always understanding about bugs and errors. Every chicken gets a turn in the fryer.
- **Attend internal postmortems.** After the incident has subsided, attend as many engineering meetings about the issue as you can. These are great opportunities to learn from your engineering team and learn more about how your product is built and maintained.

SUMMARY

A strong developer brand isn't built through traditional marketing tactics. It's built through credibility, trust, and authenticity. This chapter explores how to create a brand that developers respect, engage with, and advocate for.

- **Developer brands are built on authenticity and technical credibility.** Developers don't trust marketing fluff. They trust well-built products, clear communication, and transparent messaging.
- **Trust is earned through expertise, not slogans.** Developers respect brands that demonstrate technical excellence through content, contributions, and interactions.
- **Your brand exists whether you define it or not.** Developers are talking about your product in forums, on GitHub, and in Slack groups.
- **Consistency matters.** Your messaging, visuals, documentation, and product experience should feel cohesive across all touchpoints.

- **Your documentation is your brand.** For many developers, the first interaction with your company isn't your website; it's your API docs or README file.
- **Your brand should have a clear point of view.** What problem do you solve? How do you approach it differently? Your messaging should reflect this consistently.
- **Developers are allergic to hype.** Avoid exaggerated claims and stick to facts, technical proof, and real-world use cases.
- **Community engagement is part of your brand.** How you respond to questions, feedback, and issues in forums or GitHub shapes how developers perceive your company.
- **Developer advocates are an extension of your brand.** Your team members, their credibility, and their ability to educate and inspire directly impact how your brand is viewed.
- **Measure brand perception.** Track developer sentiment through NPS, social mentions, community discussions, and survey feedback to refine your positioning.

Building a great developer brand is an elusive goal. Many have tried, most have failed. Ultimately, respect for your audience is essential. Give developers tools, avoid marketing fluff, and enable them to build with you, unfettered by obstacles that slow them down.

CHAPTER 11

Developer Documentation

Throughout my career, I've held a hypothesis that your developer documentation is your greatest and most effective sign-up vector. In my experience in evaluating developers and analyzing how they use websites, I've noticed that they will spend an inordinate amount of time on your landing page (if they came from an ad or somewhere else); your homepage; perhaps your products page (but not always); your pricing page; and finally, your documentation. Your documentation is typically the last place a developer goes before they elect to sign up.

The first advice I have to give you is to get your documentation right. Don't expect your developers (internal or external) to write it and for it all to be good. Invest in a quality documentation platform; a dedicated web developer for docs (at least in the initial stages); and an excellent technical writer (or several, if you can afford it). The best tech writer I ever worked with was also a web developer, and she was a force to be reckoned with.

WHAT MAKES GOOD DOCUMENTATION?

This isn't a book on developer documentation, so I won't spend too much time belaboring what I believe good documentation looks like. But I think it's worth highlighting a few qualities:

- clear navigation paths that indicate to developers where they should go to get started, for API reference, for tutorials and how-to guides, and so on
- clear and simple writing using concise, jargon-free language
- excellent working code examples that can be copied and pasted and applied to all common use cases
- cross-linking throughout the entire documentation corpus, including tutorials, troubleshooting guides, and even blog posts and related website content
- a logical hierarchy where content is arranged from general to specific, beginner to advanced
- a robust, functional search mechanism

I think of documentation as fitting into four categories:

- **Learning:** getting-started guides, concepts related to the product, and features and explanations
- **Tutorials:** tutorials and how-to guides for completing common tasks or solving common problems related to your product
- **Reference:** API documentation, schema definition, configuration settings
- **Troubleshooting:** FAQs, knowledge base, common errors

Follow communities like Write the Docs and initiatives such as "docs as code" to learn more about the state of the art for documentation.

HOW TO USE DOCUMENTATION IN MARKETING

The first thing is to never mistake documentation for marketing content. What I mean is that documentation should never be full of marketing language or bombastic claims. By now you already know that *all* our marketing content as it relates to developers should be free of florid marketing language or bombastic claims, but this particularly needs to be the case for developer documentation.

Documentation should not have a fancy layout or distracting colors, as you'd find in marketing content. That doesn't mean that documentation should be the equivalent of ASCII art and lack proper layout or design. It does mean that documentation should be free of distractions and focus the user on getting information.

The inverse is also true. You should never be so precious about your documentation that it doesn't have calls to action or upsell information. If you have both an open-source and a cloud product, for example, the documentation for your open-source product should absolutely include a callout or message that the cloud product is available and has certain advantages.

DOCUMENTATION AS A SIGN-UP VECTOR

The biggest thing to remember when you're using documentation to further your marketing efforts is that it should do the heavy lifting of your most complex marketing challenge: enabling developers to imagine life with your product as an indispensable part of their daily workflow.

Enable developers to imagine their life with your product

Documentation can reduce friction in the decision-making process. Developers are more likely to sign up if they have a great understanding of what your product does, who it's for, and how they use it day to day. Once a developer can see their problems in your product documentation, they will be more likely to proceed. (Once again, note how much empathizing with the *problem* vs. jumping ahead to the *solution* helps drive conversion!)

Some actionable tips for you as you build out your documentation:

- **Include a quick-start guide** for common scenarios. For good examples, check out documentation from both Supabase and Modal.
- **Highlight the beginner-friendly path** in prominent locations on your documentation homepage. Make it obvious for new users to know where to go to get started.
- **Use in-line product demos** to give developers a view of the product when it is fully installed. This is particularly useful for complex products with long sales cycles, as we discussed in an earlier chapter.
- **Embed aspects of products in your documentation.** This is an advanced feature, and only possible if you own your entire documentation stack. But embedding terminal windows or ways for developers to interact with the product as if they had already installed it will go a long way toward helping them imagine life with your product.
- **Include "instant feedback" in your docs** and allow people to rate whether a particular page of documentation was helpful using a thumbs-up/thumbs-down or other scale.

Documentation as midfunnel content

Documentation builds trust in much the same way that case studies build trust through social proof. Use tutorials and how-to guides to emphasize your understanding of the problems that potential customers face, and where possible link back to case studies as examples of how your best customers have tackled real-world problems using those same tutorials.

Be sure to strategically highlight paid offerings, including cloud versions and higher tiers, throughout the documentation—and if your product has several paid tiers, make it clear in the documentation which features are available in which tiers. Don't frustrate your customers by getting them excited over a feature that is not available in a lower tier. Be transparent, and the transparency will drive upsells.

Documentation in product-led growth

Consider embedding documentation, especially tutorials, quick starts, and how-to guides, in your onboarding flow. Leverage work from across the company to improve successful onboarding.

Use contextual clues you gain during onboarding to present relevant information to customers. Similarly, use the same contextual clues to identify gaps in documentation and weaknesses in the product.

Good docs paper over flaws in product

Often we can use documentation to provide workarounds in scenarios for which the product is currently insufficient. This helps you test a few things, including the importance of the scenario and the applicability of your chosen solution. After all, it's a big deal if a customer willingly jumps through hoops to solve a problem. That's a huge clue as to what the product team should prioritize.

DOCUMENTATION AND SEO

Your docs can do the heavy lifting for many of your desired long-tail keywords, so making sure your tech writers are plugged into your content-marketing and SEO goals is important. You don't obviously want to stuff keywords into documentation in a blatant attempt to game Google's algorithm, but you also don't want to pass up natural opportunities for including long-tail content.

DOCUMENTATION IN THE AGE OF AI

Most AI-driven development tools now include the ability to spec-ify global and project-specific rules for how the AI should interact with various external tools, APIs, frameworks, languages, and so on. Consider writing AI prompts and making them available in your doc-umentation so that users can update their tool's rules using instruc-tions that you bless and maintain. Supabase does this well by providing AI Prompts for popular development tools, including Cursor, GitHub, and more.

Beyond writing AI prompts for users, you may be wondering why you should even bother writing documentation if an LLM could read your API reference, sample code, and GitHub repositories and deliver an answer to the end user in seconds.

But the reality is that documentation is only partly about how-to content. What you really want to do with your documentation is en-capsulate your content with a mental framework or system for think-ing about your product, and add context about when—not just how—to use your product. LLMs can advise your end users with this context in addition to how-to content.

In addition, as I've maintained, one of the main purposes of writ-ing documentation is to help customers imagine themselves using your product. Providing a well-structured contextual framework helps customers place your product in their lives, and reinforces your posi-tioning and messaging as well!

METRICS FOR YOUR DOCUMENTATION

Track engagement metrics for your documentation, including the following:

- common web metrics, such as time spent on page, most common pages viewed, etc.
- the most common "last doc viewed" before someone signs up
- The rating of the documentation from the thumbs-up/ thumbs-down widget

- number and percentage of users who signed up after viewing documentation
- the most common pages viewed by existing users of the product

SUMMARY

Developer documentation is often the most critical touchpoint in the developer journey. It serves as both an educational resource and a conversion tool, helping developers understand, adopt, and succeed with your product.

- **Your documentation is your best sign-up vector.** Developers visit your documentation right before deciding to use your product. This is where you win or lose them.
- **Good documentation requires investment.** You can't rely on developers or engineers to write great docs. When you've reached sufficient scale, hire technical writers, invest in a solid documentation platform, and prioritize clarity.
- **Great documentation is easy to navigate.** Developers should be able to quickly find what they need, whether it's a getting-started guide, an API reference, or a troubleshooting section.
- **Use concise, jargon-free language.** The best docs explain concepts in simple, direct terms without unnecessary complexity or marketing fluff.
- **Code examples should be copy-pasteable.** Every common use case should have a well-documented, working code snippet that developers can quickly test.
- **Cross-link content to create a seamless experience.** Tutorials should link to relevant API references, troubleshooting guides should reference common errors, and docs should be connected to blog posts or external resources.
- **Follow a logical structure.** Organize documentation from beginner to advanced topics, ensuring a smooth learning curve for new users.

- **Search functionality must be robust.** Developers expect to find answers quickly. Make sure your search works well and surfaces the right content.
- **There are four primary types of documentation:** Learning (getting-started guides, product concepts); Tutorials (step-by-step guides); Reference (API docs, schemas); and Troubleshooting (FAQs, error messages).
- **Documentation should be free of marketing fluff.** Developers don't want sales pitches in documentation, they want answers, clarity, and technical accuracy.
- **Your documentation should still drive business goals.** While avoiding overt sales language, it should include subtle CTAs such as links to upgrade features, cloud versions, or support plans.
- **Regularly update and maintain your documentation.** Stale documentation leads to frustrated users. Build a process to refresh and improve it continuously.
- **Measure documentation effectiveness.** Use analytics, feedback forms, and search queries to understand where developers struggle, and refine accordingly.

Section 2

PRODUCT MARKETING

CHAPTER 12

Developer Product Marketing

Product marketing sits at the nexus of nearly all disciplines in a company: product/engineering, sales, marketing, and customer success. Effective product marketing managers do the following all at once:

- conduct customer discovery and identify market needs
- develop positioning and messaging that resonate with developers and enterprises
- build go-to-market plans and drive cross-functional alignment

If developer advocacy is the heart of my developer marketing program, developer product marketing is the spine. Everything in the organization is orchestrated by product marketing. I like to call them "the ringleaders of the circus." In truth, they're the most knowledgeable in the company about the target customer and how the product or feature meets that customer's needs. As a result, they're the ones who orchestrate go-to-market by bringing knowledge of the customer to everyone in product, marketing, and sales, and program-managing all aspects of launches and campaigns.

Where marketing builds programs to reach a group of developers, product marketing defines which types of developers the programs should target. Where marketing drives awareness, product marketing focuses on helping customers understand the problems a product solves and what the product does. While marketing builds programs and campaigns, product marketing gives sales and the entire organization the tools to convert interested users into paying customers. They work together, always in lockstep.

RINGLEADERS OF THE CIRCUS

Given that product marketing sits in between a number of different disciplines, effective product marketers are exceptional communicators. They are able to synthesize viewpoints, de-escalate conflict, ensure that everyone is heard, and build consensus toward resolutions— sometimes all at the same time!

Like a ringleader, product marketing ensures that every team has a moment to shine and recognizes that each member of each team has special skills they can bring to the table. Navigating competing interests and finding common ground amid the maelstrom of day-to-day business operations makes product marketing both an exhilarating and a complicated profession.

At a high level, this is what we ask product marketing to do:

- **Drive segmentation, positioning, and messaging:** Establish who the product is for, what place it occupies in the context of the industry, and how we talk about it.
- **Work cross-organizationally to determine pricing models:** And if there are pricing changes, spearhead communication about them.
- **Run all product launches:** Be the go-to person to program-manage every aspect of the company's launches.
- **Align marketing and sales:** Make sure the entire sales-and-marketing operation is in lockstep, using consistent messaging and maintaining an identical view of the ideal customer for the product or service.
- **Drive competitive analysis:** Keep an eye on competitive products and go-to-market strategy, being the first to suggest changes or opportunities.

- **Define and articulate the go-to-market strategy:** Identify the acquisition model for customers and the programs that will be run to drive adoption.

THE DEVELOPER CUSTOMER JOURNEY

We've covered at length how developers prefer to evaluate products on their own. Indeed, developers are skeptical of traditional marketing and tend to rely on peer reviews, technical content, social media discussions among developers they trust, and ultimately a complete self-directed evaluation.

If you want to drive **awareness** of your product and enter the conversation for a given problem developers are looking to solve, your most effective route will be to build deeply technical content that offers a unique spin on the problem. As I've written throughout this book, provide Help First. Help developers learn more about the problem, the history of the many solutions designed to solve the problem, and your differentiated solution.

After creating awareness, you want to enter the **consideration** phase on good footing. So while we will talk about paid acquisition in a moment, you will earn some benefit of the doubt by pulling customers to you through content as opposed to pushing developers to you by spending money. This content could be not only technical blog posts but also case studies, benchmarks, documentation, and so on.

In these crucial early stages of the customer journey, you may be tempted to throw money at the problem through ads, events, and sponsored content, but your best bet will always be to teach developers something new through content, and focus on driving distribution of the content.

At the later stage, you want to help developers **advocate** for you by giving them the tools and opportunities to share their experience with your product or service.

In fact, as independent as developers are, they remain steadfast in their quest for new knowledge.

WEBSITE CONTENT: A TEAM SPORT

Your website is the first and best representation of your customer journey. It will help customers *imagine their life with your product*, an essential aspect of carrying your message to developers. Product marketers should take command of their website and use it as the primary megaphone for the strategy, positioning, and messaging of the company.

> **TIP:** At some point as a new marketing leader, you're going to want to redo your website. Don't worry, the temptation is natural. You want to put your stamp on things. My advice is to wait. Wait until you've been able to audit and land on consistent positioning and messaging. Wait until you've proven the messaging through at least one campaign. Wait until you've received validation from customers and your sales team.

Let's talk about the various components in a typical website and some best practices for implementing them.

Homepage

Your homepage should follow a consistent flow. People have grown accustomed to this framework, and it doesn't make sense to deviate.

- What does your product do? And what value does it provide? Include the CTA.
- Customer logos and quotes.
- How does your product work?
- What use cases are enabled via your product?
- Social proof (case study quotes, social media quotes, etc.).
- Get-started CTA.

Product page

Strictly speaking, if you are at an early stage and only have one product, you don't need a product page at all. However, if you're a more established company or have a product line, you may consider breaking your product page up into more focused, dedicated pages where you can get into the technical details of everything you offer.

This isn't to say that you can't be technical on your homepage. Some of the best websites for developer products show off code, command-line instructions, or product-user experience on the homepage. After all, if you want to appeal to developers, getting to code as quickly as possible is highly recommended.

However, you want to focus your homepage on the value you provide. Yes, show what you do, but quickly get to the "So what?" Don't leave people hanging.

In contrast, the product page is the place where you can unabashedly explain the details of your product, show a feature matrix, and so on.

Pricing page

We will cover the pricing page in a later chapter on pricing and pricing models.

Use-case and solution pages

A solution page is one that explains the use cases for your product. If you have a brand-new database, for example, you'll explain its value on the homepage and its features on the product page. But you'll use your solution page to explain what developers can do with it. How is this database used in an industry vertical, such as financial services? How can this database be used in a more horizontal scenario, such as analytics?

I once worked for a founder who refused to build solution pages. Poppycock!

Solution pages serve multiple purposes:

- They show prospects how they can imagine their life with your product. If a customer comes from a financial-services background or company, don't make them do all the work of figuring out what your product can do for them!
- Solution pages are also excellent SEO magnets . . . if you do them properly. If someone is searching for a type of product or to solve a particular problem, but not yours specifically, you could build pages that deliver topical authority for that category.

My personal belief is that the best solution pages actually live in your documentation corpus. We'll talk about documentation in a later chapter, but the idea is not just to fill the page with a description of the solution and how your product fits in, but to start building templates, starter kits, sample code, how-to guides, and any number of other technical materials that improve your topical authority and help your customers get started quickly.

I call this the Christmas Tree Model, where you build a landing page (the trunk and branches) and slowly, over time, add ornaments (links to content). Use-case pages are well suited for this approach. Focus on the customer-facing messaging first and then, based on requests from customers and your sales team, add supporting materials.

Comparison pages

Comparison pages are fantastic SEO fodder. If a prospect is further down the customer journey and actively considering different products, they are most likely comparing you to others, or they are searching for alternatives to competing products.

Comparison pages provide customers with a fast view of how your product stacks up against competitors'. Build as many comparison pages as you can, and get into the conversation your competitors have already started.

But be careful: Your comparison pages *must* be truthful. Remember, developers hate overtly marketing content, and they will especially be turned off if you make bombastic claims that you can't substantiate.

Gated content

Over time, you will want to build additional lead magnets, pieces of content or marketing tactics that provide yet another opportunity for prospects to identify themselves to you. Obviously you already have product sign-ups. But what about newsletters, webinars, ebooks, and so on? All these things are great tools for you to use.

One of my favorite tactics is to take a bunch of my existing content (blog posts, documentation, etc.) and organize it into themes (which are related to my omnichannel campaigns!). I then create an ebook and give customers an opportunity to download it after providing their email address.

> **TIP:** Developers often won't be interested in downloading something called an "ebook." Fair enough. Consider branding your bundled content differently. For example, "The Buyer's Guide to AI Retrieval Augmented Generation (RAG) Pipelines."

Landing pages

As you build your ad campaigns, you will want to have dedicated landing pages that pay off the messaging and creative of the ad. There are a lot of best practices and websites (not to mention tools) for squeezing the tiniest percentage points of improvement from landing pages.

Here are a handful of my favorite tips:

- **Eliminate all site chrome from landing pages.** No header, no footer. Distractions reduce conversions, and you want to keep the visitor focused on the goal of the page, whether that's signing up, requesting a demo, or downloading content.
- **Have only one call to action (CTA) on the website.** The landing page should guide visitors toward a single, clear action. Multiple CTAs can cause decision fatigue and reduce conversion rates. Make the CTA prominent and actionable.
- **Match messaging to the ad.** Ensure that the headline, copy, and imagery reflect the ad that brought the visitor to the page. Consistency builds trust and reassures the visitor that they are in the right place.
- **Keep forms as short as possible.** The more fields a visitor has to fill out, the higher the abandonment rate. Only ask for essential information, and if possible use progressive profiling to collect more details over time.
- **Use social proof to build credibility.** Testimonials, case studies, or recognizable customer logos can reassure visitors that your product is valuable. Developers are particularly skeptical, so real-world proof points matter.
- **Speed matters. Optimize for fast load times.** Slow pages kill conversions. Compress images, use efficient code, and leverage caching/CDNs to ensure the landing page loads quickly on all devices.
- **Test continuously.** A/B test different headlines, layouts, and CTA placements. Even small changes, like tweaking button colors or rewording CTA text, can significantly impact conversion rates.
- **Make the mobile experience seamless.** Developers often browse from their phones. Ensure that all forms, buttons, and content are easy to navigate and complete on mobile devices.
- **Reduce friction with autofill and third-party log-ins.** If you require a sign-up, allow autofill from browsers or integrate social log-ins (GitHub, Google, etc.) to minimize effort.

- **Use exit-intent popups strategically.** If a visitor moves to leave the page, a well-placed pop-up offering a free trial, discount, or downloadable resource can help salvage conversions without being intrusive.

In addition, I like to put my landing pages on a dedicated subdomain. For example, if my company domain is company.com, then my landing page domain would be something like landing.company.com or l.company.com.

BUILDING LISTENING MECHANISMS AND CUSTOMER-DEVELOPMENT PROCESSES

Product marketing's core function is to listen to the market and customers and help guide product-development decisions and determine how to speak about the product to the market. Building active listening mechanisms from within your own company (e.g., your sales and customer-success teams); outside your company (keyword and trending-content research); influencers and leaders (community research); and industry experts (analyst relations, which we discuss in a later chapter) is an essential component of effective product marketing.

Let's dive into some of these tactics now.

Customer feedback loops and market research

It's critical to collect customer feedback systematically and socialize it broadly throughout your organization. Try to ensure that you have a steady flow of customer research going at all times. That way you're always able to spot changes before they become alarming.

Here are some ways to gather feedback:

- **Surveys and feedback forms embedded in your product:** Try to get a solid understanding of how your current customers perceive your product or service. Use Net Promoter Score (NPS) to put a concrete estimate onto this perception.

- **User interviews:** Periodically work with your sales team to meet with customers and interview them about their usage of the product, how they are staying on top of current events, YouTube channels and podcasts they're listening to, blogs and newsletters they're reading, and so on. Look for changes, and also look for up-and-coming trends that you can capitalize on. Be sure to ask questions about your competitors.
- **Closed-lost interviews:** Work with your sales team to conduct the same interviews with customers you lost as well as those who did not end up using your service. Try to identify any differences between them beyond simply technical considerations.
- **Community forums and social listening:** Maintain an active ear on your Slack, Discord, and forums. Monitor social media, especially Reddit and LinkedIn, for mentions of your product. Collect these for reporting. Also, collect positive feedback for use on your website!
- **Product-usage analytics:** Use your product analytics to determine popular features and changes in usage patterns.

Open development and community transparency

For open-source and developer-centric products, transparency in development is invaluable. By adopting an "open development" approach, you're not only fostering trust but also actively encouraging community involvement that can accelerate product evolution.

- **Public roadmaps:** Some companies don't like to maintain a public roadmap of features. I think this is a mistake. Let developers know, at least at a high level, what they can expect from you in the near future. Give them an opportunity to vote for and comment on features you plan to build. PostHog does this really well. But be careful: If you publish a roadmap, let people comment, and then don't deliver on what the people want, you'll come across as tone deaf. Nearly all the BigTech companies have user forums with feature requests that are routinely ignored.

- **Open beta programs:** Permit existing customers to use new features early and solicit input and testimonials for launch.
- **Regular updates:** Publish a weekly or biweekly "changelog" on your website or in your documentation so that customers know what's new, even if it doesn't rise to the level of a product launch. Sometimes a minor feature that saves hours of aggravation can be as important to your customers as a big new feature area.
- **Social media engagement:** Post ideas and gather opinions from users (and prospective users) on social media. Indeed, some of the best products around today have product and marketing leaders who are active on social media.

Integrating feedback into product development

The final step in building effective listening mechanisms is ensuring that feedback doesn't just get collected, but is systematically integrated into the product-development process.

- **Attend product and engineering stand-ups.** Product marketers should be "honorary" members of the product team and should convey research results frequently in these staff meetings and stand-ups.
- **Encourage engineers to reach out directly to customers who've given negative feedback.** Engineers should be able to talk to customers and solicit input more often.
- **Close the feedback loop with users.** Let users know when their feedback has been acted on. If someone files a bug report, let them know when it is resolved. Be rigorous about this and you can turn negative sentiment into not simply positive feedback, but powerful community building.

Feedback and research serve a greater purpose

Don't just use this research to guide product decisions. Use it to define positioning and messaging, go-to-market strategies, community-development plans, and more. This feedback should be critical for every aspect of the company, from product definition to go-to-market.

If you run a global business with products that are intended to reach a global audience (as is the case with nearly all developer-focused products), it is essential that you solicit feedback from a geographically and demographically diverse group and that your messaging reflects that diversity.

However, collecting feedback and understanding the feedback are two different things. You have to be able to interpret it and be motivated to take action upon it.

For example, we have seen in recent years that some AI vision-recognition tools have blind spots with people of color. It's natural for a team that has never been asked to think about skin color to overlook this aspect of testing. However, a team that employs a diverse array of people and listens to their input would have accounted for differences in skin color during testing.

Build diverse teams that seek diverse and varied opinions and are empowered to take action upon them.

Customer design reviews

Periodically—about once a year—I like to bring several customers together to get a preview of our intended roadmap. I try to mix the industry and firmographic characteristics of this gathering. Some customers will be from large organizations, others from smaller organizations. Some from B2B SaaS startups, some from vertical industries. I try to ensure geographic and demographic diversity as well.

The hardest part of these gatherings is avoiding groupthink and encouraging everyone to voice their opinion. You want to avoid situations where people go along with the consensus even if it's contrary to their opinion. This will cloud your research and cause you to overlook customer segments who, in the privacy of their own decision making, would choose an alternative direction.

It's also natural in a group setting for some people to remain quiet while others dominate the discussion. For this reason, I appoint a moderator (usually me) whose job it is to pose questions, ensure people stay on topic, ensure we don't dwell on a given topic for too long, and ensure that even those who are quiet are afforded the opportunity to give their thoughts. The moderator specifically fishes for dissenting opinions to help counteract groupthink.

I am also deliberate about how I design the physical characteristics of the room, as well as how I structure the day.

I start by making sure that tables are arranged in a U shape. The customer guests are seated at the table, while the presenter is in the open area at the front of the room. There is a single projector and a single table at which the presenter can plug in their laptop and go through demos. All company employees, including leadership, are seated outside the U, along the walls. As moderator, I patrol the inside of the U, looking for opportunities to spur the conversation.

The most critical aspect of fostering this discussion is to let customers speak. In fact, the *best* situation you can hope for is when customers are disagreeing with one another (cordially, of course). There is *a lot* to be learned when customers present and defend their own ideas. It is important for the moderator, as well as all company employees, to remember this rule: When customers are speaking, we do not speak. Especially when customers are engaging with one another, we remain silent.

The day's agenda is also particularly designed to foster discussion.

I usually open with an executive conversation where we talk about the vision and purpose of the company. I've invited the CEOs of Microsoft, Amazon, Twitter, and several startups to these types of events, and they've all gladly accepted. Aim high, and give your customers the opportunity to ask serious and difficult questions about the strategy of the company.

From there we dive into product discussions. Product leaders and engineers must present their own work. This is not a marketing exercise, where we do polished, perfect, pretty demos. This is a product exercise, where engineers meet the customers they're building for and get direct feedback. Everything is fair to present: imminent releases, working prototypes, design mocks, even slides with just a handful of bullets indicating potential ideas.

The stack rank exercise

Customer design reviews certainly spark amazing and fascinating discussions. But what will customers ultimately choose? In every election in every democracy on earth, there is always a poll conducted that shows one party's policies are "deeply popular," which prompts people to wonder why voters will elect a different party's candidates who act against their best interests. But ideas are inexpensive, and it's possible that an idea will be popular and still not garner any support.

Likewise with technology products. Naturally, every customer wants every feature. But it's not feasible for any product team to build every possible feature, nor is it practical. When products get bloated, value propositions get muddied and the user experience ends up looking like a trash can of buttons and sliders. It's important to prioritize our work and, as with voters in politics, it can be difficult to discern what is truly a necessity vs. what is a nice-to-have.

To better understand what customers will support in our product roadmap, I always close the day with a ranking exercise. By then everyone has seen our product roadmap directly from our product and engineering team, so I recap the day and the big ideas and then ask the customers to rank them.

We make trade-offs every day, mentally calculating the risk and reward of certain decisions before we proceed. Some people are better than others at making this calculation, which I've long believed is an indicator of personal success.

In life we make a risk-and-reward calculation before deciding on a meal. In business we make a risk-and-reward calculation before embarking on a strategic initiative. In political science this is called *preference falsification*, where voters may publicly support popular policies while privately rejecting them due to hidden personal costs. Similarly, customers may vocally support a roadmap idea during discussions but not back it when forced to allocate tangible resources.

Thus, the calculation must be visceral. If you were asked to choose between a slice of pizza for lunch or a green salad, you'd calculate in your mind the relative healthiness of your meals that week, as well as the quality of said pizza and salad. On paper, the decision is easy. But standing in front of a delicious, gooey, fresh-smelling slice of pizza and making the decision is a different matter entirely. Indeed, people in a rational, detached state often misjudge how they will behave in an emotionally engaged state.

In order to help the attendees at the design review make a consequential decision, I hand each of them three crisp one-dollar bills straight from the bank. I then tell them that we will anonymously vote for the key projects of most interest to them. At the front of the room are boxes representing each of the big ideas. Attendees are invited to place as many of their dollar bills as they want in any box—or, if they don't see anything worth spending on, to keep the dollar bills for themselves.

After the voting exercise, we then discuss the results as a group. I've found that the physical act of holding the money, inhaling that distinctive "straight off the Fed printer" smell, and feeling the crispness of it in your hand forces a very different style of decision making than an academic hand-raising and voting exercise. Putting customers in an emotionally engaged state, where they have to make a tangible tradeoff in their decision making, is nearly always a great source of information.

SIMPLIFY: THE CORE ARTIFACTS OF PRODUCT MARKETING

As described above, all the activities driven by product marketing get distilled into a handful of core artifacts that live on for the life of the product:

- Market Requirements Document
- Positioning Framework
- Go-to-Market Plan
- Sales Enablement Repository

The goal isn't to create busywork or documents just for the sake of it. Rather, we want to codify decisions into long-living documents that can be shared broadly and communicated easily to existing and new employees alike. In a fast-moving business, optimizing and streamlining communication will make it easier to share decisions. As we go through the next several chapters, consider how you will fold decisions into these artifacts.

Let's examine each of these artifacts now.

The market requirements document

The MRD is the principle product-strategy document. It is primarily accompanied by the product requirements document (PRD), or product specification. Sometimes, companies skip the MRD and PRD and go straight to listing out features, writing user stories, and prioritizing them. But done properly, both the MRD and PRD can provide guiding principles that shape the product direction in an intelligent manner.

The MRD (or whatever you may call it) includes information for market and customer analysis, product requirements, and success metrics.

The primary audience for the MRD is the entire product/engineering and marketing organizations. But the MRD can also be used to guide other customer-facing roles, such as sales and customer success. At minimum, the information contained in the MRD makes generating common sales collateral (such as competitive battle cards and first-meeting decks) much easier.

The positioning framework

This is the seminal document from which all messaging and outbound activities should flow. The positioning framework highlights the product and the context in which it lives. It describes the ideal audience for the product and the things that make the product unique. It outlines the features and benefits of the product that support the positioning.

And it does it all in an information-dense tool that all stakeholders across marketing and sales can reference as the definitive starting point for outbound communication.

You will almost certainly supplement the positioning framework with content that lays out messaging for certain audiences and specific circumstances—for example, how your product supports the financial services or health care industries. These will be actionable messaging documents for sales (and others) to refer to when engaging with or thinking about those types of customers. At the same time, the positioning framework is the seed of all that content and drives internal consistency across all messaging formats and channels.

The go-to-market plan

This is the complete strategy for what marketing plans to do and how sales fits in. Ideally it's a joint production with sales and customer success, and it gives everyone the benefit of knowing the goals, metrics, projects, and owners of all go-to-market activities.

My go-to-market plans are simple in their formatting (a straightforward Google Doc with standard document styles), but often dense and full of information. I lay out the goals and metrics for the team and build a mnemonic of some kind to help people group the strategies. For example, I may group our work in terms of "Awareness" and "Conversion," and within those two buckets lay out various tactics, from content creation and syndication to website optimization.

Most importantly, as a leader, I never treat my people as if they're coin-operated. The broad strategies and perhaps even top-line tactics (e.g., "Optimize the website to improve conversion of site visitors to signups from 4% to 8%") are mine to define. But I intentionally leave it up to the team to determine how we will execute these tactics. Typically, I ask people to create their own Google Doc and link to it from the main GTM plan.

Over the course of one planning cycle, we will have dissected our metrics, identified our biggest levers for moving them, articulated a plan with key strategies and top-line tactics for moving those metrics, and delegated responsibility to each member of the team. These responsibilities are associated with the metrics, so everyone ends up knowing what is expected of them and—this is important—how their work fits into the bigger picture.

Sales enablement repository

This is the internal wiki, SharePoint, Notion, GDrive (or whatever) where you organize and maintain all your content. A good marketing team steadfastly maintains top-level organization of the repository, routinely pruning outdated content and ruthlessly prioritizing important information.

There's not much to add here except there are many ways to format a sales enablement repository. I like to have sections for the following information:

- **News and information:** A bulleted list of key news items that I keep updated based on Slack conversations about competitors, industry trends, or technology areas. I also highlight new documents or resources.
- **Messaging frameworks:** The core positioning and messaging documents, linked at the top of the portal because of their importance to all subsequent work we do in sales and marketing.
- **Product roadmap:** A synthesization of the product roadmap discussions. I divide them into broader themes and provide links to roadmap slides to be used with customers.
- **Collateral:** Sections for links to slide decks, datasheets, battle cards, and videos.
- **Case studies:** Links to publicly available case studies and a summary of what the case study is useful for (e.g., a switcher from a competitor, an example of scalability).
- **Plans and programs:** Links to our marketing plans and other core artifacts, such as the Market Requirements Doc and Go-to-Market Plan.

DELIVERING STRATEGIC INSIGHT

Earlier, when discussing content, I talked about "original research"—the idea that a company with a unique product that serves a well-defined customer also has unique insight. This insight is how you drive strategy while simultaneously executing the tactics outlined in this book.

Most of what we've covered in this book is about how marketing helps sales *sell*. But when was the last time you tried to *buy* software? It's inordinately difficult. Recently I had to identify a sales-intelligence tool for a friend's company to buy. I understood the company's requirements well enough. But as I weighed the options, I realized I lacked insight into this space. I could check the boxes to see who met my needs *now*, but I lacked context about what I might need *in the future* as the company grew. I was paralyzed by indecision throughout the process and wished there was someone to call for help.

Now let's flip this around. Imagine you're a product manager or a product marketing manager in this space. If you knew that your clients were not closing because they were paralyzed by their inability to understand the space as well as you, wouldn't you want to take the time to create materials that offered background information and an informed opinion of how the space will grow over the coming years?

This is what Sharely did. They build AI relationship-as-a-service tools, but they started with a simple chatbot. Through more than one hundred customer meetings, they learned that knowledge management was keeping customers from adopting—the fear that their AI agents would relay old or outdated information as responses to customer requests. They started selling their tools using this insight in their pitches, collateral, and presentations.

This insight, borne from meeting with or conducting large surveys of many customers, is your strategic weapon as a product marketing manager. You can use it to build materials that unlock the sales process through customer education. That guides product direction to fulfill your informed analysis of the future—and that teaches and leads the entire industry. That provides an invaluable resource for buyers and vendors alike, which clarifies the market for all.

Developing this kind of insight comes from customer research, analyst conversations, and, yes, years of experience. This can be your superpower.

INTERNAL COMMUNICATION

Communication is an essential component of nearly every role in business today, from the software developer who likes to code alone in a dark room to the gregarious communications manager who lives, breathes, and owns the title for outbound communication. Simply having a great idea is insufficient. You need to communicate the importance of your idea, rally support for your idea, and motivate and inspire your team (whether or not you have direct-reporting responsibility) to deliver on the idea. Great communication is a hallmark of great product marketing.

As you read the subsequent chapters on segmentation and positioning, pricing, launch management, sales enablement, and more, recognize that all these tasks fall on the product marketing manager, and they all require exceptional levels of communication.

Build a process for communicating status. It could be a weekly or daily Slack message, a monthly roundup of activities, or something in between. When driving key initiatives, identify your core stakeholders *as well as* your leadership team and make sure you are communicating with them regularly about progress, good or bad. Executives hate bad news. So overcommunicate, and communicate early. Let them help you get unstuck.

As you read the next few chapters, think not only about the tasks being covered by your team, but how you plan on communicating progress about each task. If you've delivered progress updates the same way for a long time, take a hard look at whether you could stand to update your communication style. After all, people change, social mores change, and communication styles change. A decade ago, we weren't all conditioned to getting information in six-to-ten-second bursts on TikTok. Today? It's natural.

The most important aspect of communication isn't speaking or writing. It's being heard and listened to. Understand your audience, your team, your organization, and adapt accordingly.

SUMMARY

Product marketing for developer-focused products requires a deep understanding of both technical needs and business motivations. It's about bridging the gap between what the product does and why developers should care.

- **Product marketing bridges product, sales, and marketing.** Translate technical capabilities into messaging that resonates with developers and decision makers.
- **Developers need clear, technical messaging.** Avoid vague marketing-speak. Communicate benefits in precise, straightforward language.
- **Positioning and competitive analysis are essential.** Define your unique value, know your competition, and highlight what makes your product different.
- **Tailor messaging for developers and decision makers.** Developers focus on speed and flexibility, while executives care about ROI and security.
- **Content and documentation are core to product marketing.** Developers often engage with docs first. Ensure they reinforce your value proposition.
- **Measure product marketing impact.** Track sign-ups, adoption, and engagement to refine messaging and go-to-market strategies.

CHAPTER 13

Segmentation, Positioning, and Messaging

Without proper positioning, your product and company are lost in a wilderness of look-alikes. Positioning puts your product or service in a particular place that is unique, differentiated, and winning. It distinguishes you from the competition and makes it clear why a well-articulated segment of customers should consider it.

To get to effective positioning, we need to do our research. And that starts with segmentation.

THINKING OF POSITIONING AND MESSAGING HOLISTICALLY

Fundamentally what we are trying to do is connect the product that we're building to an audience or segment. It's all connected.

Think of it this way:

- **Product:** What we are building and want to bring to market. Product marketing should influence product direction, perhaps through artifacts such as the market requirements document (MRD).
- **Positioning:** The place within the broader market that the product occupies, and how that place differs.
- **Messaging:** How we talk about the product.
- **Messenger:** The company, brand, or person that is going to carry the messaging to the audience.
- **Audience:** The customer or segment we intend to target with the product.

Most of the time when products fail, it's because there's a disconnect somewhere in that chain. Let's dive into it more precisely. To put it in Amazon parlance, we start with the customer and work backwards.

DEVELOPER SEGMENTATION (NOT PERSONAS)

Segmentation is the foundation of marketing. As we saw in chapter 9, developers are a diverse group with varying needs, technical skills, and goals. Taking a one-size-fits-all approach will lead to boring, ineffective marketing tactics. Instead, start by homing in on the type of developer that will need your product.

Developers are unique customers who value authenticity and technical credibility. They respond better to products and messaging that align with their specific needs and interests rather than general marketing. For instance, a back-end engineer's concerns may center around database performance, scalability, and security, while a front-end engineer might focus more on UI performance, integration with popular frameworks, and user experience.

Segmentation helps product marketers prioritize these differing needs and craft communications that directly address the pain points and values of each group. Without it, messaging will feel generic and might miss the mark.

As we will see in this chapter, segmentation leads to identifying your ideal customer profile (the one segment that matters most to you) and your positioning (where your product resides in context relative to the customer).

But it all starts with a strong understanding of segmentation.

How to segment your market

You will need to do a ton of customer discovery to understand the types of customers that matter to you. If you've already got an established product in the market, no matter how small, focus on customers who already love you and get value out of you. If not, think more aspirationally. Maybe that's individual developers in large companies. Maybe that's executives at small companies. Maybe that's executives at big companies. Call them up and talk to them. You are trying to answer several questions:

- Who is this customer (level, title, signing authority, degrees/certifications, etc.)?
- What is their problem as it relates to something you can solve? They may have several!
- What do they currently use to solve the problem?
- What alternatives did they consider to solve the problem?

From there you can begin to cluster the answers and look for common themes.

Take, for example, these three ostensibly similar open-source PostgreSQL-based databases. Each focuses on a different segment of the developer population, with a different type of problem and lens on the technology choice.

Company	Who are the targets?	What is their problem?
Timescale	Senior developers in medium-to-large businesses with substantial existing investments in PostgreSQL	They've made substantial existing investments in PostgreSQL and need to get more out of them.
Neon	Startups, SMBs, and individual developers who are building new applications and want a low-cost, high-efficiency database	They are building microservices or multitier applications, and they need a database to go with it.
Supabase	Front-end and full-stack developers in startups and SMBs looking to rapidly build new applications and prototypes	They need to build an application, and time to market is more important than obsessing over each architectural choice.

A word about personas

For a time, there was a push to create human-relatable personas to encapsulate segmentation. The idea was that everyone on the team would develop empathy for a fictitious representation of their customer.

The problem is that personas are too imprecise and subject to misinterpretation. You can't take a description of a developer and reliably reverse-engineer it into, for example, a set of high-performing keywords. There's a huge difference between these two descriptions:

- **Persona:** "A seasoned developer who prefers highly technical documentation when building React applications."
- **Segmentation:** "Developers with over 5 years of experience in React, located in North America, and working at a company with between 25 and 100 people."

A segmentation-based approach, on the other hand, emphasizes specificity. It focuses on the exact attributes, behaviors, and needs of real-user segments rather than generalizing them into a fictional persona. Segmentation allows you to group developers based on measurable, actionable criteria, such as their role, level of influence within an organization, project types, preferred technologies, or even prior experience with similar tools. This approach enables product marketers to build targeted strategies that address the precise needs and pain points of each segment, leading to more relevant messaging, higher engagement, and ultimately better product adoption.

Moreover, segmentation lends itself to clear digital marketing strategies. For example, it is much easier to build a LinkedIn audience from a segmentation description than it is from a persona. In any organization where product marketing is split from digital marketing, precise communication is at a premium.

Segmentation research

Understanding the uses of your product will lead you to the people who will most benefit from it, and from there you can begin to understand your core segmentation. Here are some questions I like to ask (I've included the questions from earlier for completeness):

- Who is this customer (level, title, signing authority, all of it)?
- What are they trying to achieve?
- What is their problem as it relates to something you can solve? They may have several!
- What do they currently use to solve the problem?
- What alternatives did they consider to solve this problem?
- How acute was the problem they were trying to solve? Was there a sense of urgency to solve it?
- Who were the decision makers in each segment? What were their criteria for consideration?
- What is their budget and propensity to buy?
- What is the deal cycle in each segment? How long would it take to win? Who else needs to sign off on the deal? What objections could we potentially see?
- What would the go-to-market and full marketing plan look like for each segment?
- What is the total market size of each segment? How much could we realistically capture?

- What are the existing competitors in each segment? How do they compare to what we are offering?
- What do the customers find particularly unique about your offering?

All these questions and more have helped companies get a good idea of which segment would be most appropriate for them.

Developer segmentation by role and influence

Developers in different roles will have distinct expectations from a product, as well as varying levels of influence on purchasing decisions. Key segmentation categories in developer marketing might include database engineers, open-source contributors, front-end developers, and architects, among others. By understanding these categories, product marketers can tailor their approach to address the specific challenges and responsibilities of each group.

For instance, database engineers are typically concerned with data integrity, performance, and scalability. Messaging aimed at this group should emphasize features like transaction management, query optimization, and support for large data volumes. Open-source contributors, on the other hand, may value transparency, extensibility, and the ability to contribute to the codebase. Product marketers targeting open-source developers would benefit from emphasizing the openness of the product, community support, and opportunities for collaboration.

Influence within an organization is another factor you could consider for segmentation. Some developers, like senior architects, have a significant say in technology decisions, while others, such as junior developers, may not have direct purchasing authority but still impact decisions through usage and advocacy.

While segmentation by role and influence is interesting, it doesn't guarantee that the customer has the specific problem you're trying to solve with your product.

Developer segmentation by the job to be done

A more effective way—in fact, a more accurate way—to segment your potential market is to define them by their use case, the job they're trying to do. If you've got a vector database, you're looking for customers who are trying to create, store, and query embeddings in as high-performance and reliable a manner as possible. In this case, the job isn't to "store vector embeddings," it's to understand and address *why* they want to store vector embeddings in the first place. Are they trying to build a fast search capability in their application? Are they trying to identify malevolent actors on their system? Are they trying to identify fraud before or as it happens? It's important to correctly identify the specific task your customer is trying to accomplish.

This leads you down the path of who needs to create embeddings, who has performance problems, what kinds of people are trying to solve these problems, what they bring in terms of background and prior training and experience, and so on.

If you combine your "job to be done" segmentation with your "role and influence" segmentation, you can qualify customers based on the problems they're trying to solve, and by their ability and propensity to buy what you have to offer.

Using segmentation in product development

Segmentation is also key to building the right product for the right customer. Product managers can tailor experiences that align with each segment's workflow and technical needs by focusing on precise user groups rather than broad personas, driving acquisition, expansion, and retention. Segmentation helps focus product development on a specific (and important) group of users as opposed to building random features.

Segmentation in a product-development context also need not be used synonymously with the ideal customer profile (which we will discuss shortly). Product teams should be making bets across the spectrum of potential user segments. As product marketers, our job is to ensure that their feature development is *intentional* about which segments are being targeted, and that we use our research to help guide those prioritization decisions.

Here are some ways product teams can use segmentation, starting with the most obvious:

- **Drive feedback loop for the product:** Use segmentation insights to inform feature prioritization and improve the product, ensuring continuous alignment with user needs.
- **Identify key user groups:** Segment by measurable attributes like job role, technical skills, and usage patterns to create customized onboarding flows and in-product experiences.
- **Address specific pain points:** Use segmentation data to streamline onboarding, minimizing friction with features like setup shortcuts, targeted documentation, or tailored tutorials.
- **Pinpoint high-potential users:** Identify segments with high engagement or expansion potential and proactively offer resources like advanced tutorials or beta access to turn these users into product champions.
- **Align customer discovery:** Use segmentation to go deeper into customer discovery, asking questions that add insight and texture to existing research.

This is a good lesson for us that product marketing can have outsized impact across the organization if we are methodical, communicate broadly, and act inclusively.

SEGMENTATION IS THE PRECURSOR TO THE IDEAL CUSTOMER PROFILE

Segmentation is only the first step. Ultimately, you want a good handle on your product's ideal customer profile (ICP). Starting with segmentation is a rigorous and more scalable way to arrive at your ICP. It gives you the exact traits and helps you break down the broad developer market into specific, actionable groups based on shared characteristics.

Segmentation enables you to examine several slices of the market: job roles, technical expertise, industry vertical, organizational structure, and so on. This will help you identify where and with whom your product will have the greatest impact, and (ideally) you should be able to use tools like LinkedIn to understand the relative size of each of these slices.

Fundamentally, segmentation helps you organize your potential customers into groups that make sense for your business objectives, which helps you craft hypotheses and tactics to test them, and maintain a rigorous, data-driven approach to ICP development.

What is the ideal customer profile?

The ideal customer profile (ICP) is a detailed description of the type of company or individual that represents the perfect fit for your product. It goes beyond basic demographics or job titles, focusing instead on specific traits that indicate a strong likelihood of successful engagement, adoption, and retention.

An ICP encompasses factors such as industry, company size, technology stack, pain points, purchasing behavior, and the roles within the organization that influence product decisions. For developer products, an ICP may also include technical expertise, budget for developer tools, and openness to adopting new technologies.

The ICP is laser focused. It's a profile of the customer that will not only derive significant value from your product but also contribute to the product's growth through retention, advocacy, and expansion. The ICP gives your entire go-to-market team the alignment necessary to prioritize work.

How can segmentation guide you to defining your ICP?

The ICP is particularly valuable for product-led growth (PLG) strategies, where the product is a key driver of acquisition and retention. In a PLG context, the ICP helps identify the types of users likely to adopt and benefit from the product without extensive sales involvement.

Quality segmentation that yields a focused ICP enables you to build targeted go-to-market approaches to activate your ICP.

Put simply, your ICP is a more specific analysis of your most effective segment.

Segmentation reveals patterns and insights within your target audience. As you test each of this audience's attributes and their amenability to using your product, you get closer to narrowing the view of your ICP.

In many cases, as you narrow your segmentation into an ICP, you may let go of certain cohorts of potential customers that you may want to return to and target later, or even build a different product, SKU, or feature to address in the future.

Segmentation also enables you to test and refine your ICP over time. It will change as your company, product, and industry evolves. This is natural; nobody should be fixated on a single ICP for too long. By identifying and testing adjacent segments, you can widen or tighten the focus of your ICP accordingly.

Ensuring your ICP is actionable

One helpful strategy I use is to make sure that I can "find" my ICP using LinkedIn Sales Navigator. If my ICP includes as part of its definition traits that are not easily searchable and filterable in common sales-intelligence tools, it becomes very difficult to actually use.

There are more than twenty different filters available for narrowing search criteria in LinkedIn Sales Navigator, including the following at a person level:

- current and past company
- title
- function
- seniority level
- recent job changes

At a company level, there are some valuable filters as well:

- geography
- industry
- headcount
- annual revenues
- recent changes to senior leadership

If you use these filters to help guide the creation of your ICP, you'll be able to turn around and take immediate action on your ICP to find customers, whether as part of LinkedIn Ad targeting or creating an outbound sales list.

Using segmentation to identify your unique value proposition

Segmentation not only helps you define your ideal customer profile (ICP), but it also illuminates your unique value proposition (UVP) by revealing where your product is truly differentiated in the market. Through segmentation, you identify groups that align most closely with your product's strengths, which helps you understand what these customers value and what your product does better than alternatives. This is the foundation for crafting a UVP that speaks directly to the specific needs of your best customer segment.

Once segmentation has allowed you to pinpoint a valuable segment and develop an ICP, you can analyze what makes your product stand out for this audience. For instance, if your ICP reveals a segment of back-end engineers at mid-sized SaaS companies focused on scalability and ease of integration, your UVP may center around your product's speed in handling high volumes of data or its interoperability with popular developer tools. This process of narrowing the focus ensures that your UVP is not generic, but highly relevant to the exact users who are most likely to adopt, use, and advocate for your product.

Segmentation also brings clarity to competitive differentiation. By identifying distinct traits and pain points within a specific segment, you can see where your competitors might fall short, and then highlight how your product fills that gap. If other tools in the space require extensive configuration and your product's appeal lies in its straightforward setup, segmentation helps make that a core part of your UVP for the ICP. Understanding exactly what each segment values, and how your product uniquely satisfies those needs, strengthens your positioning and drives adoption by clearly articulating why your product is the best fit.

Ultimately, segmentation and ICP refinement are about more than finding the right customers, they're about refining and articulating why your product deserves those customers.

POSITIONING

With a solid understanding of your segments, ideal customer profile, and unique value proposition, you're ready to tackle positioning and messaging, the two foundational elements that shape how your product is perceived and adopted. Although they're related, positioning and messaging serve distinct purposes in the product marketing process.

Countless books have been written about positioning. The best of these books is *Obviously Awesome* by the legendary April Dunford. In this section, I will tell you what works for me.

What is positioning?

Positioning is a strategic exercise, a foundation that defines how the product fits into the market or market segment. It isn't a tagline or a slogan; it's what is unique about your product and describes the place in which your product lives in the market.

Positioning involves answering specific questions: What category does the product belong in? What makes it different from existing solutions? And why should a developer, engineer, or decision maker choose it over another? The key here is clarity. Positioning must clearly and unequivocally explain the product's specific advantage for a given audience and use case.

Take our example of the three PostgreSQL-based startups from earlier. Each of them ostensibly offers the same thing (albeit packaged differently): full Postgres in the cloud. But each occupies a different *place* (position) on the spectrum of developers.

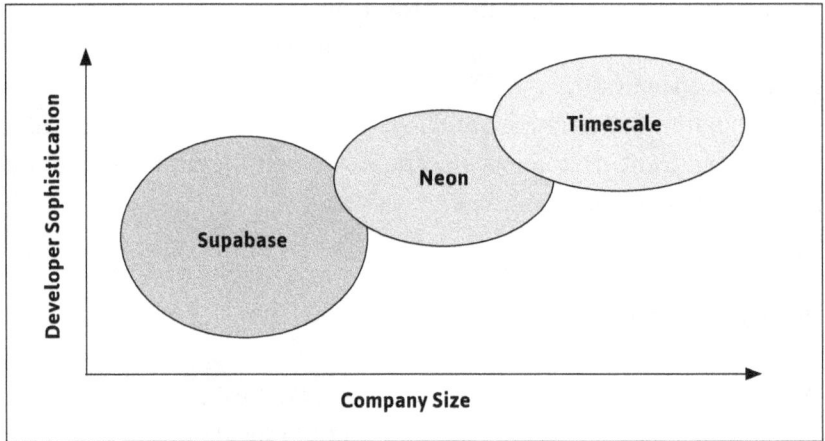

Positioning needs to answer what is unique about your product and the context in which its uniqueness really shines:

- **Supabase:** open-source Firebase alternative built on Postgres
- **Neon:** Serverless Postgres for cost-effective, efficient deployments
- **Timescale:** Postgres made powerful for high-end workloads

Here are some other ideas from companies you may know well:

- **Stripe:** payments infrastructure for the internet
- **Twilio:** the communications layer for every product
- **Docker:** build, share, and run any app, anywhere
- **Vercel:** develop, preview, and ship web applications

Finding uniqueness

You'll typically find yourself in one of two circumstances: you're building a product in a new or immature market, or you're building a product in an established market with incumbent players. For example, Cursor, the AI-assisted integrated-development environment, is disrupting the existing coding-tools market, with incumbent Visual Studio Code the established leader. Meanwhile, Stripe entered the market over a decade ago, attempting to make the process of integrating payments into an app far simpler for developers.

As you search for your position in the market, the first step is to identify this competitive alternative. In an immature market, it will often be a process or bloated series of steps across multiple tools. We forget how hard adding payments was before Stripe. In a mature market, it's often another competitor. Ironically, Stripe development today could probably be even easier, and sometimes the steps to integrate Stripe can take substantial effort. A nimble competitor that focuses on the developer experience could position themselves as an even-easier-to-use Stripe (easier said than done, of course).

When you start by identifying the alternative, you can articulate exactly why your product is better, and that goes a long way toward establishing your position in the market. It's common when describing the differentiation between your product and the alternative to land on one of two points: either you do the process better, faster, or cheaper, or you have capabilities others don't.

- Stripe eliminates hundreds of manual steps just to process a credit-card payment
- Cursor has AI code-assistance tools that Visual Studio does not
- Supabase includes all the components you'd have to build on your own for your app

And the final element of your uniqueness is explaining why this differentiation matters and why your product is the best way to achieve it. For developer products, *developer productivity* is usually the reason why it matters. Sometimes it's *cost*, but that's usually a secondary message for the bean counters who approve a platform or tool choice made by developers. It can also be *scalability and performance*, but that's usually a table-stakes feature without which your product wouldn't even be considered. With most developer products, everything comes around to making developers' lives easier. That's the productivity message.

Positioning in rapidly changing industries

The market or industry in which most tech companies reside is constantly changing. One day you're happily building a CRM alternative to Salesforce, and then the AI revolution subsumes you and changes the entire industry. Your product and company are still the same, but the market's expectation for what a good-enough product is has changed.

Understanding these broader market forces (for example, artificial intelligence) can amplify your positioning if the trend is truly complementary to your product. As we've seen with countless products, just bolting "AI" onto it doesn't come across well.

For example, Supabase added a feature that lets you store vector embeddings inside the database and write SQL queries using plain English language, both great uses of AI. Yet they didn't alter their positioning or topline messaging to incorporate AI. They're still the open-source Postgres alternative to Firebase, except they now have a handful of features related to AI.

Positioning and category creation

Where positioning is about defining the space your product occupies in the minds of customers, category creation is about shaping that space into something entirely new. Categories provide a frame of reference. A product that stores multiple types of data in a high-speed, high-scale environment can be called a "database" (an existing, well-known category) or it could be a "data lake" (a newer, different category altogether).

If you're positioning within a category, you're fighting for differentiation. You're making the case that your product is better in some fashion: speed, cost, security, scalability, etc. You're looking for separation from the incumbents. For example, Dragonfly is a fast database that is Redis-compatible. Or a new payments API could be "like Stripe, but for micropayments from online games."

Creating a new category is a much heavier lift. You are now embroiled in a battle to change how customers think about their problem altogether. Dragonfly could attempt to define a whole new type of database. Your new payments API could be "the foundation for a new type of global commerce." New categories are not for the faint of heart and are very difficult to pull off.

The best category creators educate before they sell. They produce thought leadership, industry reports, and real-world case studies that frame the problem in a way that makes their solution feel inevitable. This is why the best category creators don't start by selling their product, they sell the problem. Datadog didn't just sell a logging and monitoring tool. They sold the idea that cloud-native observability was an entirely new challenge that required an entirely new approach.

The hardest part of category creation is that early on, no one is searching for you. No one wakes up in the morning and thinks that they need a product in a category they don't know exists. Many of the traditional tactics to drive product adoption won't work.

For BigTech, category creation tends to go with the territory. It's rare for BigTech to innovate out of thin air. Most of the time they cobble together germs of ideas from smaller, more nimble companies and build a new product. Microsoft continues to add features to Office, for example, blatantly copying Slack, Zoom, Notion, and others. BigTech can subsequently reposition their product as a new category, which elevates them from the noise and forces others to follow.

For startups, category creation is risky. Unless you have rocketship traction, you're better off entering an existing category, proving differentiation, and perhaps even building features that cross category boundaries to slowly grow into something bigger. For example, Supabase has a Postgres-based database that rivals Amazon Relational Database Service (RDS) as well as an authentication product that rivals Auth0. Separately, Supabase's products successfully challenge the incumbents with differentiation centered around ease of use and cost. But combined, Supabase offers a complete backend as a service, with products across multiple categories.

Positioning is a team sport

As the ringleader of the circus, it's time to convene the cast:

- the business leader (CEO in a startup, VP or SVP in a larger company)
- product and engineering leaders
- sales leader
- marketing leader

> **TIP:** If you're in a startup and the CEO isn't taking the most active leadership role in positioning, you need to find another job. The CEO of a startup absolutely cannot abdicate responsibility for charting the company's positioning. Positioning is core to the mission of the company, and it is essential that the CEO is passionate about driving not only the results, but also broad communication of positioning across the company, to investors, and to key customers and stakeholders.

You need to include everyone in this list, because positioning affects almost everyone in the company. In fact, each person on this list provides a different lens on what the product is, who the target market is, and what is unique about the product. Bad positioning will result in a stalled business. But good positioning requires buy-in to execute.

If you're not using a third-party facilitator, product marketing can serve in that role. The goal is to seek out different points of view and agree to start fresh. Don't use past assumptions to guide the future.

The positioning framework

Summing up all your research into segmentation, ideal customer pro-files, unique value propositions, and place/context, you can begin to organize your positioning and start debating and answering questions:

- Who are your ideal customers? Who cares the most about your product?
- Who are the competitive alternatives? What makes them different from you?
- What is unique about what you offer?

The entire process concludes by answering the most import-ant question: **What is valuable about your uniqueness?** What is it about your product that stands above the competition, and why is that valuable?

This final statement becomes the fodder for messaging and all other customer-facing communication.

Positioning and the "rule" of three

Spend any time with marketing people and you'll quickly see how much they adapt to "three bullet" thinking. Broad statements are usually fol-lowed by three bullet points that support the statement. It's not a hard-and-fast rule, but there is some science and a lot of history behind it.

Somewhere around the middle of the 300s BCE, the Greek phi-losopher Aristotle devised a rhetorical framework that shapes (among many things) marketing messaging to this day. He posited that the best, most effective persuasive messaging contained three elements:

1. ethos, an appeal to credibility and authority
2. pathos, an emotional connection
3. logos, logic and reasoning

A little more recently, in 1956, a cognitive psychologist named George Miller authored a seminal paper, "The Magical Number Seven,

Plus or Minus Two: Some Limits on Our Capacity for Processing Information." Whether we consciously know it or not, all marketing people have internalized his work and use it daily. In the paper, he made a few observations:

- People can hold at most seven (give or take two) chunks of information in their short-term memory.
- Information is best when it is chunked into smaller pieces (this is why telephone numbers often have "breaks" in them and credit card numbers are grouped into four chunks of three to four numbers).
- The more items you add, the more cognitive load increases.

Over time, marketers have adopted this work and it has become the de facto model. We think in small, digestible chunks of information so as not to overwhelm our prospects' cognitive load. We try to provide logical breaking points in our messaging. In so doing, we have effectively standardized on a positioning framework that looks something like this:

- Positioning statement
  - Supporting point 1
  - Supporting point 2
  - Supporting point 3

You see this everywhere you go in marketing collateral. But with developer marketing, we take Miller's work and suffuse it with Aristotle's rhetorical framework, and our positioning frameworks often look like this:

- Positioning statement
  - An emotional point about why you will love this product
  - A logical point about what unique capabilities this product has for you
  - A credible point that explains why you can depend on this product

This is the positioning framework I created as the first director of marketing for Amazon Web Services:

- Amazon Web Services gives you a cost-effective and dependable cloud computing platform that makes it easy to provision infrastructure so you can build anything quickly.
  - Flexible: easy to use and get started
  - Cost-effective: no contracts, pay as you go, transparent pricing
  - Dependable: scalability and reliability from the company who knows how to run infrastructure at web scale

In my experience, most developer-focused products evolve their positioning into some form of the following:

- Positioning that identifies the uniqueness of a product in a market
  - A supporting point about productivity improvements or ease of use (appeal to emotion)
  - A supporting point that dives into what's unique about the product and what that enables (appeal to logic)
  - A supporting point about dependability or scalability, or both (appeal to credibility)

When I went through my Greek philosopher phase in my early thirties, I was shocked and humbled to learn that Aristotle was a far better product marketing manager than I was.

MESSAGING

Messaging is not the same as positioning. Indeed, messaging translates positioning into the words, visuals, and examples that make that positioning compelling. Messaging takes the strategic foundation of positioning and builds the story around it.

- **Supabase:** Build in a weekend. Scale to millions. Supabase is an open-source Firebase alternative. Start your project with a Postgres database, Authentication, instant APIs, Edge Functions, Realtime subscriptions, Storage, and Vector embeddings.
- **Neon:** Ship faster with Postgres. The database you love, on a serverless platform designed to help you build reliable and scalable applications faster.
- **Timescale:** Over 3 million Timescale databases power IoT, sensors, AI, dev tools, crypto, and finance apps—all on Postgres. We use Postgres for everything; now you can too.
- **Stripe:** Financial infrastructure to grow your revenue. Join the millions of companies of all sizes that use Stripe to accept payments online and in person, embed financial services, power custom revenue models, and build a more profitable business.
- **Twilio:** Drive better ROI from every customer conversation. Twilio's all-in-one platform combines powerful channel APIs with AI and data, so you can serve every customer uniquely.
- **Docker:** Develop faster. Run anywhere. Build with the #1 most-used developer tool.
- **Vercel:** Your complete platform for the web. Vercel provides the developer tools and cloud infrastructure to build, scale, and secure a faster, more personalized web.

This distinction between positioning and messaging is critical because technical audiences, especially developers, can see through superficial messaging or poorly defined value propositions. Developers need context about where a product fits into their stack, why it solves a specific problem, and how it compares to alternatives. Good positioning lays this groundwork, allowing messaging to focus on resonating with the audience's needs and interests without explaining the product's place in the market each time.

Messaging is contextual

The concept of "universal messaging" is a fallacy. One message will not resonate with all audiences. Your positioning should be consistent, of course. It defines your place in the market. But how you speak about who you are should reflect the audience to whom you are speaking.

If you are speaking with a group of startup founders about adopting your product, it's important to talk about the things that are important to them. They care about time to market. They care about easy deployment and operation. They care about cost-effectiveness.

If you are speaking with an enterprise audience, they will care about scalability and trustworthiness. You'll want to play up your SOC 2 and HIPAA compliance assessments. You'll want to emphasize things like interoperability and how easy it is to use your product alongside product investments they've already made. You may need to talk about migration from existing tools.

As you land on segmentation and positioning, you'll be able to create and frame messaging appropriate to your audience or audiences.

Crafting messaging for technical audiences

Developers are no-nonsense people. They want to know what a product does, and little else. The more you attempt to decorate your messaging with hyperbole, the more developers will tune out.

As an example, when I first joined Amazon Web Services, now-Amazon CEO Andy Jassy would routinely criticize my website copy. "Too much puffery," he would say. And he was right. Developers want the facts and just the facts.

For technical messaging to resonate, it must address specific pain points experienced by people represented by your segmentation. Database engineers want to know about performance and scalability. Full-stack developers want to know about the seamless workflow between front-end and back-end development. Tell developers exactly what your product does and why it's worth their time to try out. Avoid abstract promises.

But of course, as a marketer, you still want to make a claim about your product relative to others on the market. That claim is what differentiates you, after all. That's great. Just avoid hyperbole.

One way to ground your messaging in reality but still make bold claims is to reference customer case studies, benchmarks, or quotes from customers speaking well about your product on Reddit, Twitter, or the like. Use social and technical proof to handle your hyperbole, while you stick to the facts.

Tips for effective messaging

Messaging doesn't have to be hard. In fact, it can be quite fun and a great creative exercise. But there are some guidelines you should follow:

- **Keep it simple.** Very simple. "Postgres for everything," not "The database for metrics, traces, and logs."
- **Use direct, plainspoken language.** As always with developers, avoid florid marketing puffery.
- **Repeat it endlessly.** Good marketing is all about repetition. Identify one simple message, and repeat it across all channels.
- **Be clear about the problem.** This is the hardest thing for marketers to learn. It is essential to demonstrate an understanding of the problem. We all want to jump ahead to our solution. But first, as President Bill Clinton once said, "Feel their pain."

Another messaging tactic that is often underutilized is adhering to **consistent terminology**. If your product has a benefit, or you're trying to articulate a problem, stick to the same words everywhere: in documentation, in slide decks, in speeches, in videos . . . everywhere.

Differentiation vs. value

Ultimately, as with positioning, there are two kinds of messaging. The first kind draws a clear distinction between you and your competitors. **When you have a popular and well-understood market, you focus on differentiation.** After all, if everyone already knows that they want—say, a "vector database"—then you need to explain why yours is better.

In contrast, **slow and undeveloped markets often call for explaining what value you provide.** If you have a "real-time analytics" tool (which no one really wants or needs), then you must do the heavy lifting of explaining why people need a product from this category to begin with.

Yes, as a marketing organization you need to develop an understanding of both how you differentiate from the competition and the overall value you provide to potential buyers. But it's your market that determines which form of messaging you should focus on.

Differentiating your product in the developer space

Differentiation isn't just about comparative feature lists with beautiful checkmarks. It's about staking out and articulating what makes your product uniquely suited to solve a problem.

To find differentiation, you need to dive into user research and identify your own and your competitors' strengths and weaknesses. How can you turn a competitor's weakness into a claim of strength? And how can you turn one of their strengths into a weakness?

When I was at Timescale, one of our staunchest competitors was another database called ClickHouse. We ran benchmarks and identified that ClickHouse would beat us at some use cases, while we would handily beat them at others. In effect, it was a draw. But we chose to position using our strength (a PostgreSQL-based database for time series and metrics). ClickHouse was a specialized database for certain use cases, while Timescale built atop the world's most popular database to deliver more value across all use cases: use what you already know and love, and now you can do more.

This positioning enabled us to shore up defenses against a potential competitor; lean into a huge strength (our support of the large PostgreSQL community); and hone our overall strategy ("Postgres for everything").

Competitive differentiation is the whetstone of positioning. It sharpens and focuses positioning in a way that makes it unassailable.

How to win on value

When you articulate the value you provide to a potential customer, you need to be very explicit about two things. First, the quantifiable benefits you provide a customer. And second, a clear definition of who within an organization is affected by the problem your product solves. In contrast with differentiation messaging, where your audience is already self-qualified and interested in your category, with value messaging you are carrying the hopes and dreams of the entire category with your marketing efforts.

The worst job I ever had was in a rudderless startup that changed its goals and strategy nearly every quarter. This startup didn't just build a product that very few people wanted; it lived in a category that almost nobody knew or cared about. People in this company kept obsessing over differentiation on the website, in trade-show booths, and in sales enablement. But the market situation called for focusing on why the category mattered to begin with.

In contrast, if you look at the early days of Segment, they spent a significant amount of time defining the customer data platform (CDP) category and training people how to take advantage of it. At the time, CDP wasn't nearly as crowded a category as it is today. Segment defined, and won, the category over smaller players like mParticle.

One thing to be careful of, especially if you're an early-stage startup, is confusing the existence of ostensible competitors with the existence of a developed market. Sometimes, even if there are several "competitors" in your space, there's benefit to standardizing how you talk about the category so that when a prospect considers one vendor, they end up considering them all.

Testing your messaging

Because developers are discerning and value authenticity, it is essential that you employ numerous strategies to test your messaging from multiple angles. Here are just a few of the processes I use to test my messaging:

- **Work with sales:** Salespeople talk to customers every day, and if an experienced salesperson is having trouble landing your messaging, you should know about it. Talk with your salespeople and learn how your current messaging helps and hinders them, brainstorm ways to iterate and improve on your messaging, and collaborate on testing messaging early and often.
- **A/B testing:** Try multiple variations of messaging on your homepage and see if there's any lift. I like to use "themes" for these messaging options, such as "Apple-style pithy and fun," "Overly descriptive and practical," and "Microsoft-style impenetrable enterprise nonsense."
- **Landing-page tests:** Run different creative options on your landing pages for ads and see which ones generate relative lift.
- **Survey developers:** Use targeted surveys, in-product or otherwise, to test different messaging options with different personas of developers.
- **Interview developers:** During your periodic customer-discovery calls, you or your product team should ask developers to react to messaging options you are currently thinking about.
- **Community forums:** Ask your community in your forums, Slack, or Discord and see how they react to some of your ideas.
- **Social media:** Try different styles of messaging on social media and see which ones get the most traction and engagement.

- **Content performance:** Use your content subject matter to determine where your product is currently gaining mindshare and attention.
- **Product-usage analysis:** Your most-used features are good clues to what is resonating with developers. If you're able to identify customer intent (what they're trying to do with your features), you'll be in an even better position to evaluate what works.

And last but certainly not least, don't forget to interview your own internal developers! They will have strong opinions on the authenticity of your messaging and will be able to give you substantial feedback.

USING POSITIONING AND YOUR ICP TO WORK WITH PRODUCT

I ask all product marketing managers to be actively involved with product and engineering on the design and definition of the product itself. Given all the segmentation and positioning research already completed, product marketing has a unique lens on the customer and market that must be reflected in what is ultimately shipped.

Product marketing distills this research into the market requirements document (MRD).

> **TIP:** Note the word *market* (not marketing) is intentional. This is not marketing's requirements of engineering. It's a distillation of the market's requirements to solve problems it is facing.

Through segmentation and positioning research, product marketing has already put together background information about the market and various types of customers within it. Now we get to the fun stuff: how to solve their problems.

My MRD usually begins with a recap of the ICP and links to my segmentation and ICP research.

From there, I ask and provide a hypothesis for these important questions:

- What kind of products, features, or services will you need to build to activate customers in your ICP?
- What products, features, or services are table stakes among competitors in this space?
- Does the presence or absence of these features affect the ICP? For example, a competitor may have invested in building a feature that is unnecessary for your chosen ICP.

Ultimately, while positioning and messaging is immensely important for marketing and sales, it can be abstract for the product team. Going one level deeper and providing an analysis of the product and feature requirements for the ICP will help them understand what marketing needs to win.

Marketing cannot complain that product and engineering aren't delivering "the right features" if marketing does not provide hypotheses and data that inform product and engineering what is necessary to win in the market.

SUMMARY

"Market segmentation is the key!" read an old *Dilbert* cartoon making fun of marketers. As silly as it may sound, it's still true today.

- **Segmentation helps you target the right audience.** Define your key developer personas based on their needs, workflows, and purchasing power.
- **Positioning determines where you fit in the market.** Articulate why your product exists, who it's for, and what makes it different from alternatives.
- **Strong messaging is clear, concise, and specific.** Developers respond to factual, benefit-driven language. Cut the fluff and get to the point.
- **Differentiate with real technical advantages.** Don't just claim you're "faster" or "better." Prove it with benchmarks, case studies, and real-world use cases.
- **Your pricing should reflect your positioning.** If you sell to enterprises, align pricing and packaging accordingly. If you're PLG, make self-service easy.
- **Test messaging continuously.** Use A/B tests, interviews, and real-world interactions to refine what resonates with developers and decision makers.
- **Avoid buzzwords and vague claims.** Be direct, use specific comparisons, and let your product's capabilities speak for themselves.
- **Messaging should be consistent across all channels.** Docs, landing pages, ads, and sales decks should all reinforce the same core positioning.

CHAPTER 14

Pricing for Developer Products

Pricing should always reflect your segmentation and positioning. If you price too high for your segment, you risk choking off adoption altogether. If you price too low, you damage your brand by making it seem more like a toy.

PRICING STRATEGIES FOR DEVELOPER PRODUCTS

Most developer products are priced on either a per-seat basis (for example, tools like Atlassian and GitHub) or by consumption (for example, MongoDB and cloud computing services).

Consumption-based pricing is tricky. Inventing a unit of measurement (e.g., "processed data") will always create confusion. Customers won't know what it is or how to estimate it, and they will be understandably concerned about unexpected overages or spikes.

When adopting a consumption-based pricing model, consider providing calculators so that customers can estimate their costs. Closely monitor your customer usage, and if you detect a spike in costs, proactively reach out to help customers understand why their costs are spiking and how they can optimize or mitigate the expense. Be aggressive in providing discounts early for first-time offenders, and use your customer success team to turn a potentially negative situation into a positive one.

PSYCHOLOGY OF PRICING

As we've covered many times in this book, developers are data driven, analytical, and skeptical of traditional marketing tactics. However, they are not immune to the psychological principles that govern human decision making. Pricing psychology leverages cognitive biases and behavioral patterns to influence perceptions of value and cost. By mastering these principles, you can position your pricing as not only fair but compelling, encouraging developers to engage and convert.

The key to success lies in balancing transparency with subtle persuasion. Developers demand clear, honest pricing models, but effective pricing goes beyond clarity. It requires an understanding of how your audience perceives value and risk, and how to nudge them toward making a decision.

Anchoring the price

The first price a customer sees sets a reference point that influences their perception of almost everything about your product. For example, if your pricing page displays a premium plan at $399/month first, the basic plan at $99/month will seem like a bargain in comparison.

Part of this is your SKU design. Thinking about cohorts of customers and the features they absolutely need and the features they might stretch their budgets to obtain will help you isolate feature sets into tiers that satisfy a customer's basic needs while also encouraging them to consider whether they can afford the next tier higher.

Using decoys

Related to anchoring is the decoy—the less-attractive third option that forces the customer to consider the plan you want them to gravitate toward in a whole new light.

For example, if we had a $399/month tier that we wanted most users to select, and a $99/month tier that was good, but lacked features that professionals really wanted, we could offer a $329/month tier that also lacked a handful of very desirable features for our target customer, which would entice them to consider moving up to the $399/month offering. The pricing page would look something like this:

Starter Tier $99/month	Professional Tier $329/month	Enterprise Tier $399/month
Some features	All the features in Starter + More features	All the features in Professional + More features

This is a tactic I employed frequently at Microsoft, where I offered an Express product at $49, a Professional product at $999, and a Standard product at $199. The Express and Standard products were virtually indistinguishable, but most features of interest were in Professional. That's where most customers gravitated.

Halo pricing and Cadillac tiers

Throughout my tenure at Microsoft on the Visual Studio team, our Professional product performed very well for a long time. That is, until we offered an Enterprise product at $2,999 (which we later increased to $9,999). A certain cadre of professional developers and organizations weren't as concerned about the budget for developer products; they just wanted the best available.

In this case they were also able to negotiate the Enterprise product along with a companywide enterprise agreement. So we blended the per-seat pricing with enterprise custom-pricing models.

TIP: There is always a consumer that wants the best. The best iPhone Pro Max Ultra. The best Audi. The best toppings at Baskin-Robbins.

For this customer, the "halo" product (what I call the Cadillac tier) represents the full-featured, no-empty-button slots, every bell-and-whistle experience, and they are willing to pay for it.

The tyranny of "or"

At some point, you can offer too many choices. This leads to decision paralysis and customers who bounce.

Recall that one of Steve Jobs's first acts upon his return to Apple was to significantly streamline the SKU lineup. One could argue that one of Apple's biggest problems today is proliferation of SKUs in an attempt to capture value at each level of price sensitivity. Do you know which iPad to buy? An iPad Air, an iPad, or an iPad Pro? Maybe you just won't buy an iPad at all.

Be careful not to fatigue your customers through your pricing. Keep it simple and obvious.

Loss aversion

People fear losses more than they desire gains. You can use this principle to your advantage by emphasizing what developers risk losing if they don't adopt your product.

- **Time-limited offers:** Make your pricing page dynamic and offer pricing that will disappear if not taken advantage of quickly.
- **FOMO (fear of missing out):** A dynamic pricing page can also be built to detect the industry from which the site visitor is coming, and then show them case studies from their

competitors or others in their industry. Create a sense of urgency that if the site visitor doesn't also adopt your product, their competitors will leapfrog them.

In general, I love dynamic pricing pages, which is why I've always insisted that my marketing teams have on-staff developers and the ability to control the entire website and sign-up experience. It's a lot easier to run marketing programs knowing you have the flexibility to build dynamic features for pricing (or any other area on the website).

DIFFERENT PRICING MODELS FOR SAAS TODAY

There are a handful of tried-and-true pricing models, as well as some variants beginning to take hold among SaaS products. Let's take a look at some of these now. In most cases, you will want to mix and match pricing models.

Per-seat pricing

Basically, you charge for the number of active users, or seats, within an organization.

The pros of this model:
- Your revenue is predictable.
- Account sizing and opportunity are also predictable.
- It's very easy for teams and organizations to understand.

The cons of this model:
- You may lose money if your product or service is built on usage-based services (e.g., compute or storage) and a given customer makes heavy use of your product.

The other con is that you are limiting your adoption within organizations. If you sign an organization to five seats, you are restricting your ability to grow within the organization and show value. The more value you show, and the more indispensable you become to the workflows of many teams in an organization, the more anti-fragile you become. If your technical champion leaves, then you're stuck trying to prove your worth and re-up your subscription. On the other hand, if your product is growing organically within an organization, even if your technical champion leaves, your product is being used more widely.

Examples include GitHub Enterprise and JetBrains.

Pay-as-you-go (PAYG) and usage-based pricing

In this model, you are charging customers based on their actual usage, such as API calls, data storage, or compute time.

The pros of this model:
- It's transparent and scalable for users as they grow.
- It aligns with developer expectations for flexibility.
- It's easy to offer a free forever trial or freemium tier (which we will discuss in a moment).

The cons of this model:
- It can be really hard to predict revenue.
- It may discourage heavy use if the pricing tiers feel punitive.

There are numerous examples, including Amazon Web Services, Stripe, and Twilio.

Tier-based pricing

You offer multiple pricing tiers with increasing levels of features, support, or usage caps. This model can be applied to any of the pricing models. For example, you may want to unlock certain types of features for customers who buy more than a designated number of seats.

The pros of this model:
- ○ It appeals to a wide array of segments, from hobbyists to enterprises.
- ○ Encourages upgrades as users grow.

The cons of this model:
- ○ If the tiers are too complex, it can lead to decision fatigue.

Examples include Vercel and Netlify.

Credit-based pricing

The customer elects to buy a certain number of usage (credits) in tranches that they can draw upon as they use your product. These credits can be applied to different features or services within the product.

The pros of this model:
- ○ It can offer customers with varying needs a lot of flexibility.
- ○ It encourages experimentation with different features or services in the product.
- ○ It gives you instant, measurable, specific feedback on what customers are willing to pay for.
- ○ It's easier to provide complimentary or promotional credits.

The cons are pretty straightforward:
- ○ It's harder to lock customers into longer-term deals.
- ○ It encourages churn as credits expire and there's little incentive to continue.
- ○ It's hard to create long-term value for the product.
- ○ It's potentially confusing for customers if different features cost more credits than others (e.g., an AI product that charges more for image generation than it does for text generation).

Credit-based pricing is great when you're just starting out. It's fairly simple to instrument your code, and it's even cooler to be able to see which features your customers will spend money to use. You get some fantastic, quantifiable customer feedback. But it's hard to scale it into a business.

Custom enterprise pricing

This is the age-old "talk to us if you're big and we'll get you on an annual deal."

In this model, you negotiate a certain amount of usage with customers in exchange for an annual commit. You gain predictability and the customer gains better pricing as a result. It's always in your best interest to negotiate the right level of commitment, as customers who overcommit tend to churn at renewal time.

There are some variants here that you can consider:

- **Value-based pricing,** where your negotiated price is predicated on the value your product delivers to the customers. This value is often tied to ROI metrics, such as revenue generated or costs saved. While this can be challenging to define during the scope of negotiations, if you believe in your product and it actually delivers on its promise, it can be lucrative.
- **Consumption tier pricing,** which offers discounts to customers when they reach certain thresholds of usage. It encourages customer retention by giving them a discount before they receive a shocking usage-based bill, and it provides cost incentives for heavy users.

Nearly everyone offers this sort of model, including Databricks, Snowflake, and MongoDB Atlas.

Open-source plus cloud

One of the most popular pricing models among developer products today is to offer your own cloud-hosted version of an open-source product.

The pros of this model:
- ○ It builds trust and community among developers.
- ○ It lowers the barrier to entry for adoption and trial.
- ○ It may obviate the need for a free-forever tier.

The cons of this model:
- ○ It can be difficult to identify open-source customers and drive upsells (we will discuss strategies to do so later).

There are many examples of this model, including Supabase and Timescale.

Open-source plus support

With this model you offer an open-source product but you sell services and support for customers who want to customize and incorporate it into their business.

The pros and cons are similar to the open-source-plus-cloud model.

The best examples of this model include Red Hat and HashiCorp.

Simple flat-rate pricing

With this model you offer a single price point with no usage caps or limits.

Pros of this model:
- ○ It offers simplicity for both customers and billing.
- ○ It generates a predictable revenue stream.

Cons of this model:
- ○ It doesn't scale well with larger teams or organizations.
- ○ It limits revenue potential.

Examples of this model include Basecamp and Fathom Analytics.

AI PRODUCTS AND OUTCOME-BASED PRICING

As products begin to incorporate artificial intelligence, we will see some shifts in how they are priced. AI services and APIs are expensive to operate and therefore relatively expensive to use. In an effort to contain costs, many companies offering AI products charge for the results you get when using the product or service. For example, an image-generation API may charge based on the size and complexity of the image being produced.

Product marketers need to be aware of these changes and adjust accordingly:

- **User-based pricing:** Some end-user products (such as Google Workspace and Notion) include AI capabilities as an add-on to the core user-based pricing of these products.
- **Cost-based pricing:** Passing on the cost of tokens, queries, and so forth to the customer typically works for infrastructure products (such as OpenAI's API, Amazon Web Services, and so on) where fine-grained units of compute and storage are already de rigueur.
- **Outcome-based pricing:** New as a result of AI, some products will be priced based on the value provided or the answer computed. This new class of products (such as Zest AI for credit-risk determination and C3.ai for fraud detection) are already priced according to the impact they have on a user problem, so including AI-induced solutions as part of the pricing model makes sense.
- **Pricing based on LLM being used:** Large language models vary in complexity and size, so the price to use them differs accordingly. Products like Cursor let you have unlimited uses with lower-end LLMs, but they cap usage for higher-end LLMs.

FREE TIER VS. FREE TRIAL

PLG companies typically offer some form of a free trial (limited time usage of the product) and free tier (limited usage of the product with no time limit). The decision of which option to select should not be taken lightly. You need to have a good understanding of your customer's usage patterns and your costs before proceeding.

In recent years, many companies have rescinded their free tier to chase profitability and reduce costs. Over the last few decades, developers have grown accustomed to getting many things for free. Hence, these decisions to remove the free tier seem like "takebacks" and cause friction between a company and the developer community.

Therefore, it is important to think intentionally about the free tier. Typically, users are hobbyist developers at home (many of whom are professional developers by day) and have very small departmental workloads in a commercial environment. If a free tier is done properly, it's impossible to game it into running a full production website. The hypothesis is that some percentage of your freemium users could be persuaded to upgrade to a paid plan.

As you ponder offering a free tier, ask yourself the following questions:

- **How much does it cost to run a free tier for each customer?** This answer will be different for everyone. Supabase can offer a free tier because they use low-cost storage and run compute only when it's needed. (If your database is idle, they will wind down compute and spin it back up when your database is needed again.) Conversely, some products have value propositions that require them to make sure that your resources are always on and running at full capacity. For these companies, a free tier can be very expensive, and a free, limited-time trial makes the most sense.
- **Is there a high likelihood that free-tier customers will convert to paid users?** Supabase and Neon are products that serve the broad base of developers. It is likely that at least some hobbyist developers may want to turn their

product into a small lifestyle business or, best case, a full company. So, given they are keeping their costs low already, it may pencil out.

• **Is my product complex or in a new space, so customers could benefit from learning more background information before deciding whether to pay?** Many of the newer AI products will require some amount of training for customers to understand their true value. Providing a free tier enables them to experiment and identify the value you provide over time. In *Crossing the Chasm* parlance, you're building a slightly long-term pipeline into "Early Adopters" while you actively focus on and nurture the "Innovators."

The free tier vs. freemium decision can engender philosophical debates within companies. I've seen engineers (and even founders) irrationally hold onto "free forever" tiers simply because they believe that is what developers want and expect. But a rational analysis of both the market and the costs may provide a different answer.

Finally, if you have an open-source version of your product, you may not need a free tier at all. Customers who want to use it for free can always clone the repo and host it themselves. The downside to relying on your open-source product is that it's harder to accumulate users' contact information (as we will discuss in a subsequent chapter).

Remember, "taking back" a free tier will be a reputational hit in an industry where reputational hits are difficult to recover from. You should experiment with a free tier early in your company's lifecycle, and pay particular attention to how many free-tier customers you can convert into paid users. If the customer lifetime value (LTV) of these conversions is greater than the total cost of running a free tier, then you have a viable acquisition funnel on your hands and you should continue to invest in it. If not, you should kill it and move on. It's always easier to reconsider later and add a free tier back to your pricing suite. But make the analysis and decision early—and decisively.

BUILDING AN EFFECTIVE PRICING PAGE

In all likelihood, you will blend multiple pricing models to come up with something that works best for you, your scenarios, and your customers. For example, the AI code editor Cursor fuses these models:

- per-seat pricing
- credits-based pricing, where your seat includes a certain number of credits
- PAYG for overages beyond the initial credits threshold
- outcome-based pricing for certain features

These kinds of complex pricing models aren't bad at all. In fact, they can offer the right mix of value for all parties. However, the key is to communicate the pricing model well.

Here are some tips for building an effective pricing page:

- **Clarity is key:** Avoid jargon or ambiguous metrics in your pricing descriptions, and use visuals like tables or charts to clarify complex models like hybrid pricing.
- **Highlight features:** Create a simple table comparing tiers and emphasizing the most valuable features in each. Use labels like "Most Popular" to guide customers toward preferred tiers.
- **Be transparent about overages:** Clearly explain what happens if customers exceed their limits, and include specific dollar amounts to reduce anxiety over hidden costs.
- **Provide a pricing calculator:** Allow users to estimate their costs dynamically based on usage scenarios with tools like sliders or input fields.
- **Showcase social proof:** Include testimonials, logos, or case studies from high-profile customers to demonstrate the ROI achieved at different pricing tiers.
- **Make custom plans easy to request:** For larger organizations, include a clear CTA for contacting sales with details on what to expect.

- **Feature trials or free tiers prominently:** Highlight options like "Start for Free" or "Explore with No Commitment" to encourage sign-ups.
- **Simplify complex pricing models:** Use step-by-step visuals or real-world scenarios to illustrate hybrid pricing models effectively.
- **Focus on value-driven metrics:** Highlight benefits aligned with customer goals, such as cost savings or scalability improvements.
- **Optimize for mobile:** Ensure the pricing page is responsive and easy to navigate on mobile devices, as many developers browse on the go.

CROSS-FUNCTIONAL COLLABORATION ON PRICING

Pricing involves multiple teams, but it requires a singular leader. In a startup, that's the CEO. In a larger organization, it's the senior-most executive.

While a senior leader may be the ultimate decision maker, there are so many moving parts that ultimately marketing (specifically product marketing) needs to drive pricing changes. Why? Because pricing is not just a finance decision. It's a positioning, competitive, and customer-experience decision. Your cross-functional team will include product managers, engineers, sales, customer success, and of course the leadership team.

1. First define the pricing model or options.
2. Then build the pricing model that describes what will happen in different pricing scenarios.
3. From there, start gathering customer research and feedback into your pricing scenarios.

Don't let pricing happen in a vacuum. Interview customers and prospects, conduct live interviews, run surveys, and make sure that your customer's voice is part of any decision that is being made. In fact, your best insights may come from your sales and customer-success teams. They frequently bear the brunt of pricing objections anyway.

PRICING EXPERIMENTATION

Your pricing model should never be static. Regularly test different approaches and gather feedback to refine it. Meet with your customers and especially your closed-lost opportunities. Try to understand what their concerns are, and how similar and competitive products are priced.

Don't forget to A/B-test pricing pages. Experiment with different layouts, tiers, and messaging.

MAKING PRICING CHANGES

Invariably, you will want to make pricing changes. This could be as simple as raising or lowering prices, or it could be as complex as introducing new measurements or dimensions to your overall pricing model.

As the saying goes, "People vote with their wallets." You need to get ahead of any pricing changes by communicating directly and clearly with customers. Build communication plans for each cohort of customer you currently have:

- large-enterprise deals
- midtier pay-as-you-go customers
- free-tier or freemium customers

Each category of customers will have different concerns that you must proactively address. For example, an enterprise customer may see a pricing change and, after doing some calculations, determine that their current annual commit is way overpriced compared to the new pricing model. Here's your opportunity to extol the virtues of your customer-success team and how they help with onboarding, architectural guidance, troubleshooting, and so on. For a large company, that could more than make up for the pricing differential. But unless you communicate that with them directly before communicating broadly with the world, you will end up shooting yourself in the foot.

It has always served me well to treat communications about pricing changes in the same serious, cross-functional manner as I treat crisis communications. Assemble your cross-functional team and lead the communication effort.

SUMMARY

Pricing isn't just about setting a number. It's a reflection of your positioning, target market, and business strategy. Developer-focused products often use a mix of per-seat, usage-based, and tiered pricing models. The key is to balance transparency, flexibility, and revenue growth while minimizing friction for adoption. Pricing should evolve based on real-world data, customer behavior, and competitive dynamics.

- **Pricing should align with segmentation and positioning.** Price too high and you kill adoption; price too low and you undervalue your product.
- **Developers prefer transparent, predictable pricing.** Avoid complex, ambiguous units. Clearly define how customers will be billed.
- **Per-seat pricing is easy to understand but limits growth.** Requiring approval for more seats can slow expansion within an organization.
- **Usage-based pricing aligns cost with value but creates unpredictability.** Customers worry about surprise bills, so offer cost estimators and safeguards.
- **Freemium and free trials are useful but require careful design.** Understand the cost and conversion rate before committing to a free offering.
- **Hybrid pricing models often work best.** Many successful developer tools combine seats, usage, and premium features to optimize value for different user types.

- **Psychology plays a role in pricing.** Anchoring, decoy pricing, and tier structures can nudge customers toward higher-value plans.
- **Pricing is never "done."** Continuously test and refine based on user behavior, sales insights, and market shifts.

CHAPTER 15

Developer Product Launches

Launches are the lifeblood of a marketing team. I've been on teams that launch at truly insane velocities and frequencies. And I've been on teams that didn't launch a new feature for nine months.

Years ago, when I was just a very junior individual contributor, I was at a launch party for a product I'd worked on and was surprised to see our CEO in attendance. He took the microphone to congratulate the team and concluded with four simple words that have guided me to this day: **Those who ship, win.**

Indeed, if I can give every marketer one piece of advice, I'd say, "Run as fast as you can from any product team that can't ship. Find teams that can launch, and hang on for the rocket-ship ride."

Many things go into a successful launch, including naming, logistical preparation, packaging of the launch, and proper storytelling.

PRODUCT NAMING

Product naming can be one of the most infuriating and creative exercises a company can go through. As a developer product marketing manager, you are the ringleader of the circus, but you are not the main attraction. Your coterie will include product, engineering, your fellow marketing managers, and of course your key decision makers, such as your founders or VP.

I've been through many naming exercises in my twenty-five-year career, ranging from mundane features to products as big as Visual Studio Team and the whole litany of Amazon Web Services you probably use every day.

I have employed the following process throughout in order to solicit feedback, give everyone in the organization an opportunity to provide input, and finally make a decision and stick with it.

The process involves three rounds.

Your naming team

Before you begin, you must assemble your naming team. These are the people with the most skin in the game. The goal is to make sure all objections are heard during—not after—the naming process. Give everyone a voice, and genuinely listen to their thoughts and concerns.

In my experience, the key drivers of the process have included the following:

- Product + Engineering Stakeholder: the one person in charge of the project in its entirety
- Product/Engineering team members
- Product Marketing Manager (you)
- Founders or senior management (the ultimate decision makers)

The project + engineering stakeholder will identify approximately ten people to participate in the discussion as the "naming team." **This list of people should reflect ethnic, gender, and geographic diversity.** The ten people do not all have to be contributors to the project, though there should be substantial representation from contributors to the project on the naming team.

A true story about diversity and inclusion

Years ago at Microsoft, I had gone through a naming, branding, and packaging exercise for a product. Part of this exercise included a poster to be inserted into every product (this was back in the day when people bought packaged products in a store). We commissioned a Marvel Comics artist to produce the artwork for four posters, one of which was a comic book hero representation of "pair programming" (they looked like the Wonder Twins from the old *Super Friends* cartoon).

Thankfully, I sent this artwork out to our worldwide sales leaders before we went into production. A few sales leaders in one geographic region objected to the artwork because it perpetuated gender and cultural stereotypes in their countries. At the time, almost fifteen years ago, they were the only ones who objected. We went back to the drawing board (literally) and reworked the finished product so it passed muster with our worldwide team. Fifteen years later, I think about the artwork in question and am eternally grateful. In those intervening years, our worldwide culture has evolved to a point where, yes, the original version would be considered obviously offensive to everyone.

Today we have company and product logos, designed by male-dominated teams, that look like reproductive organs, birth-control devices, and offensive symbology. For the love of all things holy in marketing, I implore you to not be one of these companies.

Representation matters. Diversity and inclusion matter. Seek diverse perspectives across your team, especially on all your naming and branding projects.

Round 1: The Free-for-All

Preparation:

- Product Marketing will write a short one-paragraph description of what we're naming.
- Product Marketing will frame the requirements for the name (e.g., "It must look good on a drop-down menu in the homepage," "It must be on the same level as our primary brand," "It can't be over-cute and draw attention to itself," etc.).
- Product Marketing will meet ahead of time with the other key drivers (Product + Engineering Stakeholder and Founders) and identify a list of potential names.
- Product Marketing will prepare a survey with all the sample names and several blank options for people to include their own.

Process:

1. Convene as a team for 90 minutes.
2. Product Marketing provides a link to the survey.
3. Everyone votes and adds their own suggestions.
4. Product Marketing closes voting and takes the time to collate results.
5. Product Marketing provides a link to a Google Doc with all names listed in order of number of votes received.
6. Product Marketing leads a discussion of each name in the allotted time remaining.
7. With 15 minutes left in the meeting, Product Marketing will cut off discussion and make sure everyone has an opportunity to declare their overwhelming affinity to any names not yet discussed.
8. Product Marketing will prepare a survey of all names discussed and send a link out for people to vote. The top ten vote-getters advance to Round 2.

Round 2: The Winnowing

Preparation:

- Product Marketing will work with Legal and Trademark teams to eliminate problematic entries.
- Product Marketing will prepare a Google Survey with the top 10 vote-getters from Round 1.
- Product Marketing will open the meeting by having people vote on the top 10 list. People can vote for more than one at this stage.
- People may also come to the meeting with inspiration for other names, which can be added to the list at the Product + Engineering Stakeholder's discretion.

Process:

1. Convene again for 60 minutes.
2. Product Marketing will present the votes and lead a discussion of the top 4–5 finalists.
3. At the end of the meeting, Product Marketing will prepare a survey of the top 4–5 finalists and each person will vote on the ONE they like.
4. After the meeting, Product Marketing will solicit feedback on the finalists from key customers and community stakeholders.

Round 3: The Exec Decision

Process:

1. The Product + Engineering Stakeholder, the Founders, and Product Marketing will discuss the votes and decide on a name.
2. At this stage, it is possible that none of the names are selected. If this is the case, go back to Round 1 and start over.
3. The Founders will socialize the name with close allies of the company, including a diverse panel of people, and return with any objections or concerns.
4. If there are no objections or concerns, throw a party and get some T-shirts made. You've successfully named a project! (I'm not being facetious . . . Making the name "concrete" helps prevent second-guessing!)

LAUNCH STRATEGY AND EXECUTION

One thing every product marketer loves is a good launch. A launch is an opportunity to align the entire organization around a single deliverable. It is the culmination of everyone's great work:

- The product and engineering team gears up to scope and adjust in order to hit a date.
- The sales team gets ready to sell new features and capabilities to existing customers, identify closed-lost opportunities that could be revived, and identify prospects for new customers with whom new features will resonate.
- Marketing supports all these efforts with positioning, messaging, content, training, and execution.

There's nothing like a great launch!

Launch tiers

Not every launch is the same. You will alter tactics depending on the scope and impact of the release. You can come up with the nomenclature and precise categorization that works best for you and your company, but generally, this is how I apply my thinking:

- **Tier 1:** New product or service, major enhancement to an existing product or service, new major partnership
- **Tier 2:** Enhancement to an existing product or service, a partner comarketing activity (such as a joint event)
- **Tier 3:** Small changes to the product or service

Feel free to customize this for your organization. Consistency is key. Decide and stick to it.

Putting launches in context

When launching a new product or feature, it's important to give customers, sales teams, and other interested parties context about what the launch is, how it improves the state of things, and who it's intended to serve. This context helps each stakeholder gauge how and when to engage with the launch.

Here are some questions to use when working with your product team to establish context for a launch:

- What new customer scenarios are now enabled as a result of this feature?
- Are there any telltale signs that would help us identify existing customers who would benefit from this feature?
- Is there a type of customer who would absolutely not benefit from this feature?
- Are there any existing customers who have asked for this feature?
- Do any of our competitors have something like this feature? If so, how does ours compare?

- Are there any logical partners we should approach to work with us to release this feature?
- What are the step-by-step instructions to begin using this feature?

With this information, you can begin creating the materials necessary for a great launch.

The launch sine wave

Launches are not moments in time. They are ongoing processes that often overlap. I call this the "launch sine wave."

Every launch has three phases, each with distinct processes:

- **Prelaunch:** Gathering and disseminating product knowledge, identifying and preparing prerelease customers, building collateral and web pages, training sales and support, and completing competitive analyses. Depending on the launch tier, you may also need to work on positioning and messaging.
- **Day of launch:** Publishing the website materials, issuing press releases, running paid advertisements on social media, and so on.
- **Postlaunch:** Companies are made or broken by how well they execute postlaunch activities. Road tours of meetups, new content, a video series, partner comarketing blog posts, and a host of additional tactics help drive word of mouth and keep the momentum going.

Imagine a sine wave where the part above the axis represents prelaunch activities, the intersection between the wave and the axis represents the day of launch, and part below the axis represents postlaunch activities.

But the launches (sine waves) overlap. When you are wrapping up postlaunch activities for one launch, you will simultaneously prepare prelaunch activities for the next.

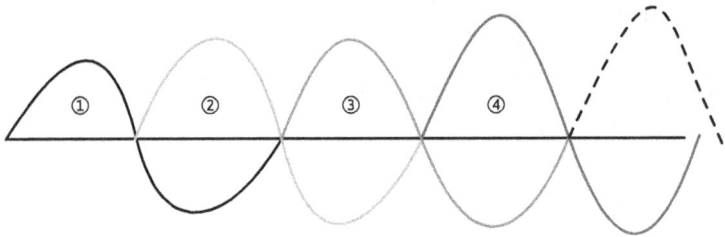

Getting and staying organized so that these processes are executed well is a key aspect of product marketing leadership.

Prelaunch preparation

Successful launches start well before the actual launch day. The prelaunch phase is where the groundwork is laid for the messaging, positioning, and operational readiness needed to create a smooth, coordinated event.

- **Drive market research and customer discovery.** Ensure that the product aligns closely with the needs of your ideal customer profile. Refine your ICP with insights from segmentation research, customer interviews, and market analysis. During this phase, work with early adopters to confirm product-market fit and refine your messaging based on real user feedback.
- **Develop positioning and messaging.** Now is a good time to revisit your positioning and messaging. Does the new feature or do new capabilities change how you stand and differentiate in the market?
- **Gather customer testimonials.** Traditionally in marketing, we think in terms of case studies—formal endorsements from customers about a product or service. For launches, you can get away with a less-formal endorsement. Perhaps a quote for a blog post, or a screenshot from

a customer of them using the feature in production. The traditional case study requires working with your sales and customer-success teams. The launch testimonial means working closely with your product and engineering team, who should already be in touch with customers for ongoing feedback during development.

- **Target all your influencers.** Remember your influencer-marketing playbook. Reach out to all the influencers you've contacted and built relationships with thus far and ask them if they'd be interested in "previewing" the feature and giving feedback. Be prepared to send them videos or links to preproduction versions of the feature.

- **Tap into analyst relations.** If you're an established company, you'll likely be working with analyst firms like Gartner or Forrester to effectively position the launch, establish industry-wide context, and provide evidence and credibility for key customers.

- **Build the collateral "bill of materials".** Create all launch assets and sales-enablement materials, including website updates, landing pages, blog posts, social media content, email campaigns, and product videos. For the sales team, build first-meeting decks, battle cards, datasheets, and FAQs. This suite of collateral ensures consistent messaging across all channels and provides sales with resources for effective conversations. Set up your spreadsheet or issue-tracking tool to assign owners, identify due dates, and track all these deliverables.

- **Develop the Getting Started Guide.** This is essential for making a great first impression. Design a detailed, visually appealing Getting Started Guide that highlights key features and takes new users through the onboarding process step-by-step. Include videos, screenshots, and animations to give users a clear path to their first aha moment. One thing I love to do for every new feature is record a two-to-three-minute "screencast" of the feature in action. You can host it on YouTube and embed it in your launch blog post to emphasize the point.

- **Align cross-functional teams.** Organize launch-readiness meetings with all relevant stakeholders. Prebrief the sales, customer success, and marketing teams about the product's capabilities, target customer, messaging, and ICP. Train customer-facing teams on positioning, competitive differentiation, and common objections.

During the prelaunch period, you should be meeting as frequently as necessary with the entire launch team, and communicating daily about deliverables and their status.

I do want to emphasize meetings that involve the entire team. Something will go wrong. Something always goes wrong. Having a diverse launch team, composed of technical and nontechnical people alike, will help you identify creative solutions. I once had a major launch issue for a two-thousand-person conference that was solved by an attorney from our legal department, whom I had included every step of the way. His solution was unique and helped us thread a needle and unblock an obstacle.

Launch activities

When launch day arrives, it's time to mobilize each team's efforts to create a coordinated impact across every available channel. Execution must be smooth and timely to maximize visibility and momentum.

- **Build the run-of-show.** Build a checklist of items that need to get done on the launch day. Often, things need to be sequenced. The blog post needs to go live so that you can refer to it in social media, for example. Have every thing in order well ahead of time,
- **Convene the launch room.** On Zoom or in person, get your entire launch team together and go through the checklist. Schedule this meeting well ahead of time.
- **Activate digital-marketing channels.** Launch your digital-marketing plan across email, social media, paid ads, and content marketing. Use SEO-optimized blog posts,

social media announcements, and email newsletters to drive awareness. Make sure all messaging is consistent with the core positioning and resonates with each target segment.

- **Don't forget Hacker News, Product Hunt, and other communities.** These are all great places to socialize your product, explain what you've built, and solicit feedback. Speak plainly and avoid overselling or marketing language. And be sure to engage with the comments. If you encounter rude comments, continue to engage with them and stay classy.
- **Use in-product prompts.** For PLG-driven products, use in-product prompts to introduce new features to existing users—a banner across the top of the product, for example.
- **Monitor social media and customer feedback.** Real-time feedback is invaluable during a launch. Track social media channels, community forums, and customer-support channels to understand immediate reactions. Assign team members to respond promptly to comments, questions, and concerns, addressing issues and showcasing engagement.

Postlaunch activities

After launch day, it's critical to maintain momentum and monitor results. This phase is where you gather insights, refine strategies, and leverage early successes to drive continued growth.

- **Analyze performance metrics.** Track key metrics like website traffic, conversion rates, product sign-ups, and revenue growth. Review the success of each channel (email, social media, ads, and content), and identify which tactics drove the highest engagement and conversions. Compile these findings into a launch retrospective to inform future launches.
- **Collect customer feedback and success stories.** Identify early adopters and top customers who can provide testimonials or participate in case studies.

- **Continue engagement with drip campaigns and targeted outreach.** Identify which customers used the product or feature, and build a campaign that reaches out to them for feedback or encourages them to continue their usage. Identify your lapsed and inactive customers and reach out to them with information about the feature.
- **Build community momentum.** Engage your biggest fans, community leaders, and online influencers to carry the story of your launch on your behalf.

Ideas for launches as a startup

Most marketing advice will work for organizations of all sizes. However, big companies have an advantage when it comes to launches: an already-large, installed base to whom they can direct their marketing efforts. Startups need to do a lot more work to get lift out of launches:

- **Focus on awareness and product-market fit.** Absolutely, you should still email your existing user base. But in a startup, the primary goal is often awareness. Use the launch to build credibility in the market, showcase early-user success stories, and drive organic engagement. Remember our messaging tip: Emphasize that you have a deep appreciation for the *problem* that customers are trying to solve.
- **Drive immediate usage.** If applicable, create a freemium or free trial offering to encourage adoption and feedback. Drive initial growth through self-service channels like SEO, developer forums, and social media.
- **Leverage influencers and community.** Startups often benefit from word-of-mouth and community support. Identify key influencers or early adopters who can amplify your message to their networks. Engage with community groups and forums to foster organic adoption.

- **Be bigger than you are.** Package several smaller launches together to create "launch weeks" or "launch months." Consider working with complementary companies in adjacent spaces on a coordinated launch week. Give customers and prospects confidence that you and your service are inevitable.

Vercel and Supabase both excel at launching developer products. Startups should study and emulate their approaches. Supabase in particular runs launch weeks consisting of ten to twelve product launches over the course of five to six days. Launch weeks are difficult grinds, but they pay off. Every company I've worked at that runs launch weeks sees consistently high social media mentions, spikes in website traffic, growth in signups, and increases in community engagement because of launch weeks. Launch weeks work and are ultimately worth the effort.

Ideas for launches as a BigTech organization

Big companies have advantages when it comes to launches, but their bigness also poses a huge challenge for making sure a launch goes well. Press, customers, and partners always recognize a disjointed story when they see it. If your story isn't complementary to the rest of the company's story, your launch will fall flat.

- **Coordinate across the organization and around the world.** BigTech launches involve larger teams across regions. Use highly coordinated digital and in-person events, along with press briefings, webinars, and customer-exclusive demos, to reach target audiences effectively. Put the effort into activating your global reach!
- **Activate your sales team.** You will already have a strong bottom-up presence, thanks to your launch news being carried broadly. But use your sales team to activate your enterprise users. Enterprise users may hear about your news, but they may not be immediately compelled to act

on it. Leveraging the existing relationships they have with your sales and customer-success teams, and providing those teams with clear marching orders for engagement, will help you maximize your launch results.

- **Engage with industry analysts.** Organizations like Gartner and Forrester have the trust and confidence of many of the top-tier customers that your sales organization is working to expand or win. It's hard not to be cynical about industry analysts, but the truth is that they have a broad viewpoint that you do not. As a marketing leader in an organization, you see your view of the world: your products, your customer's pain points, your engineering team's limitations. Industry analysts see multiple organizations, from the perspective of both the vendor and the customer. They can help you identify blind spots in your messaging, partnership opportunities, or competitive pressures you aren't yet able to ascertain. Working amicably and earnestly with industry analysts can elevate an already-successful launch.

With BigTech, the problem isn't necessarily getting attention. It's getting sustained attention and activation. Use your advantages on the ground with your global presence and your ability to speak with industry-wide influencers.

It's easy to point to Apple as an example of a company that executes launches well, but in my opinion, their follow-up with developers is nowhere near sufficiently transparent, nor are they present in developer communities. Of the BigTech companies today, I think OpenAI is doing a phenomenal job of executing launches. They lead with a consumer message, they follow up with concrete developer messaging and documentation, and they draw the connection between the two very well, thus making it clear to developers *why* they should bet on OpenAI instead of the myriad similar AI platforms.

STORYTELLING: THE CULMINATION OF EFFECTIVE PRODUCT MARKETING

I love product marketing, but the topic that is most near and dear to my heart is storytelling. The essence of any company or product is the story of why people should care. Stories engage our emotions and grab our attention. They help us remember information and make it more meaningful.

You're not just an integrated-development environment, you're a tool for greater communication and collaboration in a world where we've become increasingly isolated from one another. You're not just a super-fast database, you're the foundation of a world made better when access to and understanding of all data is available to everyone. You're not just a new JavaScript framework, you're a way for everyone, from beginner to expert, to make their ideas come to life.

As marketing professionals, we become profoundly more effective when we package our work into stories:

- Stories help build trust and credibility with developers.
- Stories help us differentiate our product from competitors' and legacy tools and processes (i.e., the "old way of doing things").
- And perhaps most important, stories help create a sense of community and connection with developers—the notion that when you use a product you're part of something new, something big, something profound.

How storytelling manifests itself in our work

Developer-focused companies—and technical founders, especially— love to lead with product. It's no secret why: it's what is intimately familiar to us. But we live in a very crowded landscape of tools, services, databases, and so on. What's the difference between your product and someone else's? Why should your product matter to me?

Going down the path of solution marketing is a great first step. You start to whittle away at the problem and get to the essence of "So what?" What benefit will customers see?

When my team launched Visual Studio 2005 back in, well, 2005, we weren't just launching a new version of the old tool. We were launching a new way of developing software. The core new functionality of the product was an Application Lifecycle Management tool, a term made up by Gartner (probably) that was, basically, "work-item tracking and functionality to manage the workflow of a project."

The easy thing to do would have been to launch the product with a new feature. But we wanted to do more and raise the price point, drive rapid upgrades, and triple already-substantial revenue from the product line. Ambitious goals required up-leveling our story.

After traveling the world and visiting with customers, we noticed a common theme emerging. The year 2005 was the height of the "offshoring and outsourcing" boom and the start of what we refer to today as "distributed teams." People found it really difficult to stay on top of all the work across time zones, geographies, languages, and cultures.

Thus when we launched the product, we launched not as a new version of a developer tool, but as a communication and collaboration platform to make creating software easier. "Communicate. Collaborate. Create." was the tagline I came up with, and I rebranded our new higher-end SKU as Visual Studio Team (instead of a typically boring Microsoft name, such as Visual Studio Enterprise).

The key to any story is to center it on the customer, not on yourself. Customers don't care about your story. They care about their own: their dreams, their pains, their goals, their desires.

Your story is that you've built a serverless database. Or a JavaScript framework. Or a developer tool.

Their story is that they want to build something quickly. Or be able to embed AI into their products in seconds. Or be faster at their job. Or defend their code from state-sponsored cyberattacks. And so on.

The creation myth: The backstory

Every good story has a backstory. This is the story that isn't necessarily told, but whose presence can be felt everywhere. I like to think of it as the texture of the story and its characters. In branding, this is "the creation myth."

Earlier I referred to Patrick Hanlon's seminal book, *Primalbranding*. Hanlon describes the creation myth this way:

All belief systems come with a story attached. In fact, a brand is often compared to a narrative. How we originated is the foundation of myth; it fulfills an innate human desire to understand how we came to be.

For startups, this creation myth looks a lot like your early-stage pitch deck.

- What is the problem you're solving, and how has it developed over time?
- Who are you, and why are you uniquely suited to solve this problem?
- Why have you yearned every day, for the bulk of your life, to solve *this* problem? Why you—and why not a different nerd down the street?

These aren't questions customers will ask of you when they go to click "Sign up for free" on your website.

Rather, the answers to these questions are present throughout your company. People who join your company aren't just there for a paycheck, they're there to go on this mission with you. Partners that elect to work with you want to be a part of solving this problem also. And customers innately feel the problem alongside you and believe you are the ones to solve it for them.

Some companies like to write their creation myth in their About Us page, and I won't disabuse you of that notion. Go for it. But also make sure that your creation myth is imbued in everyone in your company, and even though you won't ever use the exact words in marketing copy, they will still be present in the tone and tenor of your entire marketing apparatus.

How to come up with a story for your product

My first rule of thumb is that my product is not the star of the show. The star of the show is the customer and the customer's problems. The product, to borrow a phrase from Hollywood, is the MacGuffin, the object or plot device necessary to further the story.

So the first step in your story is to solicit as much customer feedback as possible. We've all seen television shows or movies that involve a software developer as either a main or supporting character. We are used to scoffing at nearly all onscreen representations of our profession. This is because writers haven't taken the time to immerse themselves in what it means to be a developer, and so their screenplays turn out to be clichés—overwrought representations of what they've read it's like to be a software developer, not what they've seen firsthand.

We talked earlier about building your ideal customer profile. The process of developing the ICP will give you the bones of your story. From here, you need to rely on your own art and creativity.

Tips for using storytelling in your developer marketing

Here are several tips for refining your story and making sure it is told in the most effective way:

- Use data and statistics to make your story more credible and persuasive. Customers don't just "need a scalable database," they need to "store millions of time-stamped records per second for consecutive days, weeks, sometimes even months."
- Keep your story concise and focused, and avoid overwhelming your audience with too much information.
- When it comes time to publish your material, consider engaging your audience with interactive elements, such as polls, quizzes, or Q&A sessions.
- Use visuals, such as images, infographics, or animations, to enhance your story and make it even more appealing.

• Measure the impact of your storytelling efforts and track key metrics, such as engagement, conversion rates, and customer satisfaction, to improve your strategy over time.

SUMMARY

A successful launch is not just an announcement, it's a coordinated effort to maximize impact, drive adoption, and sustain momentum. For developer products, launches should be tailored to how developers discover and evaluate tools. This means leveraging community engagement, clear messaging, and multiple distribution channels to ensure your product gets the attention it deserves.

• **Treat a launch as a process, not an event.** Momentum builds before, during, and after launch.
• **Developers want to see real, working products.** Skip the hype and focus on hands-on experiences like demos, docs, and trials.
• **Launch with a clear, compelling narrative.** Explain what problem you solve, why it matters, and how developers can get started immediately.
• **Use multiple distribution channels.** Blog posts, newsletters, social media, community forums, and partner promotions all drive visibility.
• **Coordinate with influencers and advocates.** Engaging developer influencers, open-source maintainers, and community leaders boosts credibility.
• **Have a technical leader or engineer communicate the launch.** Developers trust other developers more than traditional marketing voices.
• **Measure success beyond initial traffic.** Track sign-ups, engagement, and real adoption over time to gauge effectiveness.
• **Follow up with postlaunch content.** Tutorials, case studies, and community engagement help sustain momentum and deepen adoption.

Ultimately, launches are the culmination of nearly all product marketing activities. Think of them as forcing functions to get not just your product right, but to get your brand, story, customer connection, and content right as well. I've supplied a handy checklist in appendix 1 of this book so you can turn it into a launch checklist that makes sense for your organization.

Now let's turn our attention to aligning marketing with product and sales to amplify adoption of your product, and revenue as well.

CHAPTER 16

Aligning Developer Marketing with Product

Developer marketing and product teams must work in lockstep to ensure seamless messaging, adoption, and growth. Unlike traditional marketing, developer marketing must be deeply embedded in the product lifecycle to support bottom-up adoption. The key to success is ensuring that marketing understands and influences product development, while product understands and enables marketing efforts.

To put it simply, you and your product management team must be best buds. They are your tribe, and you need to be theirs.

WHY ALIGNMENT WITH PRODUCT MATTERS

As we've discussed several times, developers do not buy hype. The output of product marketing (positioning, messaging, launch management, partner enablement, sales enablement, and so on) must match a product's capabilities. "Underpromise and overdeliver" is the mantra of developer marketing, and when the mantra is inverted, developers will tune out the product and company entirely.

In fact, the more integrated marketing is with the product, the more effective marketing will be. Customers will find value in simple messaging because the messaging is aligned with the product's promise. And the inverse is true. If marketing is in touch with customers, building community-engagement tools and listening tactics, the voice of the customer will be imbued within the product from the get-go.

As I've always said in my career, it's a lot easier to market a diamond than a pile of poop. Ensuring that your marketing and product are aligned will guide the product team toward building the right products for the right customers, which will make your job easier on the other end.

SIMPLE TOOLS FOR EMBEDDING MARKETING IN PRODUCT

First of all, product marketing should be present in product and engineering leadership meetings. Be present and contribute to road-map discussions. Understand the customer and represent their interest and values.

Marketing should also use the same issue-tracking system as product and engineering. When marketing and sales teams sit in tools like Monday while product and engineering sit in tools like Jira, there will be disconnects. Marketing work items should be created as part of product releases, and they should be linked in the system so that everyone has visibility into the work necessary to launch. It's not that the product team needs to know the minutiae of marketing (or vice versa), it's that big projects are considered complete only when both product and go-to-market are represented.

You'll also run feedback loops with developers, using forums, surveys, and direct interviews. Take the time to internalize product-usage and industry-trend data and use them to guide roadmap decisions.

Last, as we've discussed, documentation is a core aspect not only of product, but of marketing as well. Use early product-design decisions to shape documentation and provide customers with straightforward information about how to use the product, as well as blog posts and introductory text in docs that shed light on why features were implemented in certain ways.

All these steps ensure that product and customers are aligned, which ultimately ensures there's no daylight between marketing and product.

USING THE MARKET REQUIREMENTS DOC

The market requirements document (MRD) is a valuable artifact when you're working with the product team, but it's often misused—or worse, ignored. Unlike a product requirements document (PRD), which defines what a product will do and how it will be built, an MRD defines why the product should exist in the first place. It gives the product team clarity about who the target customer is, what pain points they face, and what market opportunities exist. A strong MRD doesn't dictate features. Rather, it frames the problem so product teams can solve it in the most effective way.

A well-structured MRD should outline market trends, competitive landscape, customer segmentation, and key use cases. The marketing team gathers intelligence from multiple sources: customer interviews, sales feedback, analyst reports, industry trends, and so on. It then distills it into a clear, actionable document. When done right, the MRD prevents the classic trap of product teams building for an imagined customer rather than a real one. It also helps prevent feature bloat by aligning development with what will actually drive adoption and revenue, rather than chasing internally driven ideas.

For the marketing team, the MRD serves as a bridge between strategy and execution. It informs positioning, messaging, and go-to-market planning long before a product is ready to launch. It ensures that by the time engineering starts writing code, marketing has already mapped out who will buy the product, how they'll find it, and why they'll care. Without an MRD, product development becomes a guessing game, and marketing is left scrambling to retrofit a story to a product that may not align with market needs.

ALIGNING MESSAGING

We've already discussed segmentation, positioning, and messaging. One of the most important deliverables of product marketing is a strategy for how you talk about the product with your target customer, and the venues in which you will carry that message in order to reach them. Your product and engineering team should be part of that discussion. Setting the tone early that the teams are unified and contribute to each other's work will ensure that when you need help on messaging, the teams will be there to support you.

AREAS WHERE PRODUCT MARKETING CAN PUSH PRODUCT

Product marketing also has a role in pushing for changes in how products are built. Be an active voice in product onboarding. Your job isn't done at sign-ups. Make sure your strategies for driving sign-ups align with how the product turns a new user into an activated user. You should have data- and interview-driven information to guide decisions about a user's earliest steps inside your product. If you're marketing to super-technical database developers, onboarding will look quite different than if you were marketing to knowledge workers using low-code tools.

As we discussed early in this book, you will want to implement usage analytics in the product. Often, development teams will push back on server-side analytics or implementing integration with CRMs, such as Salesforce or HubSpot. These integrations are absolutely critical for a well-functioning, data-driven marketing organization. You need to make a strong case and push for it to be implemented.

You also have a strong role to play in driving the overall developer experience. Most developers in the product team have very little experience using the product end to end. In contrast, developer relations and product marketing build demos, write collateral, and create conference talks that show a complete left-to-right view of the product in a way that very few product or engineering members of the

organization ever do. As such, you have the moral authority—and perhaps the responsibility?—to represent a cohesive view of the developer
experience.

> TIP: As a side note, never stop using your product. Build
> a side-hustle app for fun, and continue adding features
> to it using features your company, your partners, and
> even your competitors ship, as they ship it. The differ-
> ence between an average product marketer and a great
> product marketer is right here in this paragraph.

SUMMARY

Developer marketing is most effective when aligned with the product. The key to success is tight feedback loops, shared goals, and data-driven insights that connect marketing with product development.

- **Respect the customer's voice.** Ensure accurate messaging based on product reality.
- **Embed yourself in the product team.** Sit in on their meetings, use their issue-tracking system, and contribute to road-map decisions. Work hard to be a part of the team that designs and develops the product.
- **Push where necessary.** You have needs from the product team as well, so don't be afraid to use your relationship with the team and the respect you gain by being present in product decisions to make sure marketing's needs are being met.
- **Developer marketing has a unique perspective on the developer experience.** Unlike engineers who work on isolated features, marketing and developer relations interact with the product holistically and should push for improvements that enhance usability.
- **Great product marketers use their own product.** Continuously building with your product (and your competitors' products) gives you the insight to create better messaging and developer experiences.

CHAPTER 17

Aligning Developer Marketing with Sales

Collaboration between sales and marketing is critical in any B2B context, but especially so when it comes to developer products. Developers are a particular audience, and any tone that reeks of marketing or sales will turn them off and hurt your brand.

As I've outlined throughout this book, marketing is focused on a Help First mentality, which builds trust and confidence among the target audience. But the target audience doesn't make a distinction between a marketing manager, sales executive, or engineer. If they see that you work for a company and they are turned off by your tone, they'll immediately flip the bozo bit on the company, and it is very hard to recover.

Thus it is imperative that marketing and sales work together to establish the right tone, stay on message, employ the positioning framework effectively, and coordinate their efforts.

WHY SALES ENABLEMENT MATTERS

Sales enablement equips sales teams with the training, resources, tools, and strategies to effectively engage with potential customers and close deals. Remember, developers value authenticity and technical expertise above all, and they dislike overt sales tactics.

Moreover, developers at *all levels* in an organization can influence purchasing decisions. So sales teams need to be trained on how to engage with developers at all levels. Focusing on economic buyers or decision makers at the expense of individual contributors often results in stalled proofs of concepts and closed-lost deals.

By aligning the team and engaging in a concerted sales-enablement process, you will realize many benefits:

- better-trained sales teams that understand the specific developer segment and positioning of the product that the company is targeting
- increased win rates through better technical insight and data on developer adoption
- a unified omnichannel message that supports the buying journey of each customer
- easier onboarding of new salespeople so they can be instantly productive

But remember, sales enablement is a two-way street. As we discussed earlier when we talked about messaging, salespeople engage with customers at the ground level, face-to-face. They will have first-hand knowledge of whether your messaging will work. Listen to them. If an experienced salesperson can't land your messaging without significant alterations, you need to go back to the drawing board.

UNDERSTANDING THE DEVELOPER-BUYER JOURNEY

Over the years, I've had a singular hypothesis about how developers buy products, and recently I confirmed it through data. By accumulating and analyzing IP addresses of visitors to my website, I was able to prove the following buyer journey:

- **Awareness:** A developer will discover your product through organic channels like blogs, forums, GitHub, events/meetups, community engagement, and social media. We've talked about all these channels throughout this book. But by having a consistent message and Help First tone everywhere, you attract developers to your brand.
- **Consideration:** Here is where it gets interesting. It is very common for developers to be intrigued by your organic presence, visit your website, view your product page, view your pricing page, perhaps even view your docs, and maybe even sign up with a personal email address (Hotmail, Gmail, etc.). But in this phase, they are not yet ready to buy. They have merely filed you away after understanding the use cases you address, and once they have an appropriate use case, they will return. Of course, some developers may jump straight into the Evaluation phase from here. It is essential to understand this mindset among developers. They are intensely curious as a rule. They were curious about your product, and now they know what it's about. But they may not be ready to use it, and the company where they currently work may not ever be ready to use it. But they have filed you away for later use.
- **Reconsideration:** Perhaps the developer now has your use case, or perhaps they now work at a different organization. Regardless, they will come back at some point—and this time they may use their work email to sign up.

Let's play the long game with this data. We know that when someone comes back after having been on your site before, and perhaps even signed up, they are more serious and more likely to engage and use your product. They are now seeking you out. Let's call it a meek "hand raise" (a stronger hand raise would, of course, be requesting a demo via your website). Be sure to capture and measure this data in your product and web analytics. Tools like Koala and Common Room are very good for this.

- **Evaluation.** Now they are in the evaluation phase. If you are running a product-led growth go-to-market motion, there are steps for how sales should engage in the later chapter on PLG. Similarly, if you are running a sales-led growth motion, you can run the playbook described in the later chapter on SLG.

Eventually you will get to a decision stage, but for now appreciate that the developer-buyer's journey can be a circuitous path with a lengthy pause in the middle before they finally get to the action. Use tools like email marketing and community engagement to keep your product top of mind with developers in the early-consideration stage.

USING POSITIONING AND MESSAGING WITH SALES

Your initial work on segmentation, positioning, and messaging should be guidelines for your sales team. These guidelines define the technical and business value for the ideal customer profile, and help narrow the field of prospects for sales teams.

Sales will also need customized messaging for their purposes:

- **For developers:** Focus on features, use cases, ease of use, and above all, a thorough understanding of the problem.
- **For decision makers:** Focus on return on investment (ROI), scalability, certifications and standards, security, risk mitigation, and so on.

Training your sales team on the problem is perhaps even more important than training them on the features and benefits of the product. If your team engages in cold outbound prospecting, the way you hook a potential customer and convince them to reply to your email or message is to demonstrate empathy for the problem they currently face.

Consider this cold email:

Hi Jane,

Most engineering teams don't realize they're overspending by 15–20% in their CI/CD pipelines. Overprovisioned resources, inefficient caching, and invisible cloud costs add up fast.

[Your Company] helps teams like [Company Name] cut CI/CD costs by 30% while improving deployment speed—without adding friction for developers.

Would it be worth a quick chat to see if we can help you do the same? Let me know, and I'll send over a few times.

Best,

Sally

The email leads with the problem the prospect faces. A problem-focused outbound email will win you more business, and it also provides the sales team with more options for how they take conversations, secure an initial meeting, drive towards a POC, and ultimately close the deal.

BUILDING A DEVELOPER-FOCUSED ABM STRATEGY

As I mentioned earlier, the developer-buyer journey often involves multiple stakeholders at all levels of the organization. A decision maker may want assurances from an individual contributor on the team that the product does what it says it can do, and a senior executive may need to sign off on the budget request. Many a deal has stalled out because an account executive didn't do their due diligence mapping out the organization and identifying champions at each level.

Account-based marketing (ABM) is an approach that coordinates outreach to all levels of a company and increases the chances of success for complex deals.

At a high level, the tactics you will employ include . . .

- identifying target accounts that fit your ideal customer profile.
- researching each account in depth and building a dossier on each one that helps personalize sales outreach.
- building and/or assembling tailored content for each account, including (but not limited to) case studies; datasheets; blog posts; and hosted demos (we talked about those in an earlier chapter). If possible, customize the data in your hosted demos and record one-off demo videos that highlight the use case for the customer. All these assets will go into the sales playbook for the account.
- engaging multiple levels of the company with a combination of outbound emails, phone calls, LinkedIn InMail Messages, and even LinkedIn Ads.

We will discuss this in detail in the sales-led growth chapter later in this book.

LEVERAGING DEVELOPER ADVOCACY IN SALES CYCLES

Developer advocates in large companies are mostly immune from being involved in the sales process. In contrast, in small and medium-sized companies, they can play an outsized role in that process. Developer advocates can act as technical translators, helping sales respond to prospects' questions and even participate in calls where sales engineers are not available. They can also build trust by acting as "independent" advisors offering technical advice and guidance.

Developer advocates routinely run webinars and training sessions, as we discussed in our content-marketing chapter. Inviting prospects to these sessions is another way for sales teams to keep the conversation flowing, adhering to the Help First mantra. Developer advocates can also help build top-flight demos using custom data for various vertical industries, which is another way for customers to evaluate their products or services.

METRICS AND FEEDBACK LOOPS WITH SALES

Ultimately, sales and marketing should share some primary metrics. Marketing should be just as accountable for the revenue metric as sales, and marketing and sales should both monitor and be held accountable for the pipeline and pipeline-velocity metrics.

Here are some other ways to measure the success of a marketing and sales collaboration:

- conversion rates for developer-originated leads
- pipeline velocity for accounts influenced by developer marketing efforts
- retention rates and expansion revenue from developer-led accounts

Marketing and sales should also hold regular syncs where they provide feedback to one another. Maintaining this tight feedback loop will help you respond to changes in market conditions, product perception, competitive pressures, and more:

- Conduct regular syncs between marketing and sales to review pipeline data and share learnings.
- Collect qualitative feedback from sales teams on what resonates with developer prospects, and whether the positioning and messaging still holds.
- Use analytics to refine messaging, content, and ABM strategies, especially target-account qualification.

ESSENTIAL SALES-ENABLEMENT MATERIALS

Marketing and sales often experience tension around the creation of sales-enablement materials, such as slide decks, datasheets, and so on. Sales always wants more, and marketing always questions whether the content they've already developed is being used.

My advice is to focus on speed and fast feedback loops and spend less time spinning your wheels, creating one-off content. In particular, you should focus on the following materials:

- **First-meeting deck:** But appreciate that every salesperson will want to tell the story their own way. As long as they are on message and maintain fidelity to the company's positioning, it's all good. Let a million decks bloom! (And don't feel bad about stealing awesome slides from other decks!)
- **Case studies:** You're already creating these, but be on the lookout for new industries and use cases.
- **Battle cards:** These are used for competitive analysis. We'll discuss this in the next chapter.
- **ROI calculator:** A spreadsheet is fine in the early days.
- **High-quality documentation:** We'll discuss this in a later chapter as well.

SUMMARY

It is critical to build a strong and vibrant (that is, ongoing and improving) relationship between marketing and sales. Marketing can help sales stay on message and on brand, and sales can help marketing stay abreast of market trends that could alter the calculus of how you talk about the product.

- **Marketing's job doesn't end at sign-up.** Developer marketing must work with sales to nurture high-intent users into becoming paying customers.
- **Enable sales with technical depth.** Give sales teams the technical education and collateral they need to have credible conversations with developers.
- **Define a clear lead handoff process.** Ensure smooth transitions, from self-service sign-ups to sales-led expansion efforts.
- **Help sales prioritize the right leads.** Use product-usage data and engagement signals to surface high-value accounts.
- **Create messaging that sales can actually use.** Avoid fluffy positioning. Instead give sales real differentiation and competitive insights.
- **Use PLG as a wedge for enterprise deals.** Many successful enterprise customers start as individual developers using the free tier.
- **Co-sell effectively with cloud and tech partners.** Hyperscaler marketplaces and partnerships can create new sales channels.
- **Regularly sync with sales leadership.** Build strong feedback loops so marketing efforts stay aligned with revenue goals.

Speaking of market trends, let's talk about how to conduct competitive analysis and market research, and how to use it in our marketing processes.

CHAPTER 18

Competitive Analysis and Intelligence

Competitive analysis provides insight into the landscape where your product operates and helps you identify opportunities for differentiation. By systematically assessing competitors' strengths, weaknesses, and strategic moves, you can craft positioning and messaging that highlights your product's unique value and resonates with your target audience.

But beyond understanding the competitive landscape, you also need to put the analysis to work. You need to imbue everyone in the organization with knowledge of how and why you beat the competition, and the tactics—all the tactics we discuss throughout this book!—necessary to cement that differentiation in the market.

Let's dive into each aspect of building an actionable competitive analysis.

IDENTIFY YOUR KEY COMPETITORS

Look beyond the obvious. Yes, some of your competitors have a brand name and a website and a product that is mentioned in deal conversations alongside yours. That's easy. But when it comes to developers, there's a lot more competition out there. Make sure you take a comprehensive inventory of your competition:

- **Direct competitors:** These are companies that offer products similar to yours, targeting the same audience. Dig deep into their technical implementation. You want your engineers to do a "teardown" of sorts, because within the choices made at the technical level lies the secret to building differentiated products and strategy. For example, focusing on databases built on Postgres versus the myriad databases not built on Postgres offers numerous avenues for intelligent positioning and comparison.
- **Indirect competitors:** They may not offer an identical product, but they solve similar problems and target much of the same customer segments as you. They may be entrenched businesses with long histories, or startups who see the space differently. For example, both Monday and Airtable saw the knowledge-worker productivity space differently. Monday built a more opinionated product aimed at teams, while Airtable was a more malleable database that could be morphed into whatever products were needed.
- **The status quo:** Developers have been building software products for over two generations now. If it works (and it's already paid for), why bother trying to fix it? If your product is about solving an old problem in a novel way, you need to get your positioning and messaging dialed in to break through developer inertia. Put another way, if you want to break through in a crowded market, you need to solve *the top problem* a key stakeholder with spending authority cares about.
- **Build-it-yourself developers:** Developers love to build complex things on company time. Is it really in the development organization's interest to imagine a whole new client-side development framework? If you have a product that *can* be built by a development organization quickly, maybe you should rethink the product.

PUBLIC DATA

Your first step will be to gather information from public sources. Look at websites, press releases, product demos, blog posts, case studies, webinars, and social media conversations to see how competitors position themselves and how customers perceive them.

- **Website and product documentation:** Review their content to understand their messaging and target audience. What is their core value proposition? Sift through support pages, knowledge bases, and forums. What are the strengths and weaknesses of the product? What do people rave about? What do they constantly ask for help with?
- **Customer reviews and testimonials:** Customer review platforms can give you some insight into how big-ticket customers view the product.
- **Press releases, launch blog posts, and news articles:** This should give you an idea of what the competitor wants to emphasize, and some indication of where they plan to direct their development efforts.
- **Job postings:** Buried within requirements for job posts (especially for software engineers) are technology choices and strategic decisions yet to be made.
- **Social media and community forums:** What do customers, unprompted, think about the competitor?

PRODUCT AND FEATURE COMPARISON

The product teardown is probably the most fun part of the competitive analysis exercise. Note that some companies will not let anyone with a competitor's email address sign up for the product. It's ridiculous, but true.

The key with a feature comparison is to be brutally honest with yourself. In this case, you are looking to tear down both products to understand where each of you stands opposite the other.

- **Do a deep feature comparison:** This should go beyond the marketing feature lists on both your websites. Go through every detail and mark things down. Your product team will love to see a series of quick wins.
- **User-experience evaluation:** Understand the full developer experience of the products and be candid about areas where they simplify things and where your product could use additional work.
- **Pricing analysis:** What is their pricing model and strategy? Can a customer view their pricing page and be able to predict their costs?

ANALYZE GO-TO-MARKET STRATEGIES

You'll look across multiple channels to see how a customer is organized for their go-to-market.

- **Content marketing and SEO:** Using Ahrefs or Semrush, you'll look at keyword strength and top-performing content. Look for trends in SEO growth and where that growth is coming from.
- **Social media strategy:** What type of content do they post, and what is the general tone? Are they more approachable, or less? How do customers engage with their content?
- **Ad campaigns:** Analyze your competitors' ad spending and messaging and look for clues about how they see and position themselves in the market.
- **Events and sponsorships:** Which events are they sponsoring, and what sessions do they give? What does their booth look like? When you attend events, be sure to put someone in charge of competitive analysis. Take pictures of their booth, check out their swag, get a demo and see what talking points they use. Be friendly and honest about who you are, but use the opportunity to gather intelligence. (Note: Sometimes competitors get acquired or fold

up shop. Make connections with employees in case you are able to hire them later.)

• **LinkedIn deep dive:** These days, account executives and sales-development representatives spend a lot of time chattering on LinkedIn. Look through all the posts from employees of your competitors to get an idea about the types of customers they're targeting and the approach their sales team is using to find customers. Remember, in LinkedIn you can look at a person's profile and see all the posts they choose to comment on.

Refine your own campaigns by examining the campaigns of your competitors.

GATHER CUSTOMER INSIGHTS

Some of the best competitive intelligence I've ever been able to accumulate is from customers who chose my product over my competitors'. It's equally important to interview customers who chose your competitor over you. You'll get a glimpse into the selling process, the willingness of the competitor to go the extra mile to win, and the pricing structure of the competitor's potential enterprise deals. In addition, you can get a deeper understanding of the technical differences by talking to customers who chose one or the other.

• **Add discovery questions to sales calls.** Work with your sales team to get answers to some pressing questions about competitors. If your account executive can work it into a conversation, they'll be able to get you some vital information.
• **Conduct customer interviews.** We talked in an earlier chapter about customer interviews. Include questions about competitors in these conversations.
• **Conduct surveys.** Use them to ask focused questions about whether the customer ever considered a competitor.

BUILD COMPETITIVE BATTLE CARDS

The first rule of sales collateral is that no one is going to read it. I speak somewhat facetiously. People are busy with their day-to-day jobs. One of the reasons I wrote this book is that marketing professionals (especially marketing executives) have so many things on their mind that sometimes it's helpful just to have a simple checklist to remind them of all the things they already know.

To that end, when you write your competitive analysis, remember there's a good chance that not many people will read it. So aim for depth, but also readability. Format the document so that the key takeaways are at the top. If an account executive is on a call and a competitor is mentioned, they should be able to quickly load your doc, glance at the key points, and see a list of short qualification questions to determine who is a better fit for their business: you or the competitor.

- **Lead with the competitor's positioning.** Describe how the competitor views themselves in the marketplace, and compare it to your own positioning.
- **Identify key differentiators up top.** Format it as a bulleted list. Short and punchy. Why do you win? Why do you lose?
- **Highlight top questions for sales to ask the customer.** Determine who's a better fit, you or the competitor. Different sales teams have different approaches to dealing with the situation when your competitor offers a superior product for a given circumstance. Some sales teams decide to cut bait and focus on easier-to-win accounts. Other sales teams are in situations where growth dictates trying to win harder, more-complex accounts. The answers to these "qualification questions" will help everyone in the go-to-market organization (sales, marketing, customer success, and so on) focus.
- **Plan how to handle objections.** If a customer has a question or problem with your product and is using a competitor as a comparison, how do you quickly respond and

de-position the competitor while establishing yourself as
the preferred choice? I typically list the common objections customers will have along with prescriptive guidance
for sales on how to address them in conversations with
prospects.

- **List value differentiators.** Going beyond features, based
  on your positioning, how can you frame the conversation
  and the customer's criteria for evaluation in a way that
  your product comes out on top?
- **Go deep, but later.** At the bottom of the document, get
  as deep and detailed as possible. Include all your research
  and citations, including screenshots, if applicable. Show
  your work. Just don't be sad if all people focus on is the key
  bullets up top.

In the past, battle cards have always been static. Product marketing creates a battle card, it lives in an intranet site, and you're at the
whims of your sales team and their willingness to look up and act on
the content. One experiment worth running is using your static battle
cards as part of an AI prompt from which you can generate personalized battle cards for sales to use when preparing for a customer meeting. For example, you could combine the battle card with information
about the customer from your CRM (and perhaps even intent signals
from your Customer Data Platform) and use AI to generate a set of
actionable talking points for sales.

SUMMARY

Competitive analysis and battle cards help you hone your differentiated positioning and the artifacts you create, provided they are easy and fast to read, and your sales team can use them to frame your product as the better fit for the customer.

- **Map the competitive landscape.** Identify direct and indirect competitors, including open-source alternatives and adjacent tools developers may use.
- **Run technical deep dives.** Go beyond marketing claims and test competitor products, document key differences, and identify weak spots.
- **Use competitive insights to refine messaging.** Focus on differentiation that matters to developers: speed, scalability, cost, or ease of integration.
- **Equip sales with battle cards.** Give sales teams clear, fact-based comparisons so they can handle objections with confidence.

Competitive analysis isn't just about reacting, it's about proactively positioning your product to win in the minds of developers and decision makers.

CHAPTER 19

Overview of Acquisition Models and GTM Strategy

Products aimed at developers can employ a variety of go-to-market models. Often companies use more than one of these approaches to build a complete customer journey. Let's look at a few ideas for bringing developer products to market:

- product-led growth (PLG)—bottom-up user acquisition
- sales-led growth (SLG)—top-down user acquisition
- combination of PLG and SLG
- open-source, community-led acquisition

We will discuss PLG and SLG in more detail in later chapters, but for now let's cover some of the basics that product marketing will be responsible for.

BOTTOM-UP ACQUISITION MODELS FOR PLG

The idea behind product-led growth (PLG) is that some substantial cohort of customers will want to try your product on their terms before deciding whether to pay for it. The hallmark of PLG is low customer-acquisition costs (CAC) and almost no burden on the sales team to try and close the deal.

At the core of PLG is the idea that a user's journey can be initiated, nurtured, and monetized with automated digital systems and minimal sales involvement. In a typical PLG funnel, users go through four primary stages:

1. **Awareness:** They discover the product through organic channels, SEO, content, events, or ads.
2. **Conversion:** They sign up for a free or trial version, with the aim of experiencing the product firsthand.
3. **Activation:** They reach an aha moment in the product, seeing value that hooks them into further use.
4. **Payment:** After seeing consistent value, they decide to pay, often via a self-service process like entering credit card details.

Each of these stages has specific levers that teams can adjust and optimize:

- **Driving awareness:** using targeted SEO, valuable content, ads, partnerships, and events to attract users
- **Optimizing for conversion:** making sign-up processes as frictionless as possible, aligning promises with actual product experiences
- **Accelerating time to value:** refining onboarding flows and in-app prompts to get users to their aha moment fast
- **Prompting for payment:** strategically nudging users to convert to paid plans when they reach key usage or value milestones.

PRODUCT-LED GROWTH WITHOUT PRODUCT IS DOOMED TO FAILURE

The first fallacy of PLG is that it is a technique restricted to the marketing team. In fact, for PLG to be successful at all, it needs to be a joint production between marketing, product, customer success, and sales. And beyond simply assembling a cross-organizational team, there needs to be a team leader who is empowered by someone in a position of power to make decisions, allocate resources, and *change the product itself* to run experiments that drive performance through the PLG funnel.

Thus, the first and most consequential challenge to executing PLG is organizational buy-in and alignment.

The second challenge of PLG is the various optimization steps at your disposal. Yes, marketing can be wholly in charge of driving awareness and optimizing the website. Even then, the promises made during awareness campaigns (e.g., the content you build, the ads you run, the trade show booths you sponsor) must resonate with your segmentation and ICP, and must be true to your positioning. So while marketing can control its own destiny, it's still at the whim of the realities of the product.

But to get a user to the promised land, you need to run fast experiments and be able to make changes in the product itself.

I cannot tell you the number of days and weeks I have spent trying to get a product team to optimize a sign-up page that is hosted "within the product" (and, therefore, not under marketing's purview) or replace the confusing dialog box all users see after sign-up with a much more streamlined version that gets developers to the aha moment immediately.

If your company is betting on PLG, but the people in charge are unwilling to assign resources to support fast PLG experimentation, you will find yourself in a bad situation very quickly.

THE RELATIONSHIP BETWEEN PLG AND ACV

The last challenge is that PLG is not enough. Let's say you have full organizational support and resources to experiment with, and you can fully optimize your PLG funnel. Run the numbers. Do your number of self-service users and the maximum amount they will pay help you achieve your revenue targets?

Most developers in small-to-medium-sized businesses will spend a maximum of $500 to $1,000 per month on a service on their credit card before thinking twice. Is $12,000 the average contract value (ACV) that will get you to your revenue goals this year?

The question to ask is if the volume of PLG customers you can convert into paid users multiplied by the ACV you are seeing will turn into the revenue numbers you seek.

PLG FOR PRODUCTS THAT ARE TOO COMPLICATED FOR PLG

One of my clients builds a product that drops into cloud-native infrastructure and immediately identifies infrastructure errors and their root causes. This software is intended for the Fortune 100 and scale-ups with demanding operational needs.

However, they still offer a PLG solution for a few reasons:

• The product simplicity implied by adopting PLG is still critical. They want their product to be easy to use and get started, with minimal forward-deployed engineering necessary to get a customer to the aha moment.
• Their target audience is still developers; they just so happen to be developers in large organizations with lots of approvals and controls to touch any infrastructure.

The solution we came up with was the microsite we discussed in chapter 4: an interactive demo that can be replayed with sample data and demonstrate the value of a fully deployed and operational solution. Now even if a prospect works in a complex organization with layers of approvals, they can experience the product using fake data in a fun and memorable manner.

We will discuss hosted demos in more detail in the next chapter.

TOP-DOWN ACQUISITION MODELS FOR SLG

So if PLG won't get you to the promised land, does that mean you need to lean on a sales team? In all likelihood, yes. But let's talk about the ramifications for product marketing and the marketing team overall.

In a top-down acquisition model, sales teams actively reach out to potential customers, develop relationships, and manage the sales process from initial contact to close. SLG is critical for enterprise customers who require more personalized interactions, custom contracts, and high-touch support.

For product marketing, adopting an SLG model requires additional focus on creating materials like this, that empower the sales team:

- **Case studies:** real-world proof of product impact that resonates with decision makers
- **First-meeting decks and battle cards:** detailed resources that help sales navigate competitive conversations
- **Product demos and trials:** tailored demo environments that highlight unique product strengths

In a top-down approach, your messaging and collateral must be tailored to meet the specific concerns of executive-level buyers. This means explaining and understanding budget, ROI, integration compatibility, and scalability. Your product's UVP must resonate with high-level business goals rather than technical features alone. Product marketers must align with sales to ensure that every interaction with enterprise customers is aligned with the product's core positioning and unique value.

COMBINING BOTTOM-UP AND TOP-DOWN APPROACHES

For many organizations, the optimal go-to-market strategy is a hybrid of bottom-up (PLG) and top-down (SLG) approaches. In this model, PLG helps drive initial awareness, adoption, and early revenue from individual users or smaller teams, while SLG targets larger deals and longer-term growth. The key is in the sequencing and alignment of these models to ensure that they support each other rather than working in isolation.

Here are a few key tactics for effectively combining PLG and SLG:

- **Don't let high-potential accounts into the PLG motion at all.** We will discuss this in the next chapter, but you could create two sign-up flows—one for smaller accounts that lets them experience the product in a self-service fashion, and another for larger accounts that requires them to book a meeting with your team.
- **Identify high-potential accounts through product.** Use data from PLG users to identify companies or teams that may be candidates for an enterprise sale. The most common signal I've seen is the "multiplayer experience," where multiple users from the same domain sign up within hours of one another.
  - In this regard, it is *essential* that your PLG motion gives you visibility into sign-ups at an *account* level. You want to know not just how many users signed up for your product, but also how many accounts signed up and the number of users per account. You also want visibility into whether an account is growing the number of users on your platform.
  - Your product must have the ability to create multiuser accounts, and any user must be able to invite other users to a "workspace" (or whatever unit of work you've settled on in your application).

- **Create a hand-raiser path.** Design the product experience so that smaller users can learn about the benefits unlocked in an enterprise engagement and easily request a consultation from a sales representative. You'd be surprised how many companies make this inordinately difficult.
- **Develop "land and expand" strategies.** Encourage initial adoption by individual users or teams (PLG) and use account-based marketing (ABM) to encourage broader, organization-wide adoption. The most successful way to execute this tactic is to turn your initial users in a large organization into your champions. Give them resources to fight their procurement teams on your behalf, and give them opportunities to become brand ambassadors within their organization (e.g., free T-shirts and so forth).
- **Align all collateral.** While you can speak differently about the benefits of your product to organizations of different sizes, the core value proposition of your product should remain the same. You should be consistent, and in this way, your outbound campaigns for PLG can support any SLG effort you have underway.
- **Build targeted content for each funnel.** Tailor content for the PLG path (guides, tutorials, forums) and the SLG path (ROI calculators, case studies, and executive-level overviews). Both paths should be aligned with the core positioning but adapted to meet the audience's mindset and decision criteria at each stage.

PLG and SLG should work closely together. Be consistent in your positioning and adapt messaging for each type of user. Use PLG to build your brand and allow users from organizations of all sizes to try your product. Encourage hobbyist usage by users of all sizes. And build onramps that allow PLG users to become enterprise users.

OPEN-SOURCE AND COMMUNITY-LED MODELS

Open-source products are common in the developer world and offer unique pathways to user growth. There are several traditional approaches to open-source. Let's cover those before we dive into the hybrid open-source, PLG, and SLG models that are common today.

- **Hosted model:** The open-source product is made available for others to clone, contribute to, and run on their own. The company also offers a hosted version of the product that it charges for using any combination of business models.
- **Open core model:** In this approach, a subset of the product's functionality is open-source, while premium features are reserved for paying customers. These premium features could be part of a cloud offering (which we will discuss in a moment) or part of a software-licensing deal (increasingly rare, though still common in situations requiring air-gapped or on-premises solutions, such as government, aerospace, etc.).
- **Paid services model:** In this approach, the open-source software is free, but services, such as support, maintenance, training, and integrations, are offered as an extra. This was the secret behind the success of Red Hat and many other software companies, but this model is also increasingly rare as these services get productized into a cloud offering.

Today it is more common to see an open-source product available for download, and the maintainer or company responsible also offers a paid hosted version in the cloud. Hosted software offers several benefits that are well known to everyone at this point: get started quickly; no installation, maintenance, or upgrades are necessary; pay only for what you use; get free support and training.

In addition, giving customers the option of running the source code themselves helps hedge against the very real risk of a startup going belly-up. A company can certainly start using a cloud version, but they can obtain their data and run the software at any time.

TIP: One risk hybrid open-source and cloud companies run is that one of the major hyperscalers (e.g., Amazon, Microsoft, or Google) elects to host and offer a cloud version of the software themselves, thus cutting the company off from potential revenue for their hard work. Companies that maintain an open-source product and a cloud (PLG or SLG) version simultaneously would be wise to use the cloud protection license (CPL) pioneered by Timescale and popularized by many other vendors in the following years. The CPL permits customers to run their own version of the software (and to view and repair the code), but it forbids anyone from running a version of the software in a way that could be competitive with the company's cloud offering.

The fundamental value of open-source

Open-source is a cultural movement every bit as much as it is a technology movement. Contributors to open-source software work collaboratively to build products. They exchange knowledge and build communities around the software. Within those communities is cachet, camaraderie, and cooperation. Disagreements are handled in the open. Software is also shipped in the open.

DeepSeek CEO Liang Wenfeng put it beautifully:

> In the face of disruptive technologies, moats created by closed source are temporary. Even OpenAI's closed source approach can't prevent others from catching up. So we anchor our value in our team—our colleagues grow through this process, accumulate know-how, and form an organization and culture capable of innovation. That's our moat.

There is tremendous value in the collective consciousness of smart, motivated people. Ultimately, the value of open-source is derived from that collective.

Turning open-source users into customers

If you have a successful open-source project with thousands of active users, you're probably wondering how you can convert even a small percentage of them into paying customers. The first thing to realize, as we've discussed throughout this book, is that developers hate overt sales and marketing tactics. You need to take a different approach.

Instead of reaching out to users with an "opportunity to see a demo of our commercial product" or "excellent pricing offering for our open-source customers," consider first reaching out to check in on their usage, get their feedback, and find out what they're trying to build. Open-source software is usually cloned from a GitHub repository, with no sign-up process involved. So you may need to do some sleuthing to find the actual person to contact. But the point remains: your first contact with these users shouldn't be a sales or marketing offer, but rather a technical conversation.

From these conversations, you should be able to determine the kind of value proposition you will need to support in your commercial product to make it more attractive than running the open-source version. It could be features, it could be user experience, or it could be something else, like technical support.

As you hone your "open-source upsell" value proposition, continue to maintain a technical-first outreach model.

Encouraging open-source users to stay in communication

Again, most open-source software is cloned from a GitHub repository. You often won't have email addresses or other contact information for them. In our chapter on sales-led growth, we will discuss some ideas for obtaining contact information from your open-source users, including publishing changelog newsletters and more.

SUMMARY

Developer products use different go-to-market (GTM) models to acquire users, often combining approaches to build a complete customer journey. Product-led growth (PLG) focuses on bottom-up adoption, while sales-led growth (SLG) targets enterprise buyers. Open-source and community-led acquisition can also drive developer adoption. Each model has unique challenges and opportunities.

- **Product-led growth (PLG) fuels self-service adoption.** Developers want to try products on their own terms before committing to payment, so optimizing the onboarding experience is critical.
- **PLG success requires cross-functional support.** If the product team doesn't prioritize sign-up and activation improvements, marketing alone cannot drive sustainable PLG adoption.
- **Sales-led growth (SLG) is necessary for enterprise deals.** Large organizations need more hand-holding, custom contracts, and procurement approvals, making SLG an essential motion.
- **PLG and SLG work best together.** Use PLG to build a broad user base, then identify high-potential enterprise customers who require a top-down sales approach.
- **Open-source models offer unique acquisition advantages.** Free and open-source software attracts developers, but converting them into paying customers requires a thoughtful approach.

No single GTM model is sufficient on its own. The best strategy combines PLG for awareness and adoption with SLG for higher contract values and enterprise expansion.

CHAPTER 20

Product-Led Growth

Previously, we covered some of the basics of product-led growth (PLG). In this chapter we will dive into more strategy, metrics, sales activation, and specific tactics to help you debug your PLG funnel.

The goal of PLG is to acquire a lot of customers at low cost. You're shifting the burden of selling the product from sales and marketing to the product and its features and user experience. Marketing will bring customers in, they'll sign up, and the product has to work its magic and drive conversion.

A WORD ABOUT PLG ZEALOTRY

Dogmatic thinking has no place in business, which is, above all, pragmatic. Our job is to find customers, get them to pay us for our products, and grow our business. PLG is in vogue for a multitude of reasons. The cost of acquisition is fairly low, it's seemingly easier to find and qualify potential enterprise customers, and it puts the product at the center of the go-to-market motion. For technical founders, PLG is the "if you build it, they will come" strategy, where product decisions affect business outcomes most directly.

But PLG isn't for everyone or every product. I do believe that *aspiring* to a PLG experience is good for every product. After all, making it easy for people to get started and onboarded is a universally positive outcome of product design. But some markets and industries are better suited for PLG than others.

When PLG does and does not make sense

Products with a clear value proposition that users can experience quickly are often best suited for PLG. If you have a product that solves a widespread problem with a large-enough audience, you may have great luck with PLG. Let's take a look at two seemingly similar databases with radically different positioning:

- **Database 1:** A PostgreSQL-based backend-as-a-service that enables developers of all skill levels to build their application in less than a weekend. (This is the Supabase model.)
- **Database 2:** A PostgreSQL-based database-as-a-service that enables developers with massive amounts of data to query and use that data most efficiently. (This is the Timescale model.)

Here we have two Postgres-based databases, but they're targeting very different audiences. The audience for Database 1 is any web or app developer who wants an alternative to Firebase (a proprietary NoSQL-based backend-as-a-service from Google). This audience is large. It encompasses hobbyist developers building personal apps, entrepreneurs building small businesses, medium-sized businesses scaling and rewriting their applications to meet new demand, and even enterprise businesses building departmental applications.

The audience for Database 2 is existing developers with massive amounts of data. You cannot get value out of Database 2 without first ingesting all your data, indexing it, and building new applications to extract value out of it. You *may* want to undergo this process by yourself, and there are certainly a few developers who will. But most developers of this type are enterprise in nature. They won't just want to prototype; they'll want assurances from the company that their database is rock-solid and the company itself has the legs to stay around.

PLG makes an inordinate amount of sense for Database 1, which can build a very large, diverse, and resilient community because of the size of its market. This will enable them to construct a top-of-funnel of thousands of sign-ups per month, identify signals within those sign-ups that indicate whether a customer is ready to start paying, and proactively reach out to promising prospects. The prospect is also probably the decision maker, and the stakes will likely be low enough that the decision can be made quickly. The average deal size for Database 1 may be smaller, but the faster deal process and the number of qualified prospects mean the number of deals will be larger.

For Database 2, PLG is a good *aspirational goal* for the product. After all, databases *should* be easy to get started with and easy to use. But the number of customers who will get value out of a database best suited for massive quantities of data is smaller. The average deal size for these customers will be much higher than for Database 1. And the process for evaluating the product will be much more involved, including teams from operations, security, legal, and more. So the total number of customers will be small and the deal cycle will be longer, but the average contract value will be much higher.

Two databases, two approaches, two different roads to the promised land.

The expectation is that Database 1 should have a very long runway off a PLG motion and should be able to transition to product-led sales (which we will discuss in a moment) with great success. Database 2 will be able to generate some leads from PLG, but most of its high-contract-value leads will likely come from a sales-led growth (SLG) motion (which we will discuss in the next chapter).

Can you bolt PLG onto an existing product?

The first thing to recognize is that self-service alone is not what makes something a PLG product. Self-service is what I mean when I say that all products should *aspire* to be PLG. So the glib answer is yes, you can (and probably should!) turn your product into a self-service product.

But PLG is much more than product features or experiences. PLG is necessarily imbued in every aspect of *the company.*

Legacy products with large sales teams and consultative sales processes will require significant investments in cultural change, which is probably much more difficult than simple product changes.

As we will soon see, the PLG team is cross-organizational. And a PLG motion means using product-level signal to drive sales outcomes. This may be an anathema to how your current sales organization runs. Transitioning and retraining them to drive sales plays from product-level signal is a process. Is it a process worth investing in?

Enterprises are just different

Let's not forget that enterprise customers are wired differently. PLG motions are great for letting departmental users or individuals kick the tires. But enterprise adoption often requires months to clear various hurdles (security, legal, procurement); pass muster with stakeholders and champions at multiple levels of the organization; and possibly be customized and reconfigured to work with software or SaaS the customer has already purchased. Sometimes a product can't be used within just one department.

Relying on a PLG motion to navigate all of the above would be very difficult. You want, and need, a sales team to shepherd your company and your product through the gauntlet.

And of course once an enterprise customer has adopted, you also need a competent on-the-ground customer-success presence to ensure the customer is happy, seek out expansion opportunities, and continue to build champions and stakeholders.

After all, just as PLG is one sign-up on the road to success, SLG is often one contract on the road to several more contracts.

Hosted demos: the PLG alternative

Let's say you have a complex product that takes time to configure and get started before seeing value. For example, Port, the internal developer portal, requires setup before seeing value. An IDP enables a platform engineering team to support their internal developer organization by standardizing request processes and configurations for cloud resources, provides aggregated views on billing for cloud resources at the individual and departmental levels, enables finance organizations to set up limits and quotas for resources, and so on.

To extract value out of this product, you need a sufficiently large team; access to cloud resources such as AWS credentials (including billing permissions); and a good chunk of time to plan out the kinds of items you will configure and make available in the portal itself. This is not something you can do in the first ten minutes of using the product.

For this reason, Port and companies like it host live demos of their product. In the live demo, customers can experience a fully set-up product and begin to imagine themselves using it to its fullest potential.

Another company, Causely, provides root-cause analysis of issues in production cloud-native environments. Installing Causely takes seconds, after which it immediately assesses the topology of all a company's resources and analyzes OpenTelemetry log-and-trace data to identify issues and propose solutions. The installation process may be easy, but it requires permissions that rank-and-file developers may not have. Further, a positive experience of the product involves seeing a problem and identifying the root cause within seconds. Your infrastructure may be running fine for now! And finally, the evaluation process will often involve some level of expertise that not all developers currently have.

For this reason, Causely staged a live demo which, after potential customers arrive at the demo microsite, *replays* data of a major outage at a North American bank. This replay is consistent for every user who starts the live demo, each time they start the live demo. As a consequence, Causely doesn't just provide a live demo of their product working in a simulated real environment, but it also teaches site-reliability engineers and DevOps professionals how to identify the root cause of a major cloud-native environment issue.

Live demos are fantastic ways to help customers see the value of your product, particularly if the product is complex or requires elevated permissions to evaluate.

YOUR PLG TEAM

When making the decision to adopt a PLG model, you should ensure that the team responsible for building PLG into the product is cross-organizational:

- **Product management and engineering:** the team with resources dedicated to running PLG experiments and implementing product features that support PLG
- **Data science:** someone who understands the schema and data of all analytics being generated and stored by the product, and who has the know-how to ask for new metrics to be measured and recorded
- **Developer growth:** the people who understand where new customers will come from, what information they will have about the product, and the problems they're trying to solve when they arrive at the website
- **Customer-success managers:** the people most responsible for making sure customers can deploy to their satisfaction
- **Sales:** the team responsible for pursuing larger contracts from your most-successful PLG customers

Your product marketing manager is responsible for positioning and messaging your product and should advise the core team on target customer and attributes, as well as ongoing competitive analysis at both a product and market level.

PLG FUNNEL AND SIGNALS TO ANALYZE

Before diving into activation signals, let's step back and put things in context. Ultimately we are trying to understand how well our PLG funnel is working and which customers show the most potential for becoming paid users. To do this, we will need to measure five things:

- **Awareness:** How many people are aware of our product, and where are they coming from? We want to be sure that we can cut all data by the *lead source* (where they learned about us).
- **Sign-ups:** Of all the people who visited our website, how many are signing up for the product?
- **Activation:** Of all the people who signed up, which ones actually used the product and saw value?
- **Conversion:** How many people who activated the product swiped a credit card and are now paying for it?
- **Expansion:** How many people who are paying for the product are growing at a fast rate?

These metrics give you a good view of your PLG funnel. It is essential that you get your product-analytics and marketing-analytics metrics aligned so that you can measure this with accuracy.

A PLG strategy that recognizes that all customers are not equal

Let's say you had a product that required a developer to add a component or JavaScript snippet to your website. Now imagine these two different types of customers came to your website:

- a startup with fewer than 50 employees that has only raised $20M in Series A funding
- an enterprise customer with more than 5,000 employees and $900M in annual revenue

The startup customer will likely want to try your product and evaluate it quickly. Their deal size is probably fairly low, and their evaluation process is likely very fast.

In contrast, the enterprise customer is not about to deploy your code to their website, and maybe the person visiting your site doesn't even have permission to do so! Before your product can be evaluated, a platform engineering team and possibly even a security team must evaluate your JavaScript snippet. When it's time to negotiate a deal, there's probably a procurement team or, at minimum, a finance team involved. The deal size could be much higher, but their evaluation process is going to involve more people than simply the person who signed up.

Now, most websites today offer two primary calls to action: "Try for free" (get started with the PLG experience); and "Request a demo" (a "hand raiser" who wants to be escorted through the product, its capabilities, and the evaluation process).

But what if we only had one call to action across the entire website: "Get started now."

And further, what if the log-in screen prequalified the size of the account and guided the customer to either self-evaluation or demo request, depending on which was most appropriate:

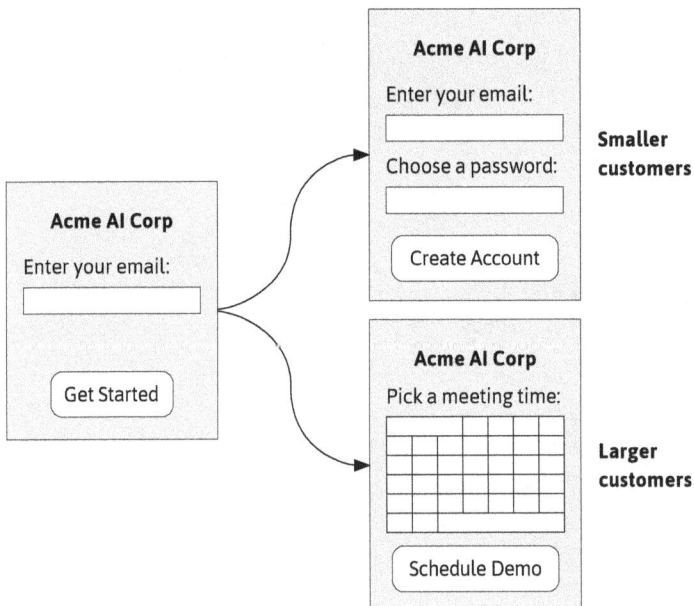

In this model, you are optimizing the entire top of funnel for either PLG or SLG (which we will discuss in the next chapter), ensuring that high-value customers get a more personalized experience while all customers have the option to try it for themselves.

> TIP: The MarTech industry is ever-changing and -evolving. Search for lead-qualification and lead-scoring tools that will work for your budget and website to help you implement a hybrid sign-up properly.

Ultimately what you are doing is making a calculation of average contract value (ACV, or the amount of money a company can pay) vs. cost of acquisition (CAC, the amount of money, time, and energy it takes to win a customer). Low-ACV customers should be pushed to low-CAC channels, which is typically going to be PLG. High-ACV customers in an ideal world would convert through low-CAC channels, but that's not usually realistic. Therefore we want to make sure we don't lose high-ACV customers and we push them to a high-touch (high-CAC) channel.

I believe it is smart to align around a single call to action, a hybrid account-creation or meeting-creation flow, and a realistic (not dogmatic) faith that people who have enough interest in your product to "get started" will follow through if you give them a way to do so.

The great Guillaume "G" Cabane writes and speaks eloquently about this topic and inspired me to run this tactic in one of my previous companies. It worked beautifully, and while overall signups declined, the percentage of signups that turned out to be qualified rose significantly. Seek out Guillaume's wisdom and experience, and you'll be in great shape.

To Gmail or not to Gmail

It's likely that one of your biggest internal debates is whether or not to accept sign-ups from people who use free/personal email accounts, such as Gmail or Hotmail.

One side of the argument is that developers love to sign up for things with their personal emails, kick the tires, and then come back to sign up with a business email if they like it. A variant of that argument is that if you choose to offer a free version of your product, people may want to build personal projects using your product using their personal email. These personal projects help developers become proficient with your product, which may lead to them recommending it as an option in their professional career.

The flip side is that cloud resources aren't free, most free email sign-ups are bots anyway, and you don't want to waste time analyzing metrics or assigning sales resources to track down free email users.

My feelings on this have evolved over the years. My experience is that permitting free emails to sign up only definitively makes sense if you have a free-forever tier.

If all you have is a time- or resource-limited trial, then you need to consider whether your product appeals to a broad base of developers, or if it's more niche.

How much setup and configuration is involved with your product? If a prospect sees value out of it only after setting up integrations with several big data or enterprise products they already have, then it doesn't make sense to permit users to sign up with personal emails.

The free email discussion is inexorably tied to ideal customer profile and product strategy, and it has significant implications for go-to-market strategy and sales processes.

Fake accounts

Hand in hand with personal emails comes the scourge of bots and fake accounts. If you have a PLG motion, you almost certainly have a fake account problem. If you allow people with personal emails to sign up, your fake account problem is probably significant.

Fake accounts affect not only your team and resources, but also your decision making. Your sales team may spend an inordinate amount of time chasing free accounts to answer emails or phone calls. Your infrastructure team may be overprovisioning cloud resources for bots. And your statistics on PLG performance may be skewed by fake accounts. This is clearly a problem you need to address early.

One option is to use specialized tools to identify and root out fake accounts before they sign up. You could also consider using CAPTCHAs or other pre-sign-up tactics, but these will add friction that could turn off legitimate buyers.

The other thing is to make sure you are discounting the importance of a raw sign-up metric. Instead focus on activated users: people who do something legitimate in your product.

PLG activation metrics and what to collect

Let's talk about the "activation" step in the funnel, because it can be the most important, and the most contentious, within an organization. After your PLG team has decided to collect metrics and make them available for analysis (ideally by everyone in the company), you will want to debate and standardize language for what constitutes an activation.

Here are some examples of activation actions:

- completing onboarding workflows or tutorials
- using a specific feature central to the product's value proposition (e.g., running a query for a data product)
- achieving a tangible outcome like uploading a dataset, sending an email campaign, or deploying an application
- inviting others to use the product with them

You will want to collect as much as possible that leads up to your chosen step, as well as all the data after. Because while you want to analyze who has activated, it is equally important to analyze who has *not* activated.

Signals to pay attention to

When sifting through your data, you want to view much of the following information:

- Track where users drop off during onboarding, and adjust the flow to reduce friction.
- Examine the time taken to complete key activation steps, such as project creation or data upload.
- Identify differences in behavior between activated and nonactivated users to refine your approach.
- Identify users who invite others on their team to use the product with them.

As you can see, the metrics you collect and the data you analyze are essential to debugging your PLG funnel. For example, you may want to optimize functionality with the following tactics:

- Automate repetitive steps in your onboarding or set-up processes.
- Provide contextual in-app guidance to steer users toward activation.
- Build personalization into onboarding flows to cater to specific user needs or industry verticals.

Mitigating failures in PLG

In PLG, the users will decide if the product is a good fit for them. If a customer signs up, swipes a credit card, and starts paying, you're golden.

Obviously, that won't be the case for every customer. So you need to examine your metrics and run experiments in the product to maximize customer self-evaluation and conversion.

Once a human intervenes (that's product-led sales, which we will discuss in the next section), it's almost impossible to get a customer back to a self-service mode.

So everything you do must be singularly focused on helping customers be self-sufficient in their evaluation and driving them to a paid plan. Marketing alone cannot do this. If you are experiencing high sign-ups and low conversion to paid, that is fundamentally a product problem. You have to work as a team to solve it: either adjust marketing to focus on customers who are a better fit, or (equally likely) work to change the product so it's a better fit for the customers coming in.

Team invitations: The golden metric for driving conversion

One important note: for most B2B products that have the ability to create "organizations," invite teammates, and assign permission-based roles to those teammates, a new user who invites other users is a key metric to investigate. Colloquially, this is referred to as "multiplayer mode."

These activation patterns are important because they give you a clue to how an organization is structured and what the role of each individual happens to be. For example, a curious technical champion may do the initial sign-up, then realize that they need a champion in their infrastructure team to provide permissions and complete the setup process.

What you will quickly realize is that activation is a team sport, and every team will choose to do it differently. To complete the evaluation, everyone on the team needs to buy into the product from their particular angle on the problem being solved. And often you will be brought into the prospect's organizational dynamics, healthy or otherwise.

You will begin to notice a few patterns as you investigate accounts with team dynamics. Some teams have a single champion who sets everything up in your product and then begins to invite collaborators. This is how I've always set up Airtable in my teams. I set up the schema and then invite people to contribute.

Other times, you will see a team where various roles are brought in to complete setup. I had to do this for Common Room, where different "signals" required specific executives and office administrators who had permissions for GitHub, Google Analytics, and so on.

The most interesting scenarios involve multiple team members who independently discover and start using your product. This has happened to me twice now, with Linear and Notion. Fortunately both products immediately recognized that I was trying to create an account with a domain name that had been set up by another person in the company, and they invited me to join the same workspace.

Handling organizational dynamics and workspaces is a critical component of both product development and go-to-market, and it's a fantastic example of why the growth team needs to be cross-functional, with everyone having the opportunity to have their opinions heard.

Asking questions during sign-up

You have a great opportunity to collect data and turn sign-ups into successful customers the moment they create an account. During the onboarding process, ask for information about the user, their goals with your product, and their team.

Many companies have concerns about asking questions during this part of onboarding. The theory is that "abandonment" can be higher if you prompt a customer to answer questions before they get to use your product. This is somewhat true. You don't want to inundate them with a bunch of questions whose answers you can either infer or get later. But it's OK to ask a handful of questions upfront.

There's also the temptation of using third-party tools, such as Clearbit or ZoomInfo, to obtain data. This third-party data can be somewhat unreliable. In my experience, this information will be accurate for only 50 to 60 percent of your users. For the remaining ones you're on your own. Thus when presented with the opportunity to ask questions and obtain information about your users, first-party data will always be preferable and more reliable than third-party data.

Given those concerns and limitations, what kind of information should you obtain from the user, and what can you infer later?

First, ask about the user:

- What is your role?
- What problem are you hoping to solve?
- How did you learn about us? (Optional)

Second, ask about their company:

- What is the size of your/the company?

You will infer the company name from their email domain unless you allow free email services. Then it's worthwhile to ask for the company name if they've provided a free email address for sign-up.

Last, if your product lends itself to multiple users in an account, then the sign-up process is a great opportunity to offer a new user the chance to quickly add their teammates:

- Do you want to invite your teammates?

That's usually all you need to help qualify a sign-up and support either automated follow-up or, as we will see shortly, product-led sales and sales-led growth motions.

> TIP: If a user signs up with an email from a domain that already has active users, work with your product team to offer the option to join their colleagues' existing workspace. This reduces friction and improves team onboarding.

Acting on PLG metrics and experiments to run

Here are some of the essential metrics you will want to track throughout your PLG journey.

Customer Acquisition Cost (CAC)

The CAC measures how much it costs to acquire a new user and serves as a critical efficiency metric for product-led growth (PLG), especially in self-serve models.

- **Why it matters:** PLG relies on keeping CAC low to achieve profitability through organic channels like word of mouth, virality, and seamless onboarding. Low CAC relative to customer lifetime value (LTV) ensures sustainability.
- **How to measure it:** Add up all marketing and sales expenses in a given period and divide by the number of new users acquired in the same period.
  - ○ **Example:** If you spend $30,000 on campaigns and onboard 600 users in a month, your CAC is $50 per user.

Time to Value (TTV)

TTV measures the time it takes for a user to experience the core value of your product. Reducing TTV is paramount in a PLG model because it directly correlates with user activation and retention.

- **Why it matters:** A shorter TTV increases the likelihood of user engagement, conversion, and advocacy. Longer TTV is also an indication that your product is too hard to use. Longer TTV coupled with higher churn rates (people who sign up but never come back) should be a warning sign for your product team.

- **How to optimize:**
  - ○ Streamline the onboarding process by removing friction and unnecessary steps.
  - ○ Use templates, preconfigured settings, or AI-driven recommendations to guide users faster.
  - ○ Introduce interactive walk-throughs and in-app tutorials that emphasize key features.

Retention and Churn Rates

Retention measures how well you keep users engaged over time, while churn shows how many users abandon your product. These metrics are core indicators of long-term success in PLG.

- **Retention rate:** The percentage of users who remain active over a given timeframe.
  - ○ **Example:** If 200 users sign up in January and 160 are still active in March, the two-month retention rate is 80%.
- **Churn rate:** The percentage of users who leave over the same timeframe.
  - ○ **Example:** If 40 out of 200 users leave, the churn rate is 20%.

Together, retention rate and churn rate should help you identify points in the typical customer workflow that frustrate or annoy users enough that they disengage. If you refine the product experience, it should follow that your retention rate will increase and your churn rate will drop.

As you improve the product, create resurrection campaigns (which we discussed in our earlier chapter on developer marketing) to bring churned users back to experience new features.

Product Engagement Metrics

Engagement metrics help gauge how users interact with your product, revealing its stickiness and adoption levels.

- **Active usage:** Measure daily, weekly, or monthly active users (DAUs, WAUs, MAUs).
- **Feature adoption:** Track the usage rates of specific features to understand their relevance.
  - **Example:** Monitor how many users try out a newly launched reporting tool within their first week.
- **Frequency of use:** Analyze how often users return to the product.
  - **Example:** A collaboration tool might measure the average number of sessions per user per week.

PLG is an ongoing experiment. It's a lot like playing whack-a-mole: you solve one problem and then see another problem to fix. The fun—indeed, the joy—of PLG is the cross-functional team all singularly focused on the customer and the daily improvements in the product that follow. Great PLG teams have instantaneous feedback loops and run fast experiments to resolve issues.

PRODUCT-LED SALES

Product-led sales is a go-to-market strategy where instead of (or perhaps in addition to) outbound prospecting, sales teams use product-usage data to identify and engage with users whose behaviors could indicate that they are ready for a larger contract. These users demonstrate high conversion potential, and unlike traditional sales models, with product-led sales there's a larger likelihood that these users will be willing to work with the sales team and be steered toward premium offerings and/or annual commits.

Remember, it's not that developers don't like salespeople. On the contrary, when a developer is ready to spend money with a company, they *want* to talk to salespeople to optimize their spend and get what they need to clear the purchase with procurement, security, and other departments that have to sign off.

With product-led sales, you are focusing on customers who are at the point where they most likely want to talk to you about a purchase.

Product-qualified leads

The most important aspect of product-led sales is respect for the customer and their current experience with the product. You never want to interrupt the self-service process just because a customer comes from a potentially large logo. If a customer abandons the product, instead of reaching out and asking why they left, use data to determine where they saw friction, address those concerns, and reach out with personalized information.

The core unit of product-led sales is **product-qualified leads (PQLs)**. A PQL is someone who has demonstrated that they know how to use and engage with the product. Before making any contact, we analyze their behavior with the product and build a personalized outreach plan.

Always use analytics to monitor user interactions, feature adoption, and even feature abandonment. Perhaps the first indicator of a PQL is their overall usage. That flags them for further investigation, upon which you want to answer a few questions:

- How quickly have they adopted the product?
- How many teammates have they invited to use the product with them?
- Are there any other people from the company who are already using the product? (Is it worth exploring a company-wide plan as opposed to departmental level only?)
- Which features are they using?
- Which features have they tried and are now no longer using?
- Which features have they never tried?

In addition, you will conduct other research into the company, the users themselves, and the industry to better understand their motivation for using your product.

Benefits of product-led sales

Once you have information about a user and their experience with your product, you can build a personalized outreach plan. This should help you in many ways, including these:

- **Better conversion rates:** You are targeting users who are already seeing value with your product, and you are doing so in a way that understands their usage and potential for expansion. Remember, always frame outreach in terms of your understanding of the problem.
- **Accelerated time to value (and revenue):** You are reducing the time it takes to turn a prospect into a paying customer.
- **Better use of resources:** You aren't spending inordinate amounts of money chasing people who aren't interested. Instead, you're focusing on users who have already demonstrated interest in your product.
- **Better customer experience:** Because you are researching and personalizing outreach, you are acting as a product advisor rather than a salesperson.

Implementing product-led sales

Assuming that you've already built your cross-organizational team and included sales from the onset, and that you've all agreed on the metrics and, specifically, the meaning of the activation metrics, you're ready to start implementing product-led sales within the sales organization.

The first order of business is to operationalize your PQLs by building a consistent process for handling a PQL once it's detected. You will also want to train your sales team on the nuances of engaging with active self-service users. Specifically, **tone down the sales rhetoric and turn up the product-consultation mindset.** You're reaching out to help a customer get more value out of your product. That's it.

I recommend starting a document with all the customer information in it (or, ideally, add it to custom fields in your CRM):

- all the background research you've done on the customer and their company
- all the metrics within the product-and-analytics stack that indicate what they've done with the product and where they might be struggling
- their spend so far and an estimate of what their spend could be in the future
- an analysis of other sign-ups from the same company and what they have or have not done with the product
- draft outreach emails

Socialize it within the cross-functional team for feedback (especially on the outreach emails), and then begin your outreach.

SUMMARY

Product-led growth (PLG) shifts customer acquisition from sales-driven outreach to product-driven adoption. It relies on a seamless user experience that enables customers to discover, try, and pay for a product with minimal sales involvement. While PLG can be a powerful motion, it requires organizational buy-in, thoughtful activation strategies, and the ability to identify product-qualified leads (PQLs).

- **PLG thrives when users can experience value quickly.** Products with a clear, immediate value proposition (e.g., Supabase) succeed in PLG, while complex products (e.g., Timescale) may require a hybrid PLG-SLG approach.
- **PLG is more than just self-service.** Simply allowing users to sign up for a product isn't enough. PLG requires a company-wide shift in how product, sales, and marketing operate together.

- **Product-qualified leads (PQLs) enable sales activation.** Instead of traditional outbound prospecting, product-led sales teams engage high-potential users based on their in-product behavior.
- **PLG doesn't work in isolation.** Many successful companies use a hybrid model where PLG fuels awareness and initial adoption, while sales teams handle enterprise conversions.
- **Activation metrics and onboarding flow are key levers.** Optimizing sign-up processes, reducing friction, and tracking engagement signals (e.g., team invites, feature adoption) dramatically improves conversion rates.
- **Live demos can replicate the PLG experience for complex products.** Companies with long setup times or enterprise constraints can create sandboxed environments that simulate real-world product usage.
- **Aligning PLG with enterprise sales requires hybrid funnels.** Companies should direct high-value accounts toward sales-assisted onboarding while allowing smaller teams to self-serve.
- **PLG is an ongoing experiment.** Cross-functional teams should constantly analyze user behavior, run product experiments, and refine onboarding flows to maximize growth.

PLG is a powerful go-to-market strategy but must be implemented pragmatically. The best companies combine PLG and SLG, ensuring that users can self-serve while high-value customers receive the personalized experience they need to convert.

Now let's talk about the opposite of PLG, sales-led growth, and how they can coexist.

CHAPTER 21

Sales-Led Growth

From product-led-growth, let's now discuss sales-led growth (SLG), sometimes colloquially referred to as "growing with enterprise customers." As its name suggests, SLG is driven by sales through a concerted cold outbound and sales-assisted model. SLG has tremendous advantages for certain types of businesses, namely those in industries with longer, more consultative sales cycles, and certain types of products, such as those that take longer to set up, install, and obtain value from.

Let's dive into what SLG is, when to use it, when to add it to a PLG model, and how to work with your sales team to build a fantastic growth engine together.

WHAT IS SALES-LED GROWTH?

Sales-led growth (SLG) is a go-to-market strategy where the primary driver of customer acquisition, expansion, and retention is a dedicated sales team. Unlike product-led growth (PLG), which relies on the product itself to convert users into paying customers, SLG focuses on human interaction to guide prospects through the buyer's journey. This approach is often necessary for complex or high-priced products or services where personalized conversations and touchpoints can speed or impact the decision-making process.

Here are some of the hallmarks of an effective SLG motion:

- **High touch:** Prospects work closely with account executives (AEs) who take the time to understand their problem and tailor the messaging of the product or service to match the customer's definition of what they need.
- **Longer sales cycles:** The more niche and specific your product, and perhaps the closer it is to the infrastructure or security concerns of a company, the longer it will take to get all the necessary approvals not just to buy the product, but to begin a proof of concept. Having humans intervene can ensure the testing and evaluation process doesn't stall out or get kneecapped by an unforeseen stakeholder.
- **Customized:** Typically the product or service you offer on your website must be modified for an enterprise customer. You may need to do some level of nonrecurring engineering to tailor an aspect of the experience or capability. A government customer may have extreme networking demands, a financial-services customer may have unique scalability requirements, a health care customer may have data-residency obligations, and so on.

In all these circumstances, the *relationship* you build between your company and the customer, specifically the technical and non-technical champions within the customer's organization, will help you overcome the hurdles necessary to win the deal. In this regard, SLG is fundamentally a game about relationships, and the best AEs on your team will cultivate relationships and partnerships with customers that get you across the finish line. Our job in marketing and developer relations is to support the process of beginning and nurturing those relationships.

WHEN TO USE (OR ADD) SLG

While PLG has become popular recently—both as a result of the pandemic and because many startup founders are averse to sales—SLG remains important in scenarios where products or services deem it necessary. We've discussed some of these already, but to recap, here are some situations where SLG makes sense:

- **A complex product:** Difficult installation steps, involved processes to see initial value, and so on, all necessitate more hand-holding through the evaluation process. If the value of the product is nuanced, that also indicates a need for someone on your team to explain exactly why it's worth the trouble.

- **Enterprise customers:** Large organizations are more demanding not just because of the big budgets they control, but also because they're more bureaucratic. In addition to the technical champion you're dealing with, other teams within the organization—like security, legal, and compliance—will have a say in whether the product will be approved.

- **High average contract value (ACV):** In addition, the negotiation-and-contract step can be more involved, as each of the other groups in an organization will have needs to be met. An experienced AE can guide you through this minefield.

- **New market:** If you are entering a new market or industry, you will likely need an experienced hand who can anticipate the obstacles that may come along the way. Each industry is governed by different regulations and norms.

- **New product category:** If you're selling an entirely new type of product or service, your technical champion may be well-versed in it but the other people with a say in contract approval may not. Being close to this decision-making process will help you win the deal—and hone your positioning and messaging in a way that simply gathering website signal will not.

- **Stalled PLG:** We'll talk in a moment about when to add SLG to PLG. But one special case to account for is when expanding your PLG product (say, from a team or departmental deployment to an organization-wide deployment) requires hand-holding on contract terms, and maybe even custom product development.

There are also times when you will want to add SLG to an existing PLG motion:

- **Your data shows that company size is a bottleneck.** If your activation-to-conversion step is stalled out with large companies compared to smaller companies, consider adding a product-led sales motion to your PLG. And if that doesn't work, add a full SLG process.
- **Upsells and add-ons are not resulting in adoption by enough customers.** Again, your data shows that customers are not adding new features and your upsell ratio is anemic as a result. You may have a messaging problem, a pricing problem, or a need for a sales-assisted motion. These are things to dig into, and we'll talk about them in a moment.
- **Similarly, cross-sells aren't getting traction.** Your initial product may target one segment (e.g., developers) but a new product targeting a new segment (i.e., testers) isn't performing well. You may have a positioning or messaging problem with the new product. You may be misunderstanding the purchase-and-consideration process of the new segment. All of these things should be investigated, and the answer may well be that your new segment fits one of the categories we described earlier, and could be prime for an SLG motion.

All of this is to say two things:

- Sometimes your problem has nothing to do with PLG or SLG and has everything to do with positioning, messaging, or pricing. Product marketers should roll up their sleeves and always start there.
- In situations where the problem does have something to do with PLG or SLG, the problem could be your assumption that either PLG or SLG is the answer, when the real answer could be both.

FAILURE MODE FOR ENTERPRISE SALES

As you look to move upmarket, think hard about the product, marketing, customer-success, and sales trade-offs that you're going to make. In some cases they may result in short-term revenue but sacrifice long-term strategy and objectives.

One classic example of these trade-offs is nonrecurring engineering, or NRE. This is when you make a special feature for one customer. You're then stuck supporting a variant of your product for one entity. Rather than thinking about NRE as a one-off, think about whether the project and the question being asked by one of your potentially top customers is something that would benefit all your customers. Or perhaps, the correct answer is that you should expose elements of your product through an API so that customers can customize it to their liking. In any event, it could be a benefit at a higher pricing tier, sure. But it could still be a benefit for everyone.

NRE will often take you down a path that will lead to failure. The short term can be a mirage. After all, you're winning a major customer. But in the long term, you fracture your product strategy. Instead of developing a long-term roadmap that is fueled by customer needs, you end up supporting one product for one group of customers and a completely different product for a different set of customers. It may not seem like it at the onset, when you first consider doing NRE, but in the end you will lose.

As a marketing team, you need to be an advocate for both the customer and the business. And while one of your customers may be asking for something, it may end up being a distraction to fulfill their wish. It will be tempting to give in and support sales in their effort to win a large deal and a large logo for your website. But think long term and take long-term actions to serve the business.

THE PEOPLE IN THE SALES ORGANIZATION

We talked earlier about my ideal structure for a developer-focused marketing organization (developer advocates, product marketing, developer marketing, developer growth, and so on).

Now let's take a look at the typical structure, roles, and responsibilities of a sales organization. The following roles often report to sales leadership (a VP of sales or chief revenue officer, or CRO):

- **Account executive (AE):** Manages the full sales cycle for *qualified* leads, from initial discovery to closing the deal.
- **Sales development representative (SDR):** The front line of the sales team. They're responsible for prospecting, qualifying, and initial contact with leads. SDRs *sometimes* report into more mature marketing organizations. Regardless, they work very closely with marketing, as we will see in a moment.
- **Sales engineer (SE):** The technical expert who addresses customer questions and demonstrates how the product fits into a prospect's existing infrastructure or workflow. A good SE will quickly build demos of products using reasonable facsimiles of sample data and be able to show the product in a "real-world" context or scenario during initial discovery meetings. It is a good idea for SEs and developer advocates to be very closely aligned.
- **Customer-success manager (CSM):** After a deal has concluded, the CSM will be responsible for making sure the customer's deployment is successful. They will hold periodic calls (greater frequency early on, after a deal has

been closed) and gauge the relative happiness of the customer with the product or service. A *great* CSM is also looking out for expansion opportunities and alerting AEs of potential new business. Product marketing and developer marketing should be very closely aligned with CSMs. CSMs can help debug positioning and messaging, identify potential case studies, and identify potential beta customers for new features or products ahead of future launches.

- **Sales operations (SalesOps):** Builds and maintains the technical systems, processes, and data that allow for accurate reporting and analysis of the pipeline and customers. SLG requires strong cross-functional alignment between marketing and sales.

DEFINING A SALES PROCESS IN AN SLG ORGANIZATION

A well-defined sales process aligns marketing, sales, and product teams on the target customer (ICP), value proposition, features and benefits, and evaluation process. It involves the following:

- pipeline generation
- lead qualification
- metrics and evaluating success
- continuous evaluation and improvement

PIPELINE GENERATION

Pipeline is the lifeblood of any go-to-market organization. Having a constant, consistent pipeline that converts is a good sign that the marketing, sales, and product engines are working in unison, and that the business will continue to grow and be healthy. Let's talk about how to build, measure, and evaluate your pipeline.

What is pipeline?

There is a big difference between lead generation and pipeline. Through various marketing activities, you may generate a large number of leads. These leads could come from product sign-ups, webinars, newsletters, ebooks, and so on. But until these leads are qualified by the sales team, they are not considered part of the pipeline. We'll discuss lead qualification in a moment.

Many people conflate leads and pipeline. The leads you obtain from all your channels *could* one day turn into opportunities for pipeline growth, but many of them will not. Maybe some of them are simply fans of your business or your space. Maybe some of them had a need but no longer have it. Maybe some changed jobs or companies and your product is no longer a fit. And maybe some were just lookie-loos who had no intention of ever converting.

Opportunities are leads that have been qualified and have a clear path to conversion. Thus, pipeline is the list of all potential revenue opportunities (new customers, expansion customers, churned customers) at various stages of the sales process. When thinking about pipeline, you want to distinguish between a few important characteristics:

- **Pipeline creation:** How many new customers are being added to the pipeline, and what is the rate of these additions? This is largely a report card metric for marketing.
- **Pipeline progression:** How fast is new pipeline moving from various stages of engagement? This is largely a report-card metric for SDRs and marketing.
- **Pipeline conversion:** How much new pipeline has signed a deal and converted into revenue? This is largely a report card metric for AEs and CSMs.

Generally speaking, pipeline is anyone who can conceivably turn into revenue. You want to evaluate the following metrics for your pipeline:

- **Lead-to-opportunity ratio**; How many leads turn into pipeline?
- **Total pipeline value:** How much revenue potential exists in your pipeline?
- **Coverage ratios:** Does each account executive have somewhere between three and five times their sales quota in available pipeline?
- **Pipeline velocity:** How quickly does the pipeline progress between stages?

When we evaluate the health of our pipeline, it's important for marketing leaders to think about it from start to finish. We don't wash our hands of the problem simply because our team attained 100 percent or more of their pipeline target for a quarter. We have to evaluate all the metrics: how much pipeline coverage we generated, how fast the pipeline is progressing, how much pipeline turns into opportunities, and how many opportunities turn into revenue. When we evaluate the whole funnel left to right, we unearth important truths: Did marketing generate *quality* pipeline? Did the pipeline conform to the ICP—and thus was sales prepared to sell to the pipeline we generated? Did our sales enablement work? And so on.

Inbound pipeline generation

Throughout this book, we've discussed many types of "inbound" marketing tactics. I've mostly grouped these into three categories: content, community, and events. In addition, we've discussed paid acquisition, which I have mixed feelings about for developer products. Each of these tactics drives engagement with customers, raises awareness of your product or services, and turns some of these customers into leads.

Over time, you can use tactics such as email marketing and other automated marketing tools to nurture these leads into higher-quality leads, meaning they spend more time either using or learning about your products or services.

It is critical that you use marketing automation tools, such as HubSpot, Marketo, and the like, to measure the efficacy of your tactics and mark your leads with attributes indicating which tactics they've expressed the most interest in. Who opened emails about tips and tricks for database optimization? Who opened emails about security considerations when deploying cloud-native services? These kinds of attributes will help you build smarter automated-nurture systems and provide your sales team with intelligence about how to approach and qualify leads of interest.

And, as we discussed in the PLG section, aspirational PLG is good for almost all products. But if you are going to add a PLG inbound flow to your website, there are a few steps we should recap from previous chapters to help you improve your lead-to-opportunity ratio and support your SLG motion most effectively:

- Implement a hybrid model for account sign-ups using a standard "get started" CTA.
- Add email nurture for high-potential sign-ups (business email sign-ups from companies in your ideal customer profile).
- Implement features in the product and analytics to go with it that give you clues about the aha moment.

Outbound pipeline generation

When sales teams proactively reach out to prospects, this is called "outbound" pipeline generation. There are several ways to drive outbound pipeline, which we will cover in a moment.

But the most important takeaway is that sales does not execute outbound in a vacuum. Marketing, especially product marketing, needs to help them every step of the way.

Your SDRs (who are largely responsible for outbound pipeline) will need to deeply internalize your customer segmentation, product positioning, and messaging. They need to understand the product, what it does, and the benefits it provides. Only then can they accurately identify prospects, hold intelligent conversations with them, and convince them to learn more (e.g., book a discovery call with an account executive and a sales engineer).

A good product marketer works with the SDR team to perfect outbound emails and call scripts. They practice with the SDRs, and they listen in on calls where appropriate. The feedback loop should be near instantaneous, and both parties should have complete confidence that the other is acting in good faith.

As a marketing team, it is essential that you are fully immersed, enmeshed, embedded, bonded, whatever term you prefer with your SDR team. Teamwork makes the dream work.

Modern outbound looks a lot like content marketing

In the old days, SDRs would cold-call or cold-email prospects, looking for a reply. It might have taken five to ten "touches" to get a prospect to return your call or answer your email.

Today, we are all conditioned to ignore unsolicited communication. We ignore calls, we ignore emails, we ignore LinkedIn messages. Approximately 1 percent of emails are returned (and most of those replies aren't happy about being interrupted). Telephone calls get about 5 percent pickup rate, and Apple and Android continue to improve their ability to filter telemarketing calls. Sure, every once in a while you might get a response. But by and large, the same old stilted conversations no longer cut it.

Today, you need to teach your prospects something. Perhaps it's an insight your company has developed in an industry or market. Maybe it's a free tool you've developed to solve a persistent pain. It could even be a revelation one of your customers made about itself that could, in turn, help a prospect. It could be an invitation to a webinar or an in-person event.

These days, the same core tenets that apply to content marketing also apply to outbound marketing. Obviously you can use your content as part of your outreach. But the tone and tenor of the outreach itself must also come from a Help First mindset.

Early-stage pipeline generation

When you're just getting started, you don't need fancy tools or methodologies. You need to invest your time early on learning what will work, and scale later. Manually identify customers who have a need for your product and write a personalized email or LinkedIn message for each one.

Here's one way to go about identifying those customers:

- Search LinkedIn for people with your target title. (Early on, you will likely want to experiment with several titles, from engineers to VPs.)
- Does their company use a tech stack that's compatible with your product or that creates problems your product addresses?
- Has their company posted job descriptions that indicate they may need your product?
- You're almost certainly using social media and participating in communities related to your product. Are people there posting about problems your product addresses?

From here, work with your sales team to construct a prospect list and identify or create key messages and content they can use with a Help First mindset.

Track the results of these outbound efforts and use that data to debug your messaging, hone your targeting, and improve your content. When you're just getting started, the more data you have, the better.

> TIP: LLMs are fantastic for identifying correlations.
> Feeding your spreadsheet of results along with call
> transcripts and email conversations into your LLM of
> choice can help you quickly identify patterns.

Once you have identified targets, messages, and tactics that work, you'll be ready to support a more scaled outbound motion. Let's discuss my favorite model next: an account-based approach to pipeline generation.

Driving pipeline through ABM

Account-based marketing (ABM) is one of the most effective tactics for generating high-value pipeline in developer-focused organizations. Instead of targeting developers en masse, ABM aligns marketing and sales efforts on a carefully curated list of target accounts. This approach allows you to focus your resources and create tailored campaigns that resonate deeply with your ideal customers.

ABM is especially relevant for developer products because their audiences are often niche and have specific needs that differ from the general population's. You are a great candidate for ABM if your product or service caters to specialized developer groups, such as data engineers at scale-ups or backend developers in fintech.

I happen to believe that all developer audiences are great targets for an ABM strategy, but they are particularly useful the more specialized your ICP is.

In contrast with traditional marketing approaches, ABM campaigns are much better researched, more focused, and have more potential for being cost-efficient. The flip side is that they are very time-consuming. You can't just decide you want to do ABM and be on your way tomorrow. It often takes weeks of preparation.

To start, you will work with your sales team (AEs and sales leadership, in particular) to build a list of target accounts. From there, you can work together to expand the list using ChatGPT: "Help me find a list of customers that resemble these, including industry type, company size, size of engineering team, and geographic location of headquarters."

You may want to further segment your ABM account list into tiers representing how much and how deeply you will research to support the outbound motion for each company:

- **High Priority (Tier 1):** custom pitch decks, account-specific landing pages, and workshops
- **Mid Priority (Tier 2):** industry-specific case studies, webinars, and semipersonalized outreach
- **Low Priority (Tier 3):** scalable tactics like newsletters and automated drip campaigns

Work with your SalesOps team to make sure this account list is represented in your CRM and that you will be able to measure the efficacy of your ABM tactics going forward.

Starting small with ABM

ABM itself is a strategy and set of tactics that is well-documented across our industry. Numerous blog posts, books, and videos round out the practice and offer useful ideas and ideas for executing your own. Vendors offer a host of very pricey ABM SaaS products, many of which are augmented by AI to provide better insight into your ICP and "look-alike" accounts that could be beneficial to you.

I encourage every marketer to dive deep into ABM. Even if you're just starting out, the principles can be adapted for your product or market stage.

Before implementing a full-scale ABM strategy, start small and build up the internal muscle as you go:

- Identify a customer that was successfully nurtured by your sales team into a closed-won deal. The best customers for ABM are "switchers," or companies that chose your product after previously selecting a competitor's.
- From there, build a list of 100 to 200 companies similar to that customer in terms of geography, size, and industry.
- Use tools like BuiltWith to narrow your list to customers with a similar tech stack to that of your successful closed-won customer.
- Now you should have a small, focused list of 25 to 100 accounts with whom you can begin to test an outbound motion: an initial email, an initial LinkedIn message, and so on.
- Create assets to support the initial ABM test (as discussed in the next section on implementing your ABM strategy).

Document everything: every email, every call, and so on. After a few weeks, take stock of your results. Did you see accounts progress through pipeline stages? How fast did they progress? Were there any commonalities in how they described their problem, your competitors, and your solution?

Sales and marketing need to be completely aligned and working very closely together every step of the way. Convene weekly meetings to review progress. Stay on top of it and keep the momentum going.

You have now built a solid base of intelligence and can make a decision:

- Was the experiment unsuccessful? If so, was it because the product didn't serve the market well enough? What features do you lack? What messaging deficiencies can you identify?
- If the experiment was successful and some of the accounts did progress far in your pipeline, can you build a larger list using expanded criteria? Or should you try a different market and repeat the same process?

You are looking for analysis that can help you decide whether to proceed with an expanded ABM motion.

Implementing your ABM strategy

From there, the most important component of an ABM strategy is research. The marketing team will compile a detailed report of each customer. You can start doing some of this with ChatGPT. For other things you may need to use Demandbase, 6sense, LinkedIn, Crunchbase, or other sales intelligence tools.

Here are some questions to answer for each account in your target list:

Account Information:

- What is the company's size (revenue, headcount, engineering team)?
- What industry and subindustry does the company operate in?
- Where is the company headquartered? Do they have multiple global offices?

Technology Stack:

- What tools, platforms, or technologies are they already using that align with your product?
- Are they known for early adoption of cutting-edge technology or for being conservative?

Business Goals and Challenges:

- What are the company's current initiatives or goals (e.g., digital transformation, cloud migration)?
- What pain points might your product solve for them?

Decision-Making Process:

- Who are the key decision makers and influencers in the buying process (e.g., VP of engineering, CTO, procurement)?
- How does the company typically evaluate and procure new technology?

Cultural and Strategic Insights:

- What is the company's public perception (e.g., developer-friendly, fast-moving startup, corporate giant)?
- What is their attitude toward open-source, SaaS, or PLG?

Competitive Position:

- Are they already using a competitor's product?
- Have they expressed dissatisfaction with current solutions in blog posts, job postings, or social media?

Start clustering these answers so that you have a good idea of the kind of content you need to build. Construct a content bill of materials and plow through it, customizing your first pitch deck, datasheet, and so forth, accordingly. Ideally you are not starting from scratch and are instead personalizing content based on the clustered answers.

Here are some additional tactics for your ABM motion, above and beyond tailored content and collateral:

- Industry-specific case studies and ROI calculators.
- Account-specific landing pages that reiterate key messages in outbound cadences and enable prospects to invite others in their organization to learn more about your company.
- Direct-mail campaigns. They're pricey, and harder in the remote- and hybrid-work era, but sending printed materials along with a swag gift is a nice way to ingratiate yourself with a prospect.
- Webinars for specific industries, with invitations included in outbound cadences.
- Workshops for specific customers. A sales engineer (or developer advocate) could host a two-to-three-hour workshop on an industry topic that your product or service addresses. Workshops are best done with a Help First mindset.

You will then work with your SDR team to build outbound cadences that are targeted for each customer. Again, ideally you are not starting from scratch each time and can personalize outbound emails.

Here are some metrics you will want to measure to help you debug your ABM motion:

- email open rates for accounts in your target account list
- if you are using webinar invites or ebook downloads in your outbound cadences, conversion from your target account list
- how much pipeline was generated from your target account list

Effective ABM is a team sport. You and your sales team—indeed your *entire* sales team and your *entire* marketing team—need to be perfectly aligned every step of the way.

Turbocharge ABM with LinkedIn

One controversial tactic that I love to experiment with is LinkedIn Ads as air cover. The hypothesis is that unless you are one of the BigTech companies with universal brand recognition, you will need to socialize your very existence with these prospects (who are by definition high-value, and therefore more discerning).

With LinkedIn, you can upload a list of customers and a list of job titles and the platform will build a list of people you can target with various types of ads. The list generated by LinkedIn needs to be at least three hundred people, but with a substantially large number of target customers, you won't have trouble meeting that threshold.

Two to three weeks before your SDRs begin account outreach, run LinkedIn ads that target your account list. Then, when the SDR does email them, there's a higher likelihood that your prospects will know about you and be willing to respond.

Be sure to build LinkedIn ads that are level-appropriate. You wouldn't target individual contributors or lead engineers with messaging about ROI. You'd focus on productivity or another value proposition true to your product. For a higher-level title, you can focus on business value messaging.

Driving pipeline through PLG (PQLs)

As we discussed in the previous chapter, product qualified leads (PQLs) are users who have had meaningful experience with your product and reached critical usage milestones that indicate they are ready to buy it or spend more. While PQLs are most often associated with PLG, they are excellent additions to an SLG motion when properly integrated into the sales context.

First, you want to identify core usage signals for PQLs. Not all these signals call for sales-team intervention. Indeed, some may call for automated nurture via the product itself. So it's up to you to determine whether a usage signal is indicative of someone who should be talking to a technical or sales resource on your team.

Here are some usage signals:

- completed a setup process
- imported a certain amount of data
- processed a certain amount of data
- created a specific artifact that your product allows for
- used a premium or advanced feature during a trial, or added it manually after becoming a paying customer

As mentioned in our PLG chapter, data collection and analysis is absolutely essential. Just as important is providing access to that data in the tools used by various roles in the nontechnical organization. Marketing people need to be able to segment users based on product-usage data in their MarTech tools, and salespeople need to be able to segment these users on the same data in their CRM or outbound sales tools.

> **TIP:** Ideally, you are creating automated triggers for these scenarios, perhaps in Slack, where everyone can see when a customer has passed one of these important thresholds.

From there you can tailor research depending on the scenarios indicated by your metric collection. For example,

- "I noticed you're near the limit of your data storage. Would you like to chat more about our enterprise plans and retention features?"
- "I love that you're using Feature FOO. This is already part of our enterprise package, and by moving to an annual commit, you should be able to save XX% per year and gain access to a bunch of other features of interest. Would you like to chat?"

Use your data collection to create archetypes of customers who could benefit from sales outreach, to tailor the outbound emails, and to measure the efficacy of the outreach.

TIP: These are your existing customers. You always want to avoid overly florid marketing or sales language, but you especially want to avoid it with your best customers.

As with all things, this is a team sport. Keep the feedback loop tight and fast. Make sure that the thresholds you're measuring are the right ones that indicate amenability to sales outreach, and that your approach in reaching out is working.

Driving pipeline through open-source

As we've discussed earlier, open-source is a powerful driver of grass-roots adoption and, if harnessed properly, can be a great way to generate pipeline. Remember that your open-source customers should always be treated as technical peers, not sales and marketing targets. Open-source products lend themselves well to community engagement, but the hard part remains getting a handle on who is using yours. After all, if someone clones and builds your repo from GitHub, you will have no idea who that individual is.

Here are some tactics for accumulating company names and email addresses from your open-source products:

- If your open-source project is on GitHub, tracking who has "starred" your project and using tools like Common Room to resolve them into actual people is one way to identify your open-source fans.
- Obviously, contributors to your project are great potential leads.
- Sometimes open-source projects "phone home" with anonymized telemetry. Depending on your project, you may be able to use anonymous data to determine industry type or solution.

- Include links to your paid product and newsletters in your GitHub README.
- Periodically publish a changelog email that does not include marketing puffery and is purely a list of bug fixes and new features. Open-source users may be more amenable to signing up for this than a newsletter.
- In any open-source command-line tools, notify the customer that they can sign up for the changelog to stay abreast of what's happening with the product.

You also want to clarify the benefits that open-source users will enjoy when they sign up for the paid product.

Partner-driven pipeline

Partner ecosystems can be effective pipeline generation tools if done properly, but they can also be massive time sinks if implemented poorly.

The term *partner* is itself often overloaded. It's worth clarifying the type of partner you want to target:

- **Technology partners:** These are sometimes called ISVs (independent software vendors). Collaborate with complementary tools and platforms. For example, if you're a database company, partnering with cloud infrastructure providers or analytics platforms can create natural integrations.
- **Channel partners:** These are resellers or distributors who sell your product as part of a larger solution.
- **Consulting partners:** These are sometimes called SIs, or systems integrators. Engage with consulting firms and systems integrators who recommend and implement your solution for their clients.
- **OEM partnerships:** Bundle your product as a feature within another vendor's offering.
- **Strategic alliances:** Collaborate with industry leaders to codevelop solutions or go to market together.

From a marketing perspective, there are multiple ways to support partners with comarketing motions:

- **Joint content:** a blog post, demo, or webinar that you collaborate on
- **Shared events:** cosponsor a conference, host joint workshops, run a hackathon together
- **Cross-promotion:** leverage one another's audiences to promote each other through your channels, including newsletters, website banners, and email marketing.

From a sales perspective, your sales team will often integrate to some degree with partner sales organizations to identify shared pipeline and opportunities.

We'll cover partner-led growth in greater detail in the next chapter.

How pipeline informs marketing strategy

We mentioned earlier how important it is for marketing leadership to see pipeline through to the end. Only then can we truly evaluate our work. When we examine pipeline, we may encounter issues that we can use to inform our marketing strategy.

If **pipeline growth is stagnant or declining**, the marketing team needs to analyze lead sources, messaging effectiveness, and target-audience segmentation. It's back to basics. Hopefully you have the instrumentation and metrics necessary in your marketing organization to analyze the customer journey and the relative quality of various marketing channels. For example, if webinars are producing junk leads and occupying sales time, you need to get into the numbers to determine if the problem is all webinars, a certain topic area, a certain format, and so on. This is why metrics *and* experimentation are so important, no matter what stage of organization you are in. Early-stage companies and large organizations alike need to be able to debug their processes.

Perhaps your problem is that **pipeline progression is slow**. Now you probably have a sales-enablement problem. You may need to improve your collateral, your competitive battle cards, or your objection-handling guides. Work with your sales team to understand what's happening. Listen in on calls (or listen to recordings) to see if certain objections keep coming up or if sales reps aren't knowledgeable about common customer questions. Get into the weeds to build the content and collateral they need to quickly follow up with answers.

Finally, maybe your problem is that **pipeline conversion is low**. Your leads are progressing into opportunities, and your opportunities are moving into proofs of concept, but they're simply not closing deals. Yes, it could be an errant sales team. But more likely the problem is far more fundamental. You may have a pricing issue or a product-market mismatch, or your buyer-engagement strategies may need reevaluation. It's time to get back to customer discovery and get some answers.

Remember, markets, companies, products, and entire industries are ever-changing. A year before I wrote this book, the AI industry was barely a thing. Now there are so many new AI tools for developers coming out every day that it's nearly impossible to keep up. Your company may also change. The brand perception of your company may diminish. Your products may be lapped by your competitors'. The entire conversation about your space may have changed.

Change is constant in our industry, and it's important as product marketing managers for us to constantly change with it. We should always value innovation over tradition.

LEAD QUALIFICATION AND STAGES

We talked earlier in this chapter about the lead-to-opportunity ratio. Now let's dive into how we evaluate and measure this ratio and the overall effectiveness of our marketing efforts.

Understanding MQLs and SQLs

Marketing-qualified leads (MQLs) and sales-qualified leads (SQLs) have long been the standard for lead qualification in B2B organizations.

- **MQLs:** Leads that meet predefined marketing criteria, such as engaging with content (e.g., downloading an ebook, attending a webinar) or meeting a demographic threshold (e.g., company size, industry). These leads are deemed worthy of further sales outreach.
- **SQLs:** Leads that the sales team has vetted and determined are ready for direct sales engagement. These leads are typically evaluated for budget, authority, need, and timeline (BANT criteria).

While MQLs and SQLs provide a basic structure for lead qualification, they often lead to inefficiencies, such as unqualified leads being passed to sales or valuable leads being overlooked due to rigid criteria.

Moving beyond MQLs and SQLs with stage-based qualification

Stage-based qualification offers a more granular, and less subjective, approach to qualified leads, allowing marketing and sales to be completely aligned on the effectiveness of marketing tactics as they pertain to pipeline generation.

Here are the generally accepted criteria for sales-qualification stages:

- **Stage 1, Discovery (S1):** The lead is in the awareness stage, engaging with content. Maybe the lead was acquired as a booth scan at a trade show. With S1 opportunities, we want to do more automated outreach until they progress on their own volition to a later stage.
- **Stage 2, Engagement (S2):** The lead shows active interest by engaging with more detailed assets, such as case studies or ROI calculators, or even signing up for the product after being prodded. From events, S2 opps can be booth scans who saw a demo and immediately expressed interest.

- **Stage 3, Qualification (S3):** The prospect showed clear buying intent through actions such as requesting a demo, responding to an email, or affirmatively booking a meeting.
- **Stage 4, Opportunity (S4):** The lead is actively engaged in the sales process by asking technical questions, watching a demo, asking about pricing, and perhaps wanting to broaden the discussion to include other teammates.

How marketing supports each qualification stage

From a marketing point of view, you want to support your sales team as they progress leads through each qualification stage. The more support you provide in terms of content and training, the more likely your lead-to-opportunity ratio will turn in your favor.

Here are some ways marketing can support each stage:

- **S1:** Marketing continues to build and distribute high-quality, technically deep content that builds awareness and interest.
- **S2:** Prod leads to engage with more content by using email marketing; invitations to webinars; and microsites, demos, and videos to give prospects more information about your products or services.
- **S3:** Provide tools and training for the sales team, including battle cards and competitive analysis (which we discussed in the product marketing chapter); FAQs; and feature walk-throughs that don't require nontechnical members of your organization to install and use the product.
- **S4:** Build case studies and other customer references. Consider writing security, SOC2, and other regulatory compliance content as required by your industry. Proactively remove objections and accelerate deals.

Debugging the qualification funnel for better marketing

Even with a well-defined stage-based qualification process, break-downs can occur. Here's how to debug common issues at each stage and ensure your pipeline remains healthy and effective.

S1: Low engagement at the top of funnel

Your problem is that few leads are entering the discovery stage, or engagement with top-of-funnel content is low.

- Start by reassessing your content strategy. What might be great for SEO or broad industry knowledge may be insufficient for customers who already have the broad knowledge and now want to go deeper. Make sure your content addresses the pain points of your ICP.
- Diversify your distribution channels. Consider newsletter sponsorship, active participation in developer forums and social media, and content syndication to reach a more varied and prequalified audience.
- As always, continue to monitor and test your entire web presence, including calls to action and website and documentation structure.

S2: Low conversion to the engagement stage

Your problem is that leads are engaging with initial content but are not progressing to deeper engagement (e.g., webinars, product trials).

- Introduce personalization and tailor outreach based on product-usage or website-engagement data. If a customer spent time on a particular solution page for an industry, identify them as someone interested in content for that industry.
- Audit your midfunnel content and ensure that your case studies, feature walk-throughs, and documentation are addressing the needs your customers have during product evaluation.

S3: Low conversion from engagement to qualification

Your problem is that leads that should otherwise be obvious opportunities are not demonstrating clear buying intent or being flagged for sales outreach.

- Tighten alignment with sales. Review the criteria that define S3 leads and make sure that your sales team has the training and product knowledge they require.
- Audit your decision-maker content and develop collateral like ROI calculators or competitor-comparison guides that encourage movement to qualification.

S4: High drop-off between qualification and opportunity

Your leads are flagged as qualified, but they are not progressing to active sales opportunities.

- Once again, tighten alignment with sales and make sure that everyone has the training and product knowledge they require.
- Revisit your ICP. Remember, what once worked is not always guaranteed to continue to work. Industries evolve, business priorities change, technologies come and go.
- Make sure you've built the battle cards, internal security and compliance materials, and other content necessary to proactively handle objections

And if there's a general slowdown in pipeline progression, consider adding time-sensitive offers or gated content (such as exclusive webinars) that add a sense of urgency for customers.

WHEN SLG OUTPACES PLG

SLG often outpaces PLG in terms of performance—or vice versa. Make sure to diagnose the problem objectively and not jump straight to blame. When salespeople talk directly to customers, they are able to ask follow-up questions in real time, read their body language, and pick up on other subtle clues. It's natural for those high-fidelity channels to yield more feedback and result in real-time adjustments in process. This is obviously harder to do with a digital motion that relies on a predefined algorithm.

I'll add one more thing: when your PLG motion performs well for quite some time but then starts to level off or drop, you will be glad that you didn't wait too long to layer in an SLG motion. Think of SLG as your forward-deployed intelligence team. Used properly, sales does not simply drive revenue. They can also help you better define your entire PLG motion.

GTM is a team sport.

Pricing

The first and most obvious problem may be that your pricing is off for your PLG motion. You may be charging too much, or the dimensions around which you're pricing may be too confusing or require too much cognitive load for the self-service customer. Adjusting pricing is easier said than done, but if your customer interviews and research indicate that this is a major reason why your PLG metrics are lagging, you have to bite the bullet.

Selection bias

The second reason is a natural consequence of the difference between the SLG and PLG motions. With SLG, your sales team is targeting customers they know to be qualified. They're using tools like LinkedIn, Common Room, and Koala to selectively choose customers well defined within your ideal customer profile. This selection bias results in better SLG performance.

In contrast, PLG attracts a broad base of prospects, many of whom will disqualify themselves for any number of reasons, many of whom are simply lookie-loos with no intention of buying, and many of whom were not qualified to begin with.

Use the data you've obtained from your SLG success stories to hone your ideal customer profile and your audience targeting. Your sales team may be automatically disqualifying cohorts of customers from learned experience while your PLG motion still considers them potential customers. Hopefully you've maintained a healthy two-way dialogue between marketing and sales so that you can adjust in real time. But in case you haven't, there's no time like the present to get started.

Sales guidance

Your sales team works hand in hand with prospects to identify the right features based on customer qualities, handle objections that arise from numerous stakeholders throughout the process, and tell an engaging story about the company and product. It's natural for this process to evolve over time within the sales organization, and even from one account executive to another.

Staying in close contact with sales, participating in their staff meetings, listening to closed-won and closed-lost debriefs, and using sales team feedback to guide sales collateral generation all help you gather the same intelligence in real time to adjust your PLG motion.

Maybe your PLG motion needs to offer a security whitepaper, an onboarding guide, or some other piece of content regularly during product adoption or when the customer achieves a milestone in product usage. Or perhaps you need to build new features to help the self-service customer accomplish something that all SLG customers have had white-glove help completing.

Regardless, the clues your sales team offers will help you adjust your PLG motion.

METRICS AND EVALUATING SUCCESS

Modern sales and marketing is built on data. Having a good way of collecting and analyzing sales and marketing data will help you optimize your funnel for growth. Here are some common sales metrics, and ways that marketing can help diagnose and improve them:

Pipeline Coverage

*   **What it measures:** the ratio of pipeline value to sales quota
*   **Lesson for marketing:** Insufficient pipeline coverage indicates a need for more or better-qualified leads. Marketing should focus on campaigns that target high-value accounts or optimize lead scoring criteria.
*   **How marketing supports:** Build targeted ABM campaigns or run demand-generation efforts that focus on high-propensity segments.

Win Rate

*   **What it measures:** the percentage of qualified leads that convert to closed deals
*   **Lesson for marketing:** A low win rate can signal misalignment between messaging and customer expectations or poor ICP targeting.
*   **How marketing supports:** Revisit ICP definitions, refine positioning, and provide sales-enablement materials like objection-handling guides and competitor comparisons.

Sales Cycle Length

*   **What it measures:** the average time it takes to close a deal
*   **Lesson for marketing:** Long sales cycles can indicate that leads lack urgency or that the sales process is too complex.
*   **How marketing supports:** Develop content that accelerates decision making, such as ROI calculators, case studies, and technical deep dives.

Lead-to-Opportunity Conversion Rate

- **What it measures:** the percentage of leads that move from qualified to sales opportunity
- **Lesson for marketing:** A low conversion rate suggests poor lead quality or inadequate nurturing.
- **How marketing supports:** Optimize nurture sequences and ensure sales outreach is tailored with high-value touchpoints.

Customer Acquisition Cost (CAC)

- **What it measures:** the cost of acquiring a new customer
- **Lesson for marketing:** High CAC can indicate inefficient allocation of resources or underperforming channels.
- **How marketing supports:** Focus on more cost-effective acquisition strategies, like PLG or organic content, and refine targeting to reduce waste.

Churn Rate

- **What it measures:** the percentage of customers who stop using the product after a specific time
- **Lesson for marketing:** High churn often reflects mismatched expectations set during the sales process.
- **How marketing supports:** Provide clear, consistent messaging during acquisition and support postsale education to reinforce value.

CONTINUOUS EVALUATION AND IMPROVEMENT

Sales and marketing is not a "set it and forget it" dynamic. You need to constantly work at getting and staying aligned.

Be present for one another. Leaders should attend one another's staff meetings. Marketing should always be invited to sales meetings, and vice versa. Hold weekly or biweekly leadership syncs to review performance metrics, share feedback, and discuss upcoming initiatives.

Use data to guide your discussions. Break down problems into metrics and work together on debugging those metrics. Use metrics to gauge the effectiveness of solutions.

Don't lock information in a silo. Create channels (Slack, etc.) to communicate fearlessly with one another. Share wins and losses, lessons learned, and tactics employed for each. Run postmortems on every account until you have so many that you can't keep up. Encourage SDRs to share winning outbound cadences that resulted in meetings.

Iterate on content together. Playbooks, slide decks, datasheets. Get feedback early and often.

Encourage experimentation. Try new things. Be bold. The businesses of tomorrow invented new ways of doing things.

PULLING IT ALL TOGETHER INTO A SINGLE CAMPAIGN MOTION

We've discussed many tactics in this book, from content to product-led growth to sales-led growth. When all these pieces are assembled, magic happens.

For example, let's say we wanted to run a campaign that drove the "attach rate" of a product in our portfolio. An "attach" is when a good customer elects to use a complementary product. For a database, it could mean encouraging a large storage customer to start using a feature called read replicas, which replicates read-only copies of the database in real-time to data centers around the world, reducing latency and increasing availability. In the database world, read replicas are often a high-value feature that is typically priced such that each read replica is considered its own database. Thus, when a customer adds one read replica, it effectively results in two databases, which doubles your revenue.

To execute this campaign, we need to pull together everything we've covered in this book:

- Metrics, including product usage metrics, that help us identify the best candidates for our campaign. In the case of a read replica upsell campaign, we would look for customers who have a high propensity to buy, high storage levels, and a large number of database reads from around the world. If you were running more of a greenfield campaign instead of an upsell campaign, you would translate your market segmentation and ideal customer profile into a LinkedIn or Google target audience.

- Content, including documentation. What kind of problems would a customer who needs read replicas face? What information do they require about the feature? Having a good combination of video content, blog posts, and documentation will help you execute your campaign across multiple channels.

- Product-led upsells. Using the data we've gathered, we should pop alerts or banners subtly within the product to encourage users to learn more about the feature. You will need to work closely with your product team to enable this, which may require substantial lead time.

- Sales-led upsells (or, more accurately, customer success–led). We need to build resources for the sales team, including sample outbound emails and LinkedIn messages, datasheets or technical materials, and landing pages to direct customers for more information. Usually, this will be run by your customer success team and framed as offering a "performance optimization session" to help customers get the most out of your product.

- Email campaign. Whenever I run a sales or customer success–led 1:1 outreach project, I like to "pre-load" customers with information via email. That way, they're socialized to the subject before they get a meeting request.

- Ad campaign. In some cases, you may want to run a LinkedIn campaign that targets the campaign cohort with information about the product or feature.

Of course, it may seem like magic to an outsider when it all works. But to marketing professionals, this is the circus we love to be a part of.

SUMMARY

Sales-led growth (SLG) is a go-to-market strategy that relies on a dedicated sales team to acquire, expand, and retain customers. Unlike product-led growth (PLG), which emphasizes self-service, SLG thrives in complex sales cycles, high-contract-value deals, and enterprise customers with multiple stakeholders. Effective SLG requires strong alignment between marketing, product, and sales to drive pipeline, convert leads, and optimize the buying experience.

- **Marketing exists to support sales.** Revenue is our top-line metric in marketing, and our mission is to help our sales team close deals.
- **SLG is ideal for complex products and high-value enterprise customers.** When onboarding requires hand-holding, legal/security approvals, or deep customization, a sales team is necessary to guide the process.
- **Sales and marketing must be tightly aligned.** Marketing provides sales-enablement materials, content, and messaging to ensure AEs, SDRs, and SEs effectively communicate product value.
- **Pipeline generation requires both inbound and outbound efforts.** Inbound marketing (content, community, events) generates leads, while outbound sales (cold outreach, ABM, and PQL-driven sales) proactively targets high-value accounts.
- **Lead qualification ensures sales prioritizes the right opportunities.** MQLs, SQLs, and product-qualified leads (PQLs) must be clearly defined, with sales and marketing teams aligned on conversion metrics.

- **Account-based marketing (ABM) is a powerful SLG tool.** Targeted campaigns tailored to key accounts help increase engagement, accelerate deal cycles, and improve conversion rates.
- **Continuous iteration and feedback between sales and marketing is essential.** Data-driven insights, regular syncs, and shared learnings optimize SLG motions, refine messaging, and improve sales efficiency.

SLG is critical for companies targeting enterprise customers or complex sales cycles. A well-executed SLG strategy, combined with marketing-driven demand generation and tight sales alignment, creates a sustainable engine for long-term growth.

CHAPTER 22

Partner-Led Growth

There are multiple ways to amplify your go-to-market strategy through partners. Before you embark on any of these partner strategies, it's important to understand what you hope to gain. Here are a handful of objectives you may consider. A typical organization could use any combination of these to justify a partner program:

- greater brand awareness and distribution by drafting off a larger partner's complementary user base
- improved pipeline generation via a partner's sales and go-to-market engine
- improved pipeline velocity through a partner's sales-engineering and customer-success organization
- faster and deeper adoption by customers through a partner's technical expertise

There are a few partner strategies that assist with these goals:

- **Technology partners:** working with other companies to build a more comprehensive solution for your customers
- **Cloud partners:** plugging into the hyperscaler marketplace (e.g., Amazon Web Services, Microsoft Azure, Google Cloud Platform, etc.)
- **Channel partners:** co-selling with partner sales organizations
- **Strategic partners:** comarketing with complementary partners
- **Integration partners:** building a network of consulting partners to help your customers build with your product

Each of these approaches requires substantial investment to execute properly. But remember, the operative word is *amplification*. Partner programs will not save a mortally wounded business or failed product. If you have your go-to-market engine working well, layering in a partner program can help accelerate your growth. Tread lightly and test small initiatives before scaling rapidly.

With that as background, let's dive into each strategy in more detail, and highlight the aspects of developer marketing that make them even more challenging . . . and impactful.

TECHNOLOGY PARTNERS

Typically, you'll look at the landscape of technology at your disposal and find not only products to build on, but also products that complement your strategic goals. You may find a database vendor with a unique capability or pricing model that helps you build a fast and cost-effective product. You may find a data provider that gives your customers valuable information within your product. You may find an API that helps you deliver functionality your customers have been asking for.

Negotiating favorable terms

A key component of establishing technology partnerships is negotiating favorable pricing. This includes volume discounts, comarketing credits, or even free-usage tiers for joint go-to-market campaigns. Many technology providers are open to discounted or trial-based pricing if they see potential in a long-term relationship or exposure to a broader user base.

Beyond pricing: Collaboration opportunities

But the true value of a technology partnership goes far beyond pricing. Collaborating with your partner opens doors to comarketing and codevelopment opportunities that can drive awareness, adoption, and innovation. Consider these initiatives:

- **Joint content:** Write a joint blog post, whitepaper, or case study that showcases how your product integrates with the partner's technology. Focus on a compelling use case that benefits both your user bases, such as solving a common developer pain point or optimizing workflows.
- **Webinars and events:** Cohost a webinar or an event to educate users about the combined value of your partnership. For example, demonstrate a seamless integration in action or provide step-by-step guidance on implementing the solution.
- **Developer tools and SDKs:** Collaborate on building developer tools, SDKs, or plug-ins that make it easier for customers to integrate your joint technologies. This can significantly reduce friction for users and accelerate adoption.
- **Mutual ecosystem promotion:** Cross-promote your products in each other's partner ecosystems or marketplaces. For instance, if your partner has a popular app store or integration marketplace, being featured prominently can expose your product to thousands of potential users.

- **Lead sharing and account mapping:** Share sales leads and customer accounts that could benefit from the combined solution. Use tools like Crossbeam or Reveal to map accounts and identify overlap, ensuring that your partnership directly supports business growth.
- **Certification and training:** Partner on creating certification programs or training materials to help developers and customers get up to speed with your combined technologies. This reinforces customer confidence and positions both of you as thought leaders in the space.
- **Custom integration:** Work together to develop unique features or integrations that exclusively serve customers using both your platforms. This can differentiate your partnership from competitors' and create stickiness among shared customers.

Measuring success

Like any partnership, success should be measured to ensure the collaboration delivers value for both sides. Here are some important numbers to track:

- **Adoption metrics:** Monitor how many customers are using the joint integration or functionality and whether it's driving increased usage of your product.
- **Revenue impact:** Track upsell opportunities or net-new customers resulting from the partnership.
- **Marketing reach:** Measure the effectiveness of comarketing campaigns, including webinar attendance, blog post traffic, or ecosystem engagement.
- **Customer satisfaction:** Survey shared customers to understand how the partnership has improved their experience or addressed specific pain points.

CLOUD PARTNERS

The major cloud hyperscalers—Amazon Web Services (AWS), Microsoft Azure, and Google Cloud Platform (GCP)—have well-curated and actively managed partner programs. These programs are designed to help customers find technology solutions that complement their cloud services, while also enabling partners to reach broader audiences through established ecosystems.

A key advantage of partnering with these hyperscalers is access to their marketplaces, where customers can discover, procure, and deploy third-party solutions directly. Many enterprise customers have annual spend commitments (often referred to as "enterprise discount programs" or "cloud commitments") with their cloud provider. These commitments typically require customers to consume a set amount of cloud services over the course of a year. By integrating your product into a hyperscaler's marketplace, customers can apply their committed spend to your product. This reduces procurement friction by allowing them to transact through the cloud provider's existing billing and invoicing systems, eliminating the need to onboard a new vendor into their accounts-payable workflows.

While the benefits of marketplace integration are clear, the process can require significant effort. Integration typically involves technical work to meet marketplace requirements, adherence to compliance and legal standards, and creating product-specific documentation for customers. Despite these challenges, the payoff is worth it for many SaaS and software providers, as enterprise customers often insist on being able to transact through their cloud provider.

Leveraging hyperscalers' sales teams

Beyond marketplace integration, working with a hyperscaler's sales organization offers tremendous upside. Cloud providers incentivize their account executives and sales teams to drive customer adoption of cloud services, including those sold through their marketplaces. When your product is listed and transacted through the marketplace, it can contribute toward the AE's quota attainment. This alignment can turn the hyperscaler's sales team into an extension of your own, helping you scale through co-selling motions.

It's important to note that quota policies and incentive structures often change annually, and sometimes even quarterly. Staying on top of these changes is critical to ensuring your product remains an attractive option for hyperscaler sales teams to recommend. Building strong relationships with the partner sales organization and participating in quarterly business reviews (QBRs) with your cloud partner can help you maintain visibility and alignment with their sales objectives.

Marketing with cloud partners

Product marketing is typically responsible for setting up the proper verbiage and catalog content for inclusion in the hyperscaler's marketplace. It can be tempting to copy and paste your standard positioning and messaging brief.

Instead, take the time to write new content, build new architecture diagrams, and customize existing slide decks to really make the value proposition of the joint partnership sing.

In all likelihood, you will be the smaller of the two partners. As such, the onus is on you to tell the story well. AWS isn't going to spend a single minute writing your marketing copy for you. You need to help them help you by explaining why joint customers should care about you in addition to the hyperscaler, and also why the hyperscaler benefits by working with you.

Benefits of working with cloud partners

While cloud-marketplace integration and collaboration with hyperscaler sales teams requires up-front investment, the long-term benefits can be substantial. By reducing procurement friction, accessing vast customer bases, and aligning with the incentives of cloud-provider sales organizations, your business can significantly amplify its reach and revenue potential. In the next section, we'll explore specific strategies and tactics for coordinating with partner sales teams on co-selling motions to maximize these opportunities.

CHANNEL PARTNERS (AND CO-SELLING)

Co-selling is one of the most powerful strategies you can employ when working with partners, particularly large organizations like cloud providers, technology vendors, and system integrators. When done effectively, co-selling aligns your sales efforts with those of your partner's sales teams, unlocking access to new customers, amplifying your reach, and driving revenue growth. However, co-selling is not without its challenges. Success requires careful planning, coordination, and ongoing relationship management across both sales organizations.

Co-selling enables your organization to tap into a partner's existing customer relationships, leveraging their credibility and established presence to accelerate deal cycles. Partner sales teams can help you several ways:

Identify opportunities.

Partners often have deep insight into their customers' needs and priorities, which can help identify new opportunities for your product or service.

Build trust.

Selling alongside a trusted partner reduces friction with customers, who are often more willing to engage when a known vendor advocates for your solution.

Navigate procurement processes.

Partnering with larger sales teams, especially those from cloud providers, can streamline procurement by enabling transactions through familiar systems (e.g., AWS Marketplace or Azure Marketplace).

Building (and maintaining) alignment with your partner

To maximize the potential of a co-selling relationship, you need to expend significant up-front and continuing effort on alignment between organizations. If you're the smaller of the partners in the relationship, you'll also need to do quite a bit of evangelism—and, depending on how small you are, that could be a deal-breaker. In fact, in my experience, I've found that if you find yourself in a situation where every meeting with the partner begins with a recitation of what your company does and other background information, you may actually be too early to benefit from a co-selling relationship.

Nevertheless, here are some elements of a successful co-selling strategy:

Start with messaging alignment on goals and incentives.

Ensure that your product or service aligns with your partner's strategic goals and the incentives of their sales teams. In one case, I had a marketing organization that worked with a partner sales organization whose goals focused on "consumption" of their services. Sales reps whose new and existing accounts drove more consumption would meet quota. So, I ensured that our product-level messaging was all about how we helped drive consumption and "new opportunities" for the partner. All our normal top-line messaging was secondary or even tertiary when it came to working with this partner, and I ensured that our slides, datasheets, and landing pages reflected their messaging.

Create collateral that is tailored and on message.

The goal is to develop materials for the partner's sales teams to use and incorporate. In one case, I noticed that a partner organization we worked with used Microsoft software. I begrudgingly downloaded Microsoft PowerPoint and Microsoft Word and built materials in .ppt and .docx formats that could be added to the partner's sales-enablement portal.

Designate a point person for the relationship.

Someone senior in your organization needs to be dedicated to serving the partner's needs; representing their requirements with marketing, product, and sales; and championing the relationship with senior management. For early-stage startups, it's better to start by assigning a senior member of the exec team to be this point person. For larger companies, you'll obviously have a dedicated partner organization.

Plan accounts jointly.

Sales teams will need to get together to identify shared customers and potential accounts where co-selling makes sense. From a marketing perspective, it's useful to join these meetings or at least review the output, as product marketing collateral and go-to-market initiatives may arise from them.

Establish a regular communication cadence.

Biweekly or monthly meetings are necessary to stay aligned. While I am nearly always a proponent of asynchronous messaging channels like Slack and GDocs, in the case of two *companies* working together, nothing beats a live conversation. If possible and if the partnership is critical, plan on periodic in-person alignment.

Measuring co-selling success

Ultimately, it's all about revenue, and that takes time to prove out. But there are some metrics to help you evaluate the effectiveness of your co-selling efforts more immediately:

- **Number of joint opportunities:** Measure how many opportunities are being generated through co-selling motions.
- **Pipeline contribution:** Track the dollar value of pipeline created through co-selling partnerships.

- **Conversion rates:** Analyze the win rate for deals involving co-selling versus deals without partner involvement.
- **Partner engagement:** Monitor how frequently your partner's sales team engages with your product or solution (e.g., training participation, joint calls).

STRATEGIC PARTNERS (AND COMARKETING)

Strategic partnerships are formed with companies whose products or services complement your offering. These partnerships aim to create a win-win scenario where both parties benefit by addressing broader customer needs, extending reach, and enhancing market positioning. Strategic partners are often chosen because their customer base overlaps with yours, or their product fills a gap that strengthens your value proposition.

These are the goals of strategic partnerships:

- **Expand your market reach.** Tap into a partner's existing customer base to introduce your product to them. For example, you may want to be included on a list of partners in the Grafana or Vercel websites.
- **Enhance the value of your product.** Combine the strengths of your and your partner's products to deliver a more comprehensive solution. For example, your database product and another company's user-management system may be perfect fits to help web developers build new applications.
- **Amplify your marketing impact.** This is more of a short-term play, where you share resources, audiences, and platforms to comarket and colaunch a marketing initiative or product introduction, building joint campaigns, events, and content. A good example is when several startups join together to execute a "launch week," amplifying one another and growing the audience for the launch.

Many of the same principles of alignment for co-selling apply to comarketing. You'll want to make sure you have aligned on goals and incentives. You'll want to create complementary messaging. You'll want to make sure you have a coordinated plan and regular communication.

But with comarketing, the onus will largely fall on you as a marketing organization, as opposed to sales. Here are some quick tips to make marketing alignment easier:

- Set clear success metrics between organizations, such as content engagement, social sharing, and event attendance.
- Synchronize attribution mechanisms, UTM parameters, and other metrics so that you have clean data on the efficacy of the partnership.
- Coordinate branding and landing pages to perpetuate a similar look and feel.
- Follow all legal practices on sharing contacts and user information, and make sure these agreements are finalized up front.
- Promote the partnership publicly through a series of blog posts, webinars, social media assets, and so on.
- Align on joint case studies and showcase the partnership and the "better together" nature of the customer's achievements with both products.

With this information, you'll be able to track your core metrics:

- leads generated through comarketing campaigns
- joint deals closed or influenced by the partnership
- growth in shared customer accounts
- revenue attributed to the partnership

INTEGRATION PARTNERS

Integration partners play a critical role in helping customers adopt and maximize the value of your product. In particular, developer-focused products often require the customer to take significant steps to maximize value. Integration partners are consulting firms, systems integrators, or third-party developers who specialize in implementing, customizing, and integrating your solution into complex customer environments.

There are three main goals of integration partnerships:

- **Drive customer success.** Ensure customers can implement your product effectively and realize its full potential.
- **Expand market coverage.** Integration partners are a great way to gain a foothold in new regions or markets, prove the viability of your product there, and gather requirements from new types of customers.
- **Accelerate adoption.** Lower the barrier for customers and reduce the time to adoption by enabling integration partners to build a corpus of repeatable knowledge, templates, and other content.

Integration partners pose unique challenges, however. Remember, everyone you recommend, whether it's in a "catalog" on your website or via communication with a customer, is someone you are vouching for. I have seen situations where integration partners represent themselves poorly and are unable to complete a project for a customer. Because the integration partner was in a catalog on my company's website, my company drew the ire of the customer, who went public with their dissatisfaction.

Here are some tips to help you get the most out of an integration partnership:

- **Training and certification:** Develop a robust training program to ensure the partner can deliver on their (and your) promise, and vet them financially and morally for their ability to follow through. Note that this process alone may be prohibitive for most companies. We didn't launch training and certification until year four of Amazon Web Services, for example.
- **Programmatic branding:** Build a program brand ("CompanyX Certified") that enables partners to demonstrate that they are aligned with you.

- **Joint customer engagement and case studies:** Feature integration partners where applicable in all case studies, and ensure that your sales and customer-success teams are involved in customer planning and engagement.

The last thing to mention is **revenue sharing**. At some point, integration partners will expect and/or demand revenue share. This isn't something to be afraid of, particularly if they bring in enough new business to make it worth your while. Just know that when you embark on a crawl-walk-run strategy with partnerships, the walk-to-run stage will come at you fast with integration partners if they find success quickly. Be prepared for this conversation.

SUMMARY

Technology partnerships are more than just tactical integrations. They are strategic alliances that can amplify your product's reach, utility, and value. By choosing the right partners and leveraging comarketing and codevelopment opportunities, you can create an ecosystem that benefits your customers, strengthens your market position, and drives growth for both parties.

However, just because you *can* enter into a partnership doesn't mean you *should*. A partnership takes time. If you're an early-stage startup, that may be a luxury you don't have or one that takes away from critical progress in other areas. If you are just getting started, working with partners can be fraught with enough details to not be worth it.

If you are a later-stage company, you may have different considerations. Launching a partner program or engaging with one of the hyperscalers may be a level of investment that simply doesn't pencil out at your current average deal size, or could even stall your momentum.

There are no hard-and-fast rules about partnerships. In the famous Jeff Bezos "two-way door" framework, in which some decisions are worth deliberating over (a "one-way door" in which the decision is difficult to reverse) and others are not (a "two-way door" in which the decision can be easily reversed), partnerships are one-way doors. Even if you can terminate a partnership, the amount of time invested and wasted may be mortal for a young or fast-growing company.

Tread carefully. Deliberate well before proceeding.

CHAPTER 23

Public Relations and Analyst Relations for Developer Products

Public relations (PR) and analyst relations (AR) play a crucial role in how developer-focused companies establish credibility, gain media attention, and position themselves within industry conversations as leaders. Unlike traditional consumer or B2B software, developer products rarely receive standalone media coverage. This means you need to think strategically about how you engage with journalists, influencers, and analysts, and identify the bigger narrative while building long-term relationships that can pay off in the end.

PUBLIC RELATIONS

To repeat: It's rare for developer products to warrant standalone coverage from media outlets. If you want to get written up for a product launch or partnership, unless you are at Google, OpenAI, or another BigTech firm, your best bet is to focus on smaller influencers, bloggers, YouTubers, and the like who will want to cover your news. Even if you *do* work for a BigTech company, the chance of you getting journalists to cover your *product news* is low. If you seek coverage in larger outlets, you need to up-level your story and become *part* of a larger narrative.

Finding the bigger story

At the time this book went to print, nearly every major journalist who covers tech was focused on the artificial intelligence beat. Different journalists care about different topics. For example, within AI, there are multiple angles:

*   doomsday AI scenarios
*   AI displacing workers
*   AI in health care
*   how to use ChatGPT
*   and so on . . .

As you read coverage of these articles, whether it's AI doomerism or the effect of AI in the labor market, you should take note of the broader story. Journalists are people, and journalists—at least the ones we're referring to in this chapter—work for large corporations (which, in the United States, are people too). What this means is that a given journalist working a specific beat and covering a certain story will bring to bear their personal biases as well as those of their employer.

Business trade publications will report a story from the perspective of the employer, while a more traditional newspaper may report the story from the perspective of its effect on the local community. To the extent that there are technology reporters covering pure technology, they may cover the story from a very slightly more technical angle.

Your mission is to understand the story, and to identify how your product or company fits into that narrative.

Let's say you were the CMO of a popular vector-database company. *The Wall Street Journal* isn't going to cover the landscape of databases, much less the landscape of vector databases. The *Journal* is a right-leaning, employer-focused publication. They will cover AI from the perspective of businesses finding cost and labor efficiencies. Your best bet as a vector-database company is to take one of your case-study wins and place it with the journalist. The company featured in your case study will talk about their business successes, and in the process, they will mention your company.

Here are some examples of how you can make developer products newsworthy:

- **Align with industry trends.** Your product should fit within a larger movement (e.g., DevOps, cloud native, AI/ML).
- **Leverage current narratives.** If AI is trending, frame your product within the AI landscape (e.g., "The AI-powered DevOps tool").
- **Use data as PR fuel.** Use internal usage stats, developer behavior trends, or industry research to pitch stories.
- **Share customer stories.** Highlight compelling case studies that demonstrate real-world value.
- **Initiate partnerships and integrations.** Announcements involving major tech players can elevate credibility.
- **Launch industry initiatives.** If you're a larger organization, you can gather a group of companies working together on an industrywide initiative that addresses a problem or trend.
- **Share fundraising or acquisition news.** If you've recently raised money or acquired another company, this is news. But don't let the news devolve into "Company X raised Y million dollars." Make sure you are positioning your overarching strategic objective: "Company X raised $40M from the investor who backed Dropbox to help build the AI platform for everyone."

Positioning your company within a larger narrative is critical to gaining traction in media and analyst reports.

Stories are relationships

Journalists get hundreds of pitches per week. In my early days at Microsoft, I took a media training course with our external PR counsel. The first exercise during this course was to take all the technology press releases from *that day* and pretend we were a journalist looking for a story to cover. In one day—and keep in mind, this was 1998!—there were *hundreds* of technology press releases.

Journalists don't pore through press releases. They rely on ongoing relationships with key professionals to surface important stories and trends. These professionals understand what journalists are covering and help match them to sources who can provide background, texture, and quotes for the stories they plan to write. PR professionals also track the sweet spots (and biases) of each journalist so that when a company positions its story, it matches the journalist's preferences.

When you hire a PR professional or agency, expect them to bridge the gap between the stories the journalists in their network are covering and the news you may have. Your PR professional will help identify what you need to flesh out your story—case studies or partnerships, for example—because, again, most journalists will not cover straight-up technology news.

Relationships are based on trust

Trust is the foundation of any successful engagement with journalists. If you burn that trust by embellishing, misleading, or outright lying, you won't just lose coverage; you'll damage your credibility for good. The best PR professionals and spokespeople understand that their job isn't to "sell" a story but to help journalists tell theirs.

Here's how to build trust with journalists:

- **Be truthful, even when the truth isn't flattering.** Journalists can smell spin from a mile away. If your company is struggling with adoption or a launch didn't go as planned, acknowledge it and provide real context about what's happening. A measured, honest response always plays better than corporate double-speak. If you try to gloss over bad news, they will find out anyway and the result will be worse.

- **Be direct.** Answer the question asked, not the one you wish was asked. Nothing frustrates journalists more than getting vague, dodgy, or robotic responses. If you don't know the answer, say so. If you can't comment on something, say why. Respect their time, and they'll respect yours.

- **Don't embellish.** Avoid exaggerated claims, unverified statistics, or grand pronouncements about how your company is "revolutionizing" an industry. If your product is truly good, you don't need hyperbole. Stick to real, verifiable value. For example, customer stories, hard data, and tangible results.

- **Never, ever lie.** Lying to a journalist, even on minor details, is career suicide. If you get caught (and you will), you'll never be trusted again. If you don't have an answer, it's always better to say, "I'll get back to you" than to make something up.

- **Provide value, not just pitches.** The best relationships with journalists are two-way streets. Instead of always pushing your own announcements, send them useful insights, trends, or expert analysis they might find valuable. Sometimes the best and most impactful long-term conversations with journalists won't even involve you or your company. You're just providing trustworthy background information. When they see you as a helpful, knowledgeable source, they'll be more likely to cover your stories in the future.

Journalists aren't just looking for news; they're looking for reliable sources. If they trust you to be honest, responsive, and knowledgeable, they'll keep coming back. The best media coverage doesn't come from one-off pitches, it comes from long-term relationships built on credibility.

Developer-focused media

We've spoken earlier about influencers and community leaders. The principles of building and maintaining relationships over time, keeping track of hot-button topics, and building on past content released by the influencer still apply.

If you want pure technology coverage, your best bet will be to build an influencer program and take it every bit as seriously as you do *The Wall Street Journal* or *TechCrunch.*

In addition to connecting with influencers, which we covered earlier, make sure you're engaging on social media, particularly Reddit, LinkedIn, and possibly Twitter, as well as the various Discord and Slack communities that apply to you. That will help you stay top of mind where the technical conversations are happening. Supabase is exceptional with their social media presence, and while their meme-centric approach isn't for every business, their prolific content posting and engagement is.

ANALYST RELATIONS

Most startups will not need analyst relations, and most large organizations will have dedicated analyst-relation organizations. Put simply, analysts are industry experts who look at a technology space from a high level and then engage with top customers—the customers you want—to understand their business problems, use cases, and needs.

How analysts work

Think of an industry analyst as a trusted advisor to you and to the customers you want. Customers ask analysts for advice on big buying decisions and the technology landscape. Suppose you work for a company building an AI platform. You live, breathe, and sleep AI platforms. You know every one of your competitors and you have put in the work (maybe with the help of this book!) to define your ICP. You do this because it is your job.

But your customers have a different job. Let's say you are trying to win a deal with a large online gambling company. They are not in the AI-platform business. They are in the business of finding new players, getting a handle on fraud and abuse, ensuring they identify problem-gambler behavior, and building new features and games. They may work with an analyst who can give them a quick overview of the AI-platform landscape and give them ideas on how each option can best help them achieve their goals.

The analyst's job, then, is to understand *your* job and simultaneously understand *your prospective customer's* job.

I've seen and heard many reductive statements about industry analysts. ("They're pay to play" being the most common.) But in reality, your prospective customers trust the relationship they've built with industry analysts. It's not uncommon to hear the C-suite of a large company say something to the effect of, "We're a Gartner shop." They know Gartner will give them sound advice.

With that in mind, your mission is to know all the analysts who cover your technology space and to build relationships with them. Now, if you're an early-stage startup, I strongly advise against procuring a formal analyst contract (their sales teams will pester you about this incessantly though!). It can cost upwards of USD 125,000 or more, and there simply is no ROI for an early-stage startup. Send analysts emails and links to docs, keep them apprised of your launches, and do this all yourself for the time being.

Remember, you want to tell a compelling story without overpromising. Analysts value clarity, differentiation, and proof. They aren't impressed by hype, and if you misrepresent what your product can do, it will backfire. Instead, follow these rules:

- **Frame your strengths honestly.** Maybe you're not a leader yet, but you're pushing the category forward.
- **Back up claims with real-world data.** Share customer-adoption numbers, performance metrics, and honest feature and product comparisons as appropriate.
- **Stay engaged.** Regular analyst briefings (even before you think you need them) keep you in the loop.

It's different, of course, as you grow. You'll need dedicated analyst-relations people, and you will want to stay on top of the hot topics and technology areas each analyst cares about.

Navigating analyst reports

If you're selling into enterprises, analysts like Gartner, Forrester, IDC, and so on can make or break your credibility. Many large buyers trust their reports to shape procurement decisions, which means getting included, or even just mentioned, can give your company serious validation.

Each firm has its own methodology, but the high-level takeaway is the same: analysts group vendors into categories based on their capabilities and market presence. Gartner's Magic Quadrant ranks companies in four buckets (Leaders, Challengers, Visionaries, Niche Players). Forrester's Wave is more of a sliding scale of performance. Either way, being listed in these reports puts you on enterprise buyers' radar.

The goal isn't just to get ranked, but also to be part of the conversation. Analysts influence enterprise-buying decisions, and even a footnote in a major report can open doors.

SUMMARY

PR and AR aren't about instant wins. They're about building long-term credibility and influence with people essential to spreading the word about your company and product. To work with press and analysts, your best marketing asset is trust.

- Position your company within a larger industry narrative rather than pushing pure product news.
- Build relationships with journalists rather than blasting them with generic press releases.
- Prioritize accuracy and transparency over spin.
- If you are looking for broad awareness, engaging with influencers and developer communities is a more effective tactic than traditional PR.
- If you are looking for specific credibility and social proof, then relying on press and analysts is a better bet for you.

Section 3

MARKETING LEADERSHIP

CHAPTER 24

Building and Managing Your Marketing Budget

Building and managing a marketing budget is both art and science. The science follows well-established metrics for SaaS or software products, while the art determines the "marketing mix," or the ratio of budget to different programs. Science gives you some informed guard-rails, while art gives you freedom to experiment and try new tactics for old strategies.

START WITH YOUR METRICS

Your top-line business metrics should dictate your ultimate budget number. As we have discussed numerous times, I'm a firm believer that marketing and sales should share the same metric: revenue. All the marketing qualified leads (MQLs), sales qualified leads (SQLs), and so forth are good waypoints and leading indicators to determine progress toward metrics, but marketing teams should carry a revenue number and work in concert with sales.

Typically, to meet a revenue number you need to see a 3–4X pipeline number. In other words, for every dollar in revenue, you need to generate three to four dollars in pipeline. If you're carrying a $5 million revenue target, you need to generate $15 to $20 million in pipeline.

> Pipeline-revenue target should be 3–4X your revenue target.

Marketing should be responsible for a percentage of that pipeline-revenue target, while sales (and outbound tactics) should be responsible for the rest. In early-stage companies, marketing will be responsible for less of it, as the sales team will also be running experiments and should shoulder some of the burden. As you progress through later stages of growth, the entire go-to-market operation should be more efficient, and marketing should be able to take on more of the pipeline target.

- **Early-stage startups:** Marketing should be responsible for 50%–60% of the pipeline-revenue target.
- **Established scale-ups:** Marketing should be responsible for 70% of the pipeline-revenue target.
- **Well-established companies:** Marketing should be responsible for 80% of the pipeline-revenue target.

From here, you need to determine the ratio of marketing spend to pipeline. If you're an early-stage company, you will likely see a lower ratio, as you'll need to spend more money to determine what works. If you're a later-stage company, you've likely run a bunch of experiments and determined the channels most effective for you and your ideal customer profile, meaning you can be more efficient with your marketing spend (thus lowering your cost of acquisition, or CAC).

The following are general guidelines, and you need to work across your organization to determine what is best for you:

- **Early-stage startups:** Allocate ⅕ to ⅛ of pipeline target to marketing budget.
- **Established scale-ups:** Allocate ¹⁄₁₂ of pipeline target to marketing budget.
- **Well-established companies:** Allocate ¹⁄₁₅ of pipeline target to marketing budget.

So, pulling it all together, if you're an early-stage company looking to generate $5 million in revenue, you will need to generate $15 million in pipeline. Marketing should be responsible for 60 percent of that target, or $9 million in pipeline. At a ratio of 5:1, marketing should be budgeting somewhere between $1.8 million and $2 million for various tactics and experiments.

ALLOCATING YOUR BUDGET TO DIFFERENT PROGRAMS

From here, you need to allocate your budget. Every company and market is different. Some companies can drive tens of millions of dollars in inbound pipeline through product-led growth. Other companies have products and markets where that's impossible. Sometimes you'll find that events work exceptionally well in terms of driving pipeline, other times you'll find that social media engagement works best, and still other times you'll find that paid acquisition works. In the early days you want to experiment, and over time you'll find the right marketing mix for your budget and needs.

Early-stage startups need to experiment across the spectrum of options. You need to gather data and make future decisions based on that data. The biggest mistakes I've made in early-stage companies is getting comfortable with a tactic that's working instead of proactively disrupting myself and trying new experiments in parallel.

At one company, I relied for far too long on content to drive leads. At another company, I left ads running far beyond their expiration date. You have to stay on top of it and mix it up before things get stale.

Later-stage companies have a good idea of which tactics work and which do not. You can run experiments to see if old tactics that didn't work are suddenly panning out, or you can focus your efforts on optimizing the ones that are working. (Hint: Go with the latter, no matter how much of a creative genius you think you are. Don't swim upstream!)

Regardless, with your data on which tactics are most effective, you can work backwards into a good marketing mix.

ITERATING ON YOUR BUDGET AND PLANNING FOR NEXT YEAR

We covered metrics and measurement early in this book for a reason: being able to measure progress and effectiveness of programs in real time is essential for a modern marketing engine. And now we come full circle.

Being able to ascribe wins (leads, revenue, etc.) to specific tactics enables you to be an effective and discriminating marketing manager. You can now assign marketing budget (if necessary) to tactics you know will work for you.

Ideally, you are finding ways to use people to scale your marketing efforts. I've always believed people are infinitely more scalable than programs. A human—a thinking, actual flesh-and-blood human—can deliver output that far outstrips that of other paid channels. A great developer advocate can write the right content, connect with the right people in the community, and speak at the right events using their judgment and knowledge of your market, and they will almost certainly outperform your paid channels.

Thus, as you identify hypotheses and test them, you can determine where best to apply marketing and personnel budget most effectively.

SUMMARY

Your budget practices are the culmination of everything in this book up to now. Your ability to experiment and identify the marketing tactics that work most effectively, your ability to optimize "free" channels, your ability to hire and motivate your team to fill in the go-to-market gaps, and so on, all determine how efficient your marketing expenditures will end up being.

Speaking of finding efficiency, let's spend the next chapter looking into the myriad ways artificial intelligence can help you maximize your marketing budget and effort.

CHAPTER 25

AI and Marketing

It's difficult to be a nontechnical person working in a technical industry. I've always held firm that in order to market developer-focused products, you need to have at least a modicum of background as a developer. I started my career as a software engineer and nearly (not quite!) received a degree in computer science. Not only is the organization and algorithmic thinking of software development useful in building and running marketing programs, but the ability to write code has become essential in an AI-driven world.

In the last week, as I've been writing this chapter, I've had to . . .

- build an ETL script in Python to move data from one system, normalize and transform it, and put it in another system.
- modify a website so that it rendered data stored in Airtable.
- build a landing page for a campaign.
- write a script to turn links in a newsletter into short links with UTM parameters.

These are tasks one would normally assign to a junior member of the team. But as a leader you are faced with two truths. First, team sizes are smaller than they used to be. Second, the larger your team gets, the slower it gets. Being comfortable with code is the difference between moving fast and . . . not. As I'll explain in my next chapter, senior leaders on the team should be careful not to get too much in the weeds of execution. At the same time, being comfortable with code, and insisting your team build their skills so they're comfortable with it too, is almost certainly a net positive when marketing to developers.

As is the case with every industry, AI is transforming marketing at a rapid pace. From automating content creation to providing deep customer insights, the most successful marketers today will be those who embrace AI as a copilot rather than fear it as a disruptor.

STAYING ON TREND

In order to plug yourself into the latest technology waves, you must, even as a marketer, be willing to go deep into the weeds. I'm not saying you need to contribute code to the project. But the early days of any technology are full of hype, some warranted and some not.

As I've emphasized throughout this book, crafting a strong narrative for developer products requires a fealty to truth, honesty, and integrity. Developers can sniff BS a mile away. They can tell when something is overpromised and will be underdelivered.

Thus, you must be able to understand the technology deeply and find the narrative throughline that speaks truthfully to the benefits developers will enjoy when using your product.

The best way to thoroughly understand a technology is to use it. It's fairly trivial to use a tool like Lovable or Bolt, or, if you're more comfortable with code, Cursor or GitHub Copilot, to write an application that takes advantage of an LLM. In a weekend, you can build a simple application to ingest data from a source of your choice, store it in a database like Supabase, use an LLM to categorize it, and write a Next.js application to display it. You can then layer in your own product or service and start learning how it fits into the overall landscape.

By actually using these technologies, you may not be able to express the insights you gain with the eloquence of a seasoned engineer. But as you write down your thoughts and impressions, you'll be able to ask more intelligent questions of your engineering team. You'll learn the vocabulary engineers use when approaching similar problems. You'll get a feel for the landscape of complementary and competitive tools to your own. You'll get immersed in the communities where these technologies are discussed daily. And you'll earn immeasurable street cred with your product and engineering team.

The work you put in during this discovery stage will set you apart from all your peers.

You will be "the CMO who codes."

AI TOOLS SAVE THE DAY

The good news is that the barrier to software development has been completely eradicated. Tools like Cursor and Lovable can imbue mere mortals with software development superpowers. Does your website stink? Does your web developer move too slow?

Through a combination of Cursor, Vercel, and Supabase, you can have a fully functional website live in a weekend. Tools like v0 can turn a Figma diagram into functioning code in minutes. It has never been easier to become a developer and optimize your entire marketing process. It's about time we held technical marketers to a high standard of technical aptitude.

You can use AI-powered ad targeting such as Meta Advantage+ to reach your target audience with compelling creative that drives conversion.

AI-powered social-listening tools like Brandwatch help you surface conversations that matter to you and your business.

Sales enablement gets the AI makeover with tools like Gong and Drift to surface the critical moments out of sales calls and help customers connect with your sales team faster.

AI tools help you do your job better and faster.

AI FOR CUSTOMER INSIGHTS

You can now use AI to understand trends and hidden motivations in large datasets. You can easily find patterns in product-usage data. You can automatically segment data into actionable cohorts. You can quickly combine, reformat, transform, and normalize massive datasets, or have AI write a Python script to do it for you.

Already, we're seeing the rise of AI SDRs who can do warmoutbound prospecting easily (cold-outbound is still, at this moment, the exclusive domain of humans). We're seeing ABM tools enriched by AI-driven insights into companies and customers, and ABM itself becoming much more approachable thanks to AI-driven research. Vertical marketing is enhanced when AI can provide data and background information on entire industries and the web of competitive and complementary partnerships therein.

AI-driven content helps personalize all customer touchpoints. You can set up email personalization in minutes and send content that is tailored for how prospects have interacted with your website and product.

In this modern AI-driven world, everything moves lightning fast. You don't have time to ask a developer to put work in their queue or take on mundane tasks yourself. You need to seize the moment and take advantage of AI tools and a technical background to solve problems.

AI PERSONALIZATION

AI enables developer marketers to deliver tailored, relevant experiences at scale without manually segmenting audiences. Instead of treating all developers the same, AI can personalize content, recommendations, and outreach based on real-time behavior, product usage, and context. Used thoughtfully, AI personalization enhances the developer experience without feeling intrusive or gimmicky.

Here are some ways to use AI for personalization:

- **Dynamic website content:** Show different docs, case studies, or tutorials based on a visitor's industry, past engagement, or known tech stack.
- **AI-powered email personalization:** Adjust email subject lines, content, and recommendations based on past interactions with your product or website.
- **Feature and API recommendations:** Suggest relevant integrations, settings, or optimizations based on real-time usage data.
- **Intelligent onboarding:** Adapt the onboarding flow based on a developer's experience level and previous actions.
- **Chatbots:** Build domain-specific LLMs and serve fresh, accurate data based on your corpus of presales and technical support information.
- **Smarter retargeting ads:** Serve hyper-relevant ads that reflect where a developer left off in their journey (e.g., API documentation views but no sign-up).

AI removes friction, boosts engagement, and helps developers discover value faster, but it must be used carefully. Developers dislike intrusive marketing, so personalization should feel helpful, not manipulative. Keep it subtle, focus on real utility, and always allow an opt-out.

AI FOR SEO

We've talked about the death knell of SEO in previous chapters. But there are some great tools, such as Clearscope, for identifying keywords and writing content to rank for those keywords.

But while AI is killing SEO, it's also great for programmatic SEO.

You can build pages that render information assisted by AI APIs. For example, you can render a page for every Postgres error, and within the page you can use AI to write the contents for you dynamically: What is the error, how do you fix it, give me sample code, etc.

Instead of manually creating content for thousands of database errors, you can dynamically generate pages that provide AI-curated solutions. However, these pages must be fact-checked and structured well to avoid becoming low-quality AI spam.

What used to take an army of writers now can be accomplished with one proofreader and an OpenAI subscription.

SUMMARY

The technology industry has fully succumbed to AI. There's no sense fighting it. Find ways to wield it effectively and with integrity. Here's a checklist to follow as your AI-in-marketing playbook:

- Identify where AI can automate vs. where human creativity is essential.
- Use AI for content generation, but always fact-check before publishing.
- Leverage AI-driven customer insights to refine targeting.
- Experiment with AI-powered personalization for emails, landing pages, and sales enablement.
- Invest in AI tools that improve efficiency without sacrificing quality.
- Treat AI as an augmentation, not a replacement for real marketing strategy.

Ultimately, as marketing leaders we need to respond to rapid changes in our profession. AI is a tectonic shift, and it is up to each of us individually to evolve our skills accordingly and lead with confidence.

CHAPTER 26

Managing a High-Performing Organization

Building a high-functioning marketing and developer relations team will directly impact the success of the entire company and every department within it. High-performing teams deliver on strategic goals without sacrificing creativity or speed. Let's dive into some aspects of leading a marketing organization with the functional makeup I've described throughout this book.

HOW YOUR ROLE CHANGES AS YOU MOVE UP

As you progress in your career, you will have more opportunities to lead teams and grow others. If you're content being an individual contributor, that's great . . . but you will still be expected to use your wisdom and experience to lead others. You'll just be relieved of the burden of people management. Leadership is the natural consequence of wisdom earned and gained. Embrace it.

But leadership is different at each level. At each level, you have increasing responsibility over the execution of and results from the marketing plan, and you have an **expanding scope of both responsibility and visibility.** Let's look at both those things across the classic leadership levels of line manager, director, and vice president/C-level.

Individual contributors

In his SaaStr Annual 2021 conference talk, the inimitable Dave Kellogg outlined the four pillars of B2B SaaS marketing. It's worth seeking out and watching in its entirety, but to summarize, he described marketing as encompassing four skill sets:

- Product marketing: launch, go-to-market, messaging, and content
- Demand generation: digital growth, programs, and events
- Communication, storytelling, and brand
- Sales development, inbound pipeline, and outbound pipeline

The thesis of this portion of his talk was that it's impossible to find a marketer who excels at both of the first two skills. Typically, a marketer exhibits mastery of only one or the other. And no marketer excels at all four. Most excel at one—or possibly two—of the four categories, and merely have sufficient background in the others.

Kellogg went on to assign up to five points for each category. "God doesn't make five-five marketers," he said, meaning there are no people on the earth (me included) who are exceptional at both product marketing and demand generation.

Instead of attempting to be all things to everyone, identify your own path. Each of these four areas is undergoing massive transformation as AI improves productivity and efficiency everywhere. AI has democratized and accelerated product development so much that it's incredibly hard for product marketing to find positioning differentiation and impactful messaging amid a crowded field of look-alikes and imitators. What used to be true about digital growth, SEO, and paid ads has now been upended by AI and LLMs. Storytelling and brand are as important as ever, but the battle for space in a prospect's mind is now waged against a sludge of AI-generated content. Sales development itself has been turned upside down by AI SDRs and other "bots" that supplement or take over your outbound motion entirely. You may be thinking that the future is bleak. On the contrary, there is tremendous opportunity to build on the foundations of the past and write the future.

Companies have a need for different skills at different stages of growth. An early-stage company probably needs significant product marketing and growth expertise. Meanwhile, later-stage companies likely need more help with storytelling and brand . . . and growth. (You can never outrun the need to keep growing!)

The path you select early in your career is the one you opt to master. That path will dictate the types of companies best suited for your expertise as you grow into leadership roles.

Line manager

Managers of other marketing professionals have a responsibility to execute the tactical requirements necessary for a marketing plan to succeed. As you begin to feel comfortable in the role, you may be asked to help put together the plan for a component of the overall go-to-market strategy. But by and large, at this level your responsibility is to execute the plan and hold your team accountable for doing what's asked of them.

In addition, your scope of visibility is more local. You understand your team and their strengths and weaknesses. You may pop up from time to time and read industry articles and internalize broader macro trends. These may or may not inform your tactical execution, but for the most part, you are an observer of the industry.

Here are a few additional tips:

- **Develop your team members.** Your primary responsibility is to provide mentorship, set personal development goals, and coach team members on handling more responsibility.

- **Start dipping your toes into strategy.** Provide feedback to directors on their plans, giving them insight into what does or doesn't work. Have positive discussions with them about the decisions they've made, and try to understand their consideration process.
- **Build relationships across the organization.** Use your position to meet other line managers and directors across the company and build your network internally. Consider doing this externally as well, meeting other line managers in other companies, including competitors. Over time you will learn to appreciate the effort you put into building your network at this stage of your career. It will not only be the source of every job you have for the remainder of your career, but also the source of your recruiting and team-building efforts going forward.

Director of Marketing

At the director level, you are responsible for a team of managers who themselves are each responsible for a team of individual contributors. At this scope, you are responsible for taking the broader marketing plan and breaking it down into logical executional units. You build a hiring plan to make sure you have the skills and background on your team to deliver results for your tactical plan.

Directors are the workhorses of most organizations. They take fancy plans from the C-suite and turn them into full-on projects. They are organized, disciplined, and mature, and they know how to get the most out of people. The first thing I advise newly minted vice presidents of marketing to do is find themselves a director they can trust. Whenever I've taken a new C-level job, I brought along a line manager I felt was ready for director-level responsibility, gave them the promotion and title they'd been looking for, and turned them loose.

As a director, you will often have company-level scope. You are making connections across the company with other directors, looking for ways to inject your team into appropriate workstreams, and making commitments with other company leaders. From time to time you may work on initiatives with directors at other companies—be they customers, partners, or even competitors. Your maturity and project management skills will earn you credibility with these other companies, and as a result they will be even more confident about working with yours.

Let me offer more advice:

- **Your biggest area of focus will be team building.** You need to learn not only how to design and implement processes that can efficiently execute the plan, but also how to determine when and whom to hire to execute the plan. Getting good at recruiting, hiring, and coaching is essential, and picking up this skill prepares you more than anything for the next level.
- **Internalize and operationalize the VP's vision.** Turn the marketing plan into actionable steps. Use it as an opportunity to mind-meld with your VP and start building your own playbook for when it's your time to take on the big chair.
- **Mentor and plan for your succession.** One day you will get tapped for the VP job. Or you will find another company that will pay you more, give you more responsibility, help you learn a new technology, or any combination thereof. Leave your current company in good shape by identifying and grooming your successor. Put yourself in great shape for your next company by identifying people you want to bring with you.

VP of Marketing/CMO

Ah, the big chair. You've finally arrived as a marketing manager and you want to make your stamp on the world. You're going to do everything differently.

The problem is that VPs don't "do" much. Your job is to understand more than do. Let me explain. As a VP of marketing, it is now your job to understand your company's business situation. It is your job to understand how your sales and product teams work, and to build effective partnerships across the organization. It is your job to understand how your project team delivers on its roadmap. It is your job to understand the competitive landscape and predict how other companies will respond to your initiatives.

Your job is to soak it all in and understand the full game board.

Only then do you get to write a plan. But even then, your job isn't to "do" anything in the plan. Your job is to hire directors, line managers, and individual contributors who can execute your plan. Your job is to . . .

- communicate your plan to everyone on your team so that they can internalize and understand it for themselves. You need to be a great storyteller, not only to customers and the market, but also internally.
- build strong cross-organizational relationships so that you can connect workstreams in other parts of the company to the work directors and line managers on your team are doing.
- set the metrics and goals that provide people with instant feedback on the plan's execution.
- bake in big bets. Always have a set of initiatives in progress that are high risk, high reward. Your team will appreciate the opportunity to stretch their creative muscles, and you'll have a great chance to see who on your team steps up to lead.
- manage performance and results across the team.
- teach and coach people to do the work the way you and the business need it done.
- go deep and understand how every workstream is connected, ensuring that communication flows within your team and to and from other teams.
- develop your successor. Plan for your replacement. Remember, even if you are involuntarily removed from the company, the success of the company will reflect back on your résumé.
- be a "shit umbrella" and maintain a strong sense of order amid all the chaos, unreasonable expectations, and change within your company and in the industry. Give your team the gift of your serenity and confidence.

The biggest mistake vice presidents can make is to roll up their sleeves and do the day-to-day work instead of delegating. I say this having worked for several startups that were underfunded and under-staffed where, yes, I had to jump in and do the work. But this was always counterproductive and is more indicative of a bad job situation than a good practice. If you're in a C-level job where your company can't (or won't let you) hire the people necessary to execute your plan, you need to find a new company. Your team *wants* the opportunity to learn from you and do the work themselves. They *need* you to trust and believe in them.

The bottom line is that you are responsible for the strategic plan *and its results.* If your strategic plan is a miss, and sales and marketing misses its numbers, you can expect to be shown the door. The marketing team will get fired first, and the sales team usually a quarter or so after that.

Vice presidents also have greater visibility into industry movements. You can seek out partnerships, customers, and comarketing opportunities that will help you execute your plan. (Indeed, these may be critical components of your plan!) You need to see and account for trends and patterns across the entire industry.

Advice for the C-suite

I have more advice for VPs and CMOs than I can fit in this book. I've made a ton of mistakes, and you will too. I've been fired before, and you probably will be too. That's all part of the game. Here's some additional advice for you:

- **Never stop managing up and across.** Master internal politics and keep a pulse on how things are changing. If your product team is struggling, you are going to feel its effects (and probably get blamed for stagnant growth). You need to know ahead of time so you can adjust the plan. If your sales team is going to add several account executives or move to a new comp model or switch to a territory model, this will affect you and you need to adjust for it.

- **Thought leadership is critical.** Don't stop speaking at conferences and getting your name out there. For far too long in my career, I "let my work speak for me." Well, my work doesn't have a mouth. It can't speak. It just sits there on a corporate GDrive. I'm the one with the mouth and the platform, and it's my responsibility to make sure my colleagues in the industry know the good work I do.
- **Thought leadership also matters internally.** Pepper your Slack with messages about critical wins. Overcommunicate. Shock and awe your company into appreciating the effort and results marketing is delivering every day.
- **Reinvent yourself constantly.** The technology industry changes rapidly. In my thirty-five years in the business, I've never seen it change faster than it's changing now. Stay close to the technology and be ever mindful of these shifts. I spoke about being wary of intruding on junior members of the teams and doing their work for them. But that doesn't mean you shouldn't go deep and learn how things work.

I always think about Microsoft CEO Satya Nadella when I think about this evolution and growth in responsibility and visibility. Nadella started as a product manager in what would eventually become the Server and Tools division at Microsoft, working for legendary leaders like Paul Maritz and Bob Muglia. Over time, Nadella's responsibilities grew, but so did his visibility into industry partnerships, competitors, and direction. Today, Nadella is arguably one of the single most important figures in the evolution of artificial intelligence, which is arguably the single most important technological movement since the growth of the internet in the 1990s. Nadella has consistently managed his performance, scope, and visibility extraordinarily well.

Across Lake Washington in Seattle, Amazon CEO Andy Jassy had a similar trajectory, working as an individual contributor, learning how to build and ship products, serving as Jeff Bezos's technical advisor, and getting a front-row seat to Amazon's early rocket-ship trajectory. Eventually Jassy helped create and run all of Amazon Web Services, one of the turning points in the history of our industry. There isn't a day that goes by that I don't take something I learned working directly for Andy and apply it to a current business problem. Jassy was tapped as Bezos's successor to lead Amazon, a position where he exerts considerable influence over not just our industry, but also consumer buying patterns, the environmental impact of capitalism as a whole, and the economic impact driven by his massive workforce.

PICKING THE RIGHT BOSS

As a marketing leader, your boss can make or break your experience and effectiveness in the role. A good boss will support your initiatives, advocate for marketing within the broader organization, and provide clarity around expectations and strategic priorities. Here are some key attributes to look for in a boss:

- **Alignment on vision and strategy:** A great boss shares your vision for how marketing should function and understands its critical role in driving business outcomes. During interviews, ask questions about their expectations for marketing and their perspective on how it integrates with sales, product, and customer success.
- **Support for marketing as a strategic function:** Look for a leader who understands marketing is more than just "leads and logos." They should value positioning, messaging, brand building, and thought leadership alongside tactical activities like demand generation.
- **Advocacy and influence:** Your boss should be a strong advocate for marketing within the C-suite. They should champion your team's efforts, secure budget and resources, and help resolve conflicts or misalignments with other departments.
- **Clarity in communication:** A good boss provides clear goals, communicates their expectations openly, and ensures alignment on company objectives. They should set the guardrails for success while giving you autonomy to execute.

- **Willingness to invest in growth:** Marketing is ever-evolving, especially in developer-focused organizations. A great boss will support ongoing learning for you and your team, whether through conferences, training, or experimenting with new tools and strategies.
- **Emotional intelligence and empathy:** A supportive boss understands the challenges of marketing leadership, from hitting aggressive pipeline targets to managing cross-functional friction. They should provide a safe space for discussing challenges and help you problem-solve effectively.
- **Openness to feedback:** Your boss should value your expertise and be open to pushback when needed. Look for someone who respects your insights and sees your relationship as a partnership.

BUILDING THE TEAM

Building a high-performing marketing team is one of your most critical responsibilities as a leader. The team you assemble will determine how well you can execute on your vision, achieve your goals, and adapt to challenges.

How to get started

As I alluded to earlier, depending on the size of your organization, your starting point will differ.

- Early-stage companies should focus on hiring a polymath marketing manager who can write content, maintain social and blog channels, run events, and do everything short of perhaps writing technical demos or materials. You're looking for a nontechnical marketing manager who has the desire and aptitude to pick up enough technical skills over time that they can grow as the company grows.

- Later-stage or established companies looking to build a developer-facing marketing program should hire an experienced developer advocate to help them understand the best content and community channels for the product or service.

Regardless of company size, the final components to add to the team are events marketing and community managers. Until the scope and number of deliverables get too involved or large, it doesn't make sense to layer in these roles when others on the team can take on those responsibilities.

Developer advocacy requires special attention

When you're looking to hire developer advocates, start by building a list of people you would like to target in the industry. When we were rebooting developer relations at Microsoft, we started by writing down everyone we wanted to work with. Then we systematically went about recruiting them to the team. Sometimes we would convince people to join, other times we couldn't, but we had a solid understanding of the archetype we were seeking and we found suitable alternatives.

It's important to keep in mind that not all developer advocates are equal. As we discussed in the developer advocacy chapter, some specialize in content while others specialize in community or events. Be aware of who you are recruiting, what their strengths are, and how they will fit into the team you are building.

Interview process

One of the more disturbing aspects of this recent turn of events as a result of AI upending the technology workforce is an almost sadistic need of employers and recruiters to put interview candidates through the wringer. This could include a prolonged wait before responses. It could also be a tendency to schedule more than five, sometimes up to ten interviews for a candidate. It could also include asking the candidate to do a take-home assignment.

Ultimately, you will make mistakes when hiring. You will hire people who aren't a good cultural fit. You will hire people who interview well, but do not execute the job very well. You will hire people who find greener pastures very quickly. And you will hire people who simply have no idea what they're doing.

Every manager knows this is a fact of life.

You cannot let the fear of hiring the wrong person cloud your judgment or create an unwelcoming interview atmosphere. If there's one thing I would implore other marketing leaders, it's to treat marketing candidates as if they will one day be your boss. In fact, it's very likely in our very small industry that a person you are interviewing and treating poorly today will one day be the person you're calling upon for a job. None of us is so important that we are entitled to treat people poorly.

So with that I'm going to offer you several tips—call them guidelines, if you will—for conducting sane and respectful interviews:

- You do not need to give every applicant an explanation for passing on their candidacy.
- You do, however, owe anyone who did a live interview the benefit of a response if you decline to proceed.
- Take-home assignments are fair requests, but you must pay people for their time. If you ask them to spend two hours preparing a presentation, demo, or other material, you must pay them for two hours of time.
- Take-home assignments may not be used unless you compensate a candidate. If you ask a developer advocate candidate to write a demo of your product as part of the interview process, you can only use the demo if you've paid them for their time and have their permission. (Also, why are you using someone's work if you're not willing to hire them?)

MANAGING THE TEAM

Over the years, through multiple management-training programs and increasingly large and complex teams, I've developed a management philosophy that I'll share with you here. The best of these management courses, taught by former Twitter CEO Dick Costolo, was a transformative moment for me as a leader. Much of that course, plus lessons from some of the many amazing managers I've worked for—Marie Huwe, Jana Messerschmidt, Jeff Sandquist, and Andy Jassy chief among them—are listed below.

As always, I encourage managers to develop their own frameworks and philosophies, and to share them broadly. Despite the numerous books, courses, and podcasts offering management advice, the fact remains that it is inordinately difficult to "teach" management because management is all about *imperfect people* leading *more imperfect people*.

To quote an old friend, "To thine own self be true." Listen, absorb, and adapt management advice to you, your personality, and your circumstances.

Management is a journey, not a destination. It's an ongoing process of learning, adapting, and growing, both for you and your team. As you refine your approach, remember that the best managers lead with integrity, prioritize their team's success, and never stop seeking ways to improve. Whether you're guiding a team of three or three hundred, the principles of good management remain the same: respect, clarity, trust, and accountability.

Be a good person

Physicians have "Do no harm." Managers should have "Be a good person." Every single one of us bears the scars of bad people doing badly at management. Thus, my first principle is to always be a good person.

- **Offer respect and behave with integrity.** People want to work for someone they respect, not a jerk. Employees often go above and beyond for their manager, not just the job itself.

- **Lead by example.** As every parent knows all too well, your behavior sets the tone for the entire team. Be transparent and deliberate in how you respond to situations. Your team is always watching—and they will emulate you.
- **Deliver and receive feedback often.** Deliver praise in public often, and offer constructive criticism in private as soon as possible after the observed behavior you want to correct. Address issues promptly and clearly. Without feedback, neither you nor your team can improve.

Start there, and you'll be halfway to being a great manager.

Listen before acting

I operate very simply when making decisions. Sometimes these decisions are straightforward: a new strategy or plan. Sometimes they are complex: termination or layoffs. In all cases, I follow these three steps, always in this order. You'd be surprised how many people screw up the order of operations.

1. **Truly listen.** Don't just wait for your turn to talk. Listen to the other party and gather as much information as you need from multiple sources. In fact, someone may have a good point during one of these listening sessions, and you may be tempted to make a decision or tell the person something to the effect of, "That's a great idea. Let me think about it, but I'm leaning toward going in that direction." **Do not do this.** Listen to everyone first before communicating *any* kind of decision.
2. **Decide.** You've listened. Now make an informed, deliberate decision.
3. **Communicate swiftly.** There should be minimal delay between the moment you decide and the time you choose to communicate. If it involves a reorg, promotion, layoff, or termination, you need to overcommunicate. If you are delivering tough news—perhaps someone didn't get a

promotion they really wanted—you can listen empatheti-
cally, but you cannot be swayed to change your decision or
equivocate. The time for that is over, and if you do so now,
you cede all future authority to make any decision.

Manage your time effectively

Many managers are taught to spend an equal amount of time with all
the people on their team. Wrong. Managers should be spending 80
percent or more of their time with their top performers.

Avoid wasting time with low performers. They cannot be "saved."
They need to be shown the door. Low performers aren't bad people.
They are simply people in the wrong situation for them. I've had to let
people go who went on to do great things in a different line of work or
industry.

Sometimes you'll have low performers who are going through personal difficulties. We are all human. And humans have ill children,
aging parents, difficult relationships, and health issues. Compassion
and empathy are always warranted. But you also have a responsibility
to your company and team. These are the hardest situations to manage, and the only advice I can give is that you're not alone. Reach out to
your management or a peer for advice.

There's one corollary to this that's worth pointing out. On your
team, you will have people who are reasonably competent performers. That's OK. Every team needs "utility infielders." These are people
who will do the grunt work, never complain, and be totally content.
Your one-on-ones with them will usually be drama free and actually
interesting.

There's also a form of low performer that's insidious and that you
should have the confidence to face. These are former all-stars who are
now poor performers. They may even be disgruntled and angry over
something that has nothing to do with you.

Some of my past roles were at companies that had recently IPOed.
There were several people on these teams who were either "resting
and vesting," or simply no longer gave a you-know-what. As someone
who had not been part of the journey to the IPO, it was exceedingly

frustrating to deal with these people who had built up so much social capital in the companies where I now worked. But they consistently brought the energy down on the team.

At great political cost, I had no choice but to let these people go. It is sometimes very difficult to be in these situations. As a manager, you will be held accountable for your and your team's performance no matter what you do. And if you have people actively diminishing the team's performance, your decision will be clear.

Delivering effective feedback

Feedback is the lifeblood of high-performing teams. Without it, progress stalls, misunderstandings fester, and teams miss out on opportunities for growth. But feedback is only effective when delivered properly, and that means mastering the art of giving and receiving it.

Here's my advice on how to give feedback:

1. **Be timely and specific.** Whether positive or constructive, feedback should be delivered as close to the moment as possible. General feedback like "good job" lacks impact. Instead, highlight specific actions or behaviors: "Your detailed analysis in today's presentation clarified the strategy and helped the team make a better decision."

2. **Separate feedback from emotions.** Particularly with negative feedback, ensure you deliver it calmly, professionally, and without frustration. Remember, the goal is improvement, not venting.

3. **Avoid the "compliment sandwich."** People focus on the negative anyway, so surrounding criticism with compliments dilutes the message and confuses the recipient. Be direct, respectful, and clear.

4. **Frame criticism as actionable.** Feedback should focus on what can change. Instead of "Your reports are sloppy," try "Your reports would benefit from more clarity. Could we agree on a checklist to ensure consistency?"

It's equally important to solicit and receive feedback. This is one of the hardest things to do *as a human being*, much less as the leader of an organization. But you need to fight through it and get to a point where you are comfortable with receiving feedback from others.

1. **Be open.** Even experienced managers can fall into the trap of defensiveness. Approach feedback with curiosity, not resistance.
2. **Seek specifics.** If someone says, "You could improve communication," ask, "Can you share an example or a specific situation where I could have handled it better?"
3. **Act on feedback.** If someone takes the time to provide constructive criticism, show that you're listening by following up and improving.

Remember, the most successful managers are those who create a culture of continuous feedback. Regularly asking for input, offering praise, and discussing areas for growth keeps everyone aligned and focused on improvement.

Building trust

Without trust, even the most skilled group of individuals will fail to collaborate effectively or achieve their potential. Building trust doesn't happen overnight. It's a deliberate and consistent effort.

1. **Lead with transparency.** Share the "why" behind decisions, even difficult ones. Explain your thought process and invite questions, particularly when delivering tough news.
2. **Follow through.** Nothing destroys trust faster than broken promises. If you say you'll do something, do it. And if circumstances change, communicate why you can't, and what you'll do instead.
3. **Be consistent.** Your team needs to know they can count on you. That means being reliable, approachable, and fair in all interactions.

4. **Admit mistakes.** Vulnerability builds credibility. When you mess up, own it. Your honesty will encourage others to do the same.

5. **Invest in relationships.** Take the time to understand your team members as people. What motivates them? What are their goals? Knowing these things helps you lead more effectively and shows that you genuinely care.

Trust isn't a one-and-done achievement. It's an ongoing process that requires consistent effort. But once established, it becomes the invisible glue that holds your team together through challenges and change.

Empowering your team

Great managers don't just manage tasks, they empower people. Your job isn't to micromanage every detail, but to create the conditions for your team to thrive.

- **Delegate with clarity.** When assigning tasks, make sure the expectations are clear. What's the goal? What's the timeline? Who else is involved? Don't just delegate tasks, delegate ownership.

- **Focus on outcomes, not processes.** Allow your team to approach problems in their own way. As long as the end result meets expectations, resist the urge to dictate how the work gets done. Give them a clear picture of success, with clear metrics, and encourage them to study prior art but find innovative ways to accomplish the task. In fact, praising innovation even if it fails is a great way to drive more creative risk-taking within your team.

- **Remove roadblocks.** Your role is to ensure your team has everything they need to succeed. Advocate for resources, streamline approvals, and address interdepartmental conflicts before they become obstacles.

- **Recognize effort and results.** Publicly celebrate wins, big or small. Recognition is one of the most powerful motivators, and it reinforces the behaviors you want to see more of.

Empowering your team isn't about being hands-off. It's about providing the right mix of guidance, autonomy, and support to help them do their best work.

Write things down

A wise person once wrote that managing people is all about managing change. When it comes to communicating change, I always start with a change document. A change document lists the following:

- what's happening
- what changes will result
- who knows now
- when it will be communicated
- a workback schedule for each step required, up to and including the change date
- communications drafts (email, Slack messages, etc.)

The change document is an opportunity to make sure that all communications are handled in a steady, deliberate manner. I'll discuss this further in a moment, when I talk about management principles.

LEADERSHIP PRINCIPLES FOR DEVELOPER MARKETING

I've been fortunate to work at some of the most iconic companies in the history of our industry. Understandably, each of these companies has different culture, leadership, process, and hiring patterns. From my combined experiences, I've put together a set of leadership guidelines that I follow in every job I take. I would encourage you to study the leadership principles of every organization you admire (they're often published for all to see) and develop your own leadership principles.

Here are my leadership principles in summary:

1. Help First
2. Think like an API
3. Managers go deep
4. Managers are right, a lot
5. Write it down
6. Respect and trust the user's voice
7. Maintain a bias for action
8. Fail fast and learn faster
9. Focus on long-term impact
10. Communicate fearlessly to build trust

Help First

We've discussed my mantra of Help First throughout this book in the context of marketing programs, messaging, growth, sales, and more. But I also take care to apply this first principle to managing teams.

My role as a leader (a "servant manager," if you will) is to help my team grow: their skills, their impact, their careers, and their ability to juggle life and work. I start by asking, "How can I help you?"

I hold regular one-on-ones and skip-level discussions with people, not just about their immediate job working for me, but about their career aspirations and goals. I then try to connect their aspirations to their current role, ensuring they're developing the skills and connections they need for later success.

It's also important to recognize that people are much more than what you see nine to five. The five-to-nine person has highs and lows in life, just like you. Early in my career, when I was twenty years old and experiencing my first significant relationship disaster, my work suffered tremendously. My boss pulled me aside and told me that he understood and was there to talk about it, but also that he expected me to deliver at work. Simply having the acknowledgment that someone saw me for who I was and what I was going through snapped me back to reality.

People go through divorces, sick children, addiction, elderly parents, and a host of other things that comprise a full, messy, wonderful life. You *can* be **both** a manager who expects high performance and a leader who helps people be at their best every day.

Think like an API

APIs (at least deterministic ones) are designed to provide predictable outputs given predictable inputs. These "preconditions" and "postconditions" form a contract with the rest of the system in that you can expect certain behaviors when the API is invoked.

Similarly, when working cross-organizationally, especially in a more "fuzzy" discipline like marketing, you will often have dependencies on other teams, and in turn, other teams will have dependencies on you. For example, your sales team may depend on you for competitive analysis and market differentiation. Your output will be a set of well-formatted battle cards that help sales teams position the product correctly and handle objections confidently. In order to deliver these battle cards, you need deep technical understanding from the product team about design tradeoffs, product decisions, and comparative product capabilities. By synthesizing these inputs with your own knowledge of the market, you can deliver to the sales team the results they need.

When you think like an API, you are building contracts with other teams in the organization so that you can deliver impactful, dependable results. Just as an API outlines what inputs it expects and what outputs it guarantees, you make clear what resources, information, or deliverables you need to succeed, and what others can expect in return. These "contracts" create mutual accountability and transparency, ensuring everyone understands what success looks like and how to achieve it together.

APIs are also processes, and good processes (like good API design) can be refined and refactored into smaller units of execution which, in turn, can be debugged more efficiently and confidently. Break complex workflows into smaller units of execution, each with its own measurable input, output, and feedback loop. This allows for easier debugging when something goes wrong and creates opportunities for continuous refinement and optimization.

Last, just as well-regarded APIs earn trust among developers, you too can earn trust by living up to your commitments and holding others accountable for theirs.

Managers go deep

I borrowed this one from Amazon. I don't believe in building a professional managerial class in an organization. Managers are always player-coaches, capable of subbing for anyone on the team. Sure, you may have weaknesses in one area or another. That's why you hire experts! But at the same time, in a pinch—prolonged illness or absence, a hiring vacancy, etc.—you can jump in and deliver.

Moreover, as you demonstrate your willingness to do hard work, you inspire your team with your leadership.

A word of caution though. Good leaders also delegate well. Trust people to become experts and do their job. There is a very fine line between "going deep" and "micromanaging," and it is critical that you straddle it every day.

Managers are right, a lot

At Amazon, it is often said that managers are right, a lot. The idea here is that people are promoted to leadership positions because they have demonstrated a career of good judgment. This judgment extends to everything: personnel decisions, product and strategy decisions, partnership decisions, and so on. Good judgment doesn't just happen by chance. It's cultivated over years of making thoughtful, data-driven decisions and learning from successes and failures alike.

As leaders, we're the ones junior employees often come to for advice and guidance on projects. Our job isn't to give them the right answers, it's to teach them *how to think*. Indeed, good judgment goes beyond knowing the right answers. It also means knowing the right way to deliver feedback, the right way to connect teams and groups, and the right way to dissect problems, frame questions, and challenge assumptions.

Being "right, a lot" isn't about infallibility. Amazon embraces a culture of constant learning, iteration, and debate. Leaders are expected to question their own assumptions, listen deeply to dissenting opinions, and change course when the data or logic demands it. In Amazon's culture, the willingness to admit mistakes and pivot when needed is just as critical as making the right calls in the first place.

Ultimately, being "right, a lot" isn't just about getting things right, it's about building trust. Employees and peers trust leaders who make consistent, fair, and thoughtful decisions. This trust is what empowers teams to move quickly and confidently, knowing their leaders will steer them in the right direction when it matters most.

Being right, a lot, means being right about a lot of things.

Write it down

This is another principle from Amazon, but one I perfected at Twitter. Amazon famously banned PowerPoint in favor of long-form documents. At first it was quite a shock for me to go from Microsoft, where stultifying PowerPoints are the norm, to Amazon and the legendary "six-page narrative," but I quickly adapted and learned to love the format. As a writer, I believe strongly in the written word, and being in an environment where cross-organizational conflict and complex problems were slowly whittled down to their essence while narrative documents were created felt very natural to me.

In short, everything I do starts with a project document. The project doc is always text based (very few diagrams) and circulated early and often for feedback. "Early" is critical. Getting input from colleagues so that you can stay on the right track is important. Nip misalignment early.

Another important aspect of having a "write it down" culture is that you can support a widely distributed, multilingual team. You can also be more inclusive of people who are shy in meetings and less likely to speak up. Documents help everyone contribute asynchronously. They can use translation tools to identify idiomatic expressions. (We Americans are famous for injecting American-specific sports metaphors into everything!) And they allow introverts to contribute as much as extroverts.

Respect and trust the user's voice

One of my favorite principles from Twitter is this: In business, and especially in marketing, the answers are not "in the building." To succeed, you must actively engage with your customers, deeply understand who they are, empathize with their struggles, and craft solutions that truly address their needs.

But listening is only part of the equation. Respecting and trusting the user's voice means internalizing their feedback and taking meaningful action based on it. I recently worked with an AI company that developed customer-facing chatbots. While their product was innovative, they kept encountering a recurring concern from customers: the chatbot's knowledge could quickly become outdated, compromising its value.

This concern speaks to a broader challenge in the AI industry: knowledge management. As AI interfaces like LLMs, chatbots, and agents become central to customer interactions, ensuring the accuracy and relevance of the underlying knowledge base is critical. One customer, a travel agency, illustrated this point vividly. When a user asked the chatbot how to prepare for an upcoming cruise, it responded with outdated COVID-19 protocols from several years earlier. For the travel agency, the chatbot was integral to their customer experience, but its utility hinged on providing timely, accurate, and controlled information.

The AI company recognized the gap. Instead of continuing to compete in the crowded chatbot space, they shifted their focus to knowledge-management solutions. By prioritizing tools to ensure up-to-date and accurate information, they aligned their offering with a critical customer pain point. The pivot was transformative. Customers immediately saw the value of a chatbot that not only facilitated conversations but reliably conveyed accurate, current information.

Respecting and trusting the user's voice isn't just about holding customer meetings or collecting feedback. It's about extracting action-able insights, drawing the right takeaways, and committing to the next steps that will genuinely address customer needs. It's a principle that transforms how companies listen, adapt, and ultimately succeed.

Bias for action

Every company likes to say they cultivate a bias for action, but it's nat-ural that as organizations grow, the pace of action slows down. People need to take the time to get aligned. Projects have more stakeholders and therefore more impact and therefore more complexity. Leaders scrutinize senior employees, who in turn scrutinize junior employees. Personal biases creep into decision making. All these things make it difficult to move fast and deliver results.

But each leader sets the tone. And it's up to you to model the be-havior of working respectfully with your colleagues, but also charting the path you know best. Amazon's famous "two-way door" decision-making framework is a good example of guidelines for helping you cut through red tape. Some decisions can be easily undone: You can go through the door but quickly come back out if it's not the right decision for the moment. And there are other, rare decisions that are harder to undo: a key industry partnership, a senior-level hire, a large cash investment in a project, and so on.

Another Amazon rubric I find helpful is the "two-pizza team" con-cept. All decisions and projects should be made by teams small enough to share two pizzas for lunch. This helps cut down the number of stake-holders while preserving the level of feedback required to make an in-formed decision. (Unfortunately for me, I really love pizza . . .)

Fail fast and learn faster

Building on several of the leadership principles so far, "fail fast and learn faster" embodies API-like thinking, where you are looking for small, executable units of process that can be attempted, measured, debugged, and if necessary thrown out altogether.

And working in small teams helps you move quickly, measure your progress, and decide whether or not it's worth proceeding.

For example, I once had an employee who wanted to spin up their own podcast about data analytics. We didn't know if a podcast, much less one of our own, would yield any results whatsoever. But once we went down the path of branding a podcast, creating and getting commitments from a guest list, publicizing the podcast, and launching it, we'd be committed without even knowing whether it was a good idea.

My advice in this case was to start small: Let's find guest spots on existing podcasts and determine if the podcast audience was useful to us. Let's recruit another partner to join us as guests on another podcast and see if the process of procuring guests and synchronizing messaging was easy and effective. Let's just post a video conversation between a customer and our founder on our YouTube channel and see if it generates views and if we know how to promote it. These baby steps required a modicum of commitment, and in the end, when we determined that this channel would not be effective, we weren't locked into seeing the project through over six months.

Focus on long-term impact

Bigger companies often think in very long time horizons. Apple famously delivers products that are years in the making. Startups rarely have the luxury of time. But it's essential for all companies to think about how each project serves their long-term vision.

Companies are rarely about products. They're about the people and the processes they build to capture inevitable changes in market conditions and customer requirements. The people and processes devise the product strategy to meet those ever-evolving needs.

Likewise, when you think about the marketing programs you build, think about the people you are assembling to build them and the processes you are creating to execute them. These processes will outlast the people, and the people will probably outlast the program. This is the long-term focus all companies need to apply.

Communicate fearlessly to build trust

And finally, let's talk about my favorite leadership principle of all time, from Twitter. Old Twitter was the best job I ever had, the best team I ever built, and the best leadership team I ever had the privilege of being a part of.

But Twitter was not a "go along to get along" culture. Twitter, much like the user base it served, was like a room of clucking chickens, all communicating fearlessly. Twitter thrived on open dialogue, candid feedback, and bold ideas. Trust wasn't built through politeness or quiet agreement; it came from the clarity of knowing exactly where everyone stood. You didn't have to guess someone's thoughts or intentions because they were willing to share them openly. Sure, as with all organizations, there were some office politics. But leaders often had no problem cutting through the nonsense and driving alignment across teams.

At Twitter, I saw attorneys contribute to product strategy, engineers deliver feedback on marketing decisions, and designers challenge executive management, simply because there was a culture and environment where everyone could speak up in a meeting. And these contributions provided valuable perspectives that were often right!

I've always believed in speaking my mind and encouraging others to do the same. My time at Twitter reinforced my conviction that organizations flourish when everyone feels empowered to contribute, challenge, and learn from one another. If you've ever had the privilege of working in an environment like that, you know just how transformative it can be. If you haven't, it's worth fighting to build one.

SUMMARY

The perfect product launch. The perfect keynote. The numbers going up and to the right.

I've experienced it all and I will tell you this: The only thing that matters is the people I did it with. I am still in touch with all my best teams. I consider them friends and I would do anything for them.

But I'll also tell you this: None of the best products I've worked on still exist. Indeed, the best company I ever worked for doesn't exist anymore at all. Such is the nature of the tech industry.

As Jimi Hendrix said, "castles made of sand, fall in the sea eventually."

There are always tough times in marketing—missed quarters, depressed pipelines. You always aim to mitigate these factors, but the days are long, the rewards are thin, and the chair is always hot.

Stay cool. Don't pass the blame. Accept reality. Fight like hell to fix what's broken.

And treat your team well at all times.

The role of VP of marketing or CMO is a short-tenured, high-stress one. It's rare to last two years in that position, not to mention three. Accept that failure is the default mode and that founders hold short leashes. Aim for the most impact you can make in the time you have. And aim to leave your people with the skills and resilience to tackle the most difficult challenges.

CHAPTER 27

Your Role in the Industry

Developer marketing and developer relations is a great genre.

Our mission is to leave the industry in better shape than we found it.

Help others wherever possible. Help developers succeed in their roles. Help developers build their careers. Help your teammates grow their skills.

Help First.

APPENDIX 1

The Developer Launch Checklist

Product launches are extraordinary opportunities to establish positioning, raise awareness, and put a stake in the ground in terms of product momentum and customer wins. Every launch needs to include a new-product release (obviously), but also customer evidence, content, and community activation.

This checklist will help you run through the list of activities you should do for every release.

Prelaunch activities: Drive market research, customer discovery, customer feedback, and content preparation that help identify product-market fit and ensure the product meets the needs of real customers.

- ☐ Develop hypotheses about target customers.
- ☐ Do customer discovery and research. (What problems do customers currently face, and how can we address them?)
- ☐ Identify customer segmentation.
- ☐ Identify market sizing and opportunity.
- ☐ Write a description of key features and benefits desired by the target customer.
- ☐ Write competitive analyses.
- ☐ Develop positioning and messaging.
- ☐ Create a customer journey map.
- ☐ Compile a collateral "bill of materials" (what we need to build for launch): website changes, landing pages, benchmarks, customer evidence, etc.
- ☐ Work closely with early adopters to write case studies, obtain quotes for use in website and sales materials, and provide references to influencers and journalists.
- ☐ Write the Getting Started Guide, a step-by-step guided tour of the product or feature, complete with screenshots, videos, and animations showing the product in all its glory.

Launch activities: Build materials, prebrief related teams, coordinate activities, and lead all aspects of the product launch.

- ☐ Build the digital marketing plan. Identify key communities, websites, and other online venues where the target customer is known to congregate. Build an outreach strategy for each.
- ☐ Identify the most common keywords the target customer will use when searching for a solution to their problem. Build a content plan (SEO) to answer each of these questions proactively.
- ☐ Use the keywords to build a paid-acquisition strategy, if this is part of your marketing mix.
- ☐ Identify the most common real-world venues where the target customer congregates: events, meetups, etc. Start submitting CFPs to speak at these events and meetups, and begin research on event sponsorship, if this is part of your marketing mix.
- ☐ Build a comms plan that outlines key influencers, journalists, and publications where information about your product or feature would be germane.
- ☐ Write the necessary collateral desired by your sales team: data sheets, first-meeting decks, battle cards, etc.
- ☐ Prebrief the sales team on all aspects of the product, probably over multiple sessions: What is the ideal customer profile? What are our customers' most common questions? And so forth.

Postlaunch activities: Identify case studies, drive the comms narrative, and inform growth activities that make a product successful in the market.

- ☐ Identify who the top customers are and check if they would be willing to write a case study or provide their logo for use in marketing materials.
- ☐ Look across customer usage and identify trends that could be used as pitches for comms outreach to journalists and publications.
- ☐ Calculate usage numbers and other "vanity metrics" that could be used in website and sales materials.
- ☐ Adjust marketing website and sales materials based on customer usage and continued customer discovery.

APPENDIX 2

Case Study Discussion Guide and AI Prompt

CASE STUDY DISCUSSION GUIDE

Here's a discussion guide for interviewing a customer about their successful implementation of one of your products or services:

Introduction

- Tell me a little about your company. What does your company do, and what is your role?
- What are the key challenges your company faces today? What specific problems are you trying to solve?

Context: Before Using Our Product

- What solutions or processes were you using to address these challenges before our product?
- What were the biggest pain points in your previous approach? Were there inefficiencies, high costs, slow processes, or other limitations?
- Can you quantify the impact of these challenges on your business—for example, in terms of lost revenue, inefficiencies, downtime, or employee productivity?

Decision to Explore New Solutions

- What made you start looking for a new solution? What was the breaking point or key event that triggered the search?
- What other solutions or vendors did you consider? What were the pros and cons of these alternatives?
- Why did you choose our product over the alternatives? Was it a specific feature, price, support, ease of use, or other factors?

Implementation and Adoption

- What did the implementation process look like? How long did it take? What challenges did you encounter?
- Who was involved in the implementation? Were there specific teams or stakeholders?
- How did the team react to the transition? Was there resistance or immediate adoption?

Product Experience and Usage

- What were the most valuable features for you? Are there specific functionalities that stand out?
- Can you share a specific use case where our product is being used today? How is it integrated into your workflow?
- What surprised you most about using the product? Were there unexpected benefits?

Results and Impact

- What measurable results have you seen since adopting our product? This could include . . .
  - time saved
  - cost reductions
  - performance improvements
  - revenue growth
  - employee productivity

- Can you share specific KPIs or metrics? What changes have you tracked?
- How has our product impacted your team, operations, or customers? Have there been qualitative improvements?

Future Outlook and Recommendations

- If you could change or improve one thing about our product, what would it be? What enhancements would make it even better?
- How do you see your company evolving, and how does our product fit into your future plans? Will you expand usage? Try new features?
- What advice would you give to other companies considering our product? Would you recommend it, and if so, why?

Final Thoughts and Closing

- Is there anything else you'd like to add? Any stories, experiences, or insights we didn't cover?
- Would you be open to participating in follow-up content (video testimonial, webinar, conference panel, etc.)?

If you plan to record your interview and make a transcript, you can use it and an AI prompt to generate the draft for a case study. You will want to attach the transcript, your positioning framework and any messaging guides, and any case studies you like. Ideally this AI prompt will get you 60 to 70 percent toward the completion of your first draft.

AI PROMPT

Here's an AI Prompt we can use to turn a transcript from the interview into a great first draft of the case study. You should consider building many AI prompts to help you be more efficient in your work.

Use this prompt with GPT-4.1 when you have:

* A transcript of a customer interview
* A messaging framework
* A completed case study to use as a reference

This prompt should get you ~60–70% of the way toward a high-quality first draft.

AI Prompt for Generating Case Study Drafts

Role and Objective

You are a professional case study writer for **[YOUR COMPANY NAME]**, trained in developer-focused B2B storytelling. Your job is to write a customer case study that blends authentic customer quotes with our company's core messaging and positioning.

Inputs

You will be provided with the following attachments:

* **Transcript**: A raw transcript of an interview with [CUSTOMER NAME] at [CUSTOMER].
* **Messaging Framework**: Our internal positioning guide for [PRODUCT NAME].
* **Reference Case Study**: A recent case study to model tone, structure, and depth.

Structure

Your output should follow this exact structure:

- ### 1. Introduction

  - Include a compelling quote from [CUSTOMER NAME] that reflects their experience or results.
  - Introduce the customer and what their company does.

- ### 2. The Challenge

  - Describe what the customer was trying to accomplish.
  - Detail their key business or technical requirements.
  - Frame the problem clearly.

- ### 3. Choosing [PRODUCT NAME]

  - Summarize the alternatives they evaluated.
  - Explain why they selected [PRODUCT NAME].
  - Highlight how our product met their specific needs better than the competition.

- ### 4. The Approach

  - Outline how they got started and onboarded with [PRODUCT NAME].
  - Describe how they implemented and used the product to solve their challenge.

- ### 5. The Results

  - Highlight improvements, wins, or key outcomes.
  - Include measurable results and performance metrics where possible.
  - Use another quote inset to showcase customer sentiment or value.

Reasoning Reminders

- **"Keep going until the structure is complete."**
- **"Use direct quotes when available instead of paraphrasing."**
- **"Think step by step when extracting insights from the transcript."**
- **"Blend in our messaging and positioning, but never at the expense of authenticity."**

Output Format

- Markdown format
- Use section headings as specified
- Bullet points only where appropriate for clarity

Final Instructions

- Do **not** fabricate quotes. Only use direct customer language from the transcript.
- Incorporate our messaging as narrative glue, not filler.
- Model tone and flow after the reference case study.
- Keep it clear, concise, and informative.

Prompt created for internal use at [YOUR COMPANY NAME]. Adapt as needed per customer or product.

This is the transcript of a case study with one of our customers. [CUSTOMER NAME] works for [CUSTOMER]. [INTERVIEWER NAME] works for [YOUR COMPANY NAME]. I want you to read this transcript and generate a case study for [YOUR COMPANY NAME].

The case study should have the following sections:

- **Introduction**, including a quote.
- **The challenge:** what is the customer trying to accomplish, what are the requirements they need in a tool
- **Choosing [PRODUCT NAME]:** why they chose [PRODUCT NAME]; how [PRODUCT NAME] met their requirements; and how [PRODUCT NAME] stacked up against alternatives
- **The approach:** how they onboarded and used [PRODUCT NAME] to solve their challenges
- **The results:** the benefits they've seen and the metrics they've been able to achieve after using [PRODUCT NAME]

I've attached the transcript file. I've also attached a PDF of a case study we recently completed. And I've attached a PDF of our messaging framework.

Where possible, use direct quotes from [CUSTOMER NAME]. Be sure to extract exact quotes when writing quote insets for the case study. Blend in our core positioning and messaging as a framework for explaining what [PRODUCT NAME] does and the benefits [CUSTOMER] has seen.

AFTERWORD

Developer tools and platforms have become some of the most valuable businesses in tech. Companies like LaunchDarkly, Chroma, Modal, and Supabase are redefining the developer experience and, in turn, reshaping entire industries. Every company is now a software company, and the tools developers use will determine how innovation unfolds.

AI and new consumption models are transforming the landscape, but one thing remains constant: the best developer-first companies know that distribution, onboarding, positioning, and brand matter as much as code, APIs, and automation.

If you're building the picks and shovels that power the next generation of developers, this book is your playbook. Good luck, and happy building.

(Astasia Myers, General Partner at Felicis)

ACKNOWLEDGMENTS

This book is the product of my thirty-five-plus-year career. I can draw a straight line from many of the points and observations I make to specific people who have helped me understand markets and launch products throughout that time. I've managed hundreds of people over the course of my career, and I'm grateful to each of them. I would especially like to thank my managers during my career for guiding me, encouraging me, and putting up with me: Fred Kuhl, Tom Button, Jon Roskill, Marie Huwe, John Case, Andy Jassy, Adam Selipsky, Doug Purdy, Jana Messerschmidt, Jeff Sandquist, Ajay Kulkarni, Paul Copplestone, and Ant Wilson.

Throughout my career, I've leaned on the expertise of my peer marketing executives and experts. I want to acknowledge several brilliant people whose own published content have led me to run experiments that led to observations that turned into passages in this book: Dave Kellogg, Guillaume Cabane, Martin Govnikas, Hank Taylor, Lenny Rachitsky, the Growth Equation Newsletter, The Growth Unhinged Newsletter, and the Product Tea Newsletter.

I'd also like to thank the many people who helped proofread drafts of this work, including April Schuppel, Jeff Barr, Jeff Sandquist, Christina Warren, Lacey Butler, Juan Perez, Oded Poncz, Astasia Myers, and several others.

Books are labors of love, but they're also extensive labors. I'd like to thank the folks at Girl Friday Productions for helping me bring these words to life, including Abi Pollokoff, Kylee Hayes, Allison Gorman, Patty Economos, and Rachel Marek.

And finally, thank you to my mother—one of the OG software

developers and the person who convinced me to give up French in high school in order to make room for computer science classes. *Je ne serais pas là sans vos conseils et votre amour.*

ABOUT THE AUTHOR

PRASHANT SRIDHARAN has more than thirty years of experience running marketing, product, and business development teams for some of the largest and fastest-growing developer platforms in the industry, including Sun Microsystems, Microsoft, Amazon Web Services, Meta, Twitter, Timescale, Tinybird, and Supabase. He is an advisor to several seed and Series A developer tools and platforms startups. He lives in Lisbon, Portugal, and San Francisco, California.